Women, Feminism and Media

Media Topics
Series editor: Valerie Alia

Titles in the series include:

Women, Feminism and Media

Sue Thornham

Edinburgh University Press

For Mike

Edinburgh University Press Ltd
22 George Square, Edinburgh

Typeset in Janson and Neue Helvetica
by Hewer Text UK Ltd, Edinburgh, and
printed and bound in Great Britain by
Antony Rowe Ltd, Chippenham, Wilts

A CIP record for this book is available from the British Library

ISBN 978 0 7486 2070 8 (hardback)
ISBN 978 0 7486 2071 5 (paperback)

Contents

List of illustrations

Acknowledgements

I am grateful to my colleagues in the Department of Media and Film at Sussex, especially Thomas Austin, Kate Lacey, Lizzie Thynne and Robbie Robb, for their support during the writing of this book. Thanks, too, go to Andrew Duff and especially to Helen Thornham, for their practical help, and to Sarah Edwards for her patience. Finally, special thanks go to Mike and Beth, who kept me going.

For permission to reproduce the illustrations in this book, I would like to thank:

Figure 2.1   *Rokeby Venus* (1649) by Velasquez: the National Gallery Picture Library, with special thanks to Margaret Daly.

Figure 2.2   *Lady Lilith* (1868) by Rossetti: Delaware Art Museum.

Figure 2.3   Estée Lauder Youth Dew: Art & Commerce, with special thanks to Jessica Marx.

Figure 2.4   Special K cereal: the Kellogg Group, with special thanks to Ben Goodman.

Figure 2.5   Snickers: Mars UK Limited, with special thanks to Dawn Palmer.

Figure 5.1   Adidas boots: Adidas, with special thanks to Sarah Talbot.

Figure 5.2   Wilkinson Sword: Wilkinson Sword and EMAP/FHM, with special thanks to Gerhild Freller.

1 Introduction: thinking women/media/feminism

In 1983 E. Ann Kaplan ended the Preface to her book *Women and Film* with a plea: 'I hope that teachers unfamiliar with feminist approaches to film will be inspired to undertake courses on women in film, or to build the perspective into their current courses'. Despite ten years of feminist film theory and criticism, she continues, 'undergraduate film students rarely learn much about it' and the work is 'virtually unknown' to students and academics in other, related disciplines (1983: ix, 1). Twenty years on, such tentativeness feels odd and even uncomfortable. In 2001, the journal *Feminist Media Studies* opened its launch issue in very different style: 'Over the past few decades,' it states, 'feminist media scholarship has flourished, emerging from a barely perceptible public presence to become a profound influence on the field of communications and across a range of disciplines, and gaining particular authority in cultural and critical studies' (McLaughlin and Carter 2001: 5). But there are other shifts too. We might now feel uneasy about some of the assumptions Kaplan makes: that 'women *and* film' and 'women *in* film' are the same thing; that women can be discussed as a more or less homogeneous category; that the relationship between feminism and women is a straightforwardly explanatory one; and that this new perspective can be unproblematically 'built in' to existing courses.[1] All of which is to say that the three terms of this book's title – women, feminism, and media, together with their relationship – present us both with a number of immediate issues for discussion and with some already existing, but not always unproblematic, histories. In this introduction I shall trace these issues and histories, and also seek to place them within some of the broader discussions within feminist theory – about subjectivity, identity, culture, and narrative – of which they have formed a crucial part.

Women and . . .

The title of Kaplan's *Women and Film* is itself very much of its moment. In Britain the 1970s saw conferences on 'Women and Socialism' and

'Women and the Media' (Women's Studies Group 1978: 12–13) and the establishment of a Women and Film Group in London.[2] The first book called *Women and Media*, edited by Helen Baehr, appeared in 1980. All of these can be seen as part of what Charlotte Brunsdon calls the 'political project of Women and . . .' (2000: 103). It was a project, as Ann Kaplan's Preface illustrates, which was determined to force the consideration of women *in* to already existing fields of study, and one which had its roots in the activism of the 1970s Women's Movement rather than in the academic fields which it was determined to open up. Though many of the women involved were working in academic contexts, usually as postgraduate students, others were not, and in both cases it was the politics of second-wave feminism (the 'Women's Liberation Movement') which brought them together.[3] In the USA, too, 'Women and . . .' was a preferred title which signalled political intentions. The journal *Women and Film* appeared in 1972, opening with a manifesto which declares its position 'as part of the women's movement'. Women, the editors state, suffer a threefold oppression within film: they are oppressed as workers within the film *industry* (they are 'receptionists, secretaries, odd job girls, prop girls' and so on); they are oppressed by being packaged as images (sex objects, victims or vampires); and they are oppressed within a male-centred and exclusionary film *theory*. 'The struggle', therefore, 'begins on all fronts', and in it women will unite with 'other oppressed peoples' (1972: 5).

Women and Media, then, emerged from a quite specific political and intellectual moment and carrying certain assumptions, many of which now seem outdated. The women's movement has fragmented, so that it can no longer be written of as a political movement with a mass following. The assumption that the politicised intellectual can speak on behalf of all women can no longer be made. The category 'all women' has itself become suspect, as 'sisterhood' reveals itself to be fractured by power differences along lines of class, race, age and sexual orientation; and women as a group can no longer line up so easily with 'other oppressed peoples'. Finally, 'women's image' can no longer be seen as a simple matter of 'misrepresentation', to be corrected by the more 'realistic' portrayals to be produced by women themselves.

We shall return to these issues later in this book. Here, however, I want to address some of the other questions raised above. As we have seen, these early projects of 'Women and . . .' seem now to be both overstated and oddly tentative. The phrasing assumes a category, 'women', whose identity can be understood and whose characteristics traced. These characteristics, those of 'real women', can be clearly differentiated from the false glossy images as which they are 'packaged'. They are the shared characteristics of a gender or social group which suffers a common oppression under a global patriarchal capitalism. Such an assumption presumes a commonality of experience which transcends differences of class, age, 'race', ethnicity and culture, so that 'we' white Western women can, in this respect, speak for all women. It also presumes a model of identity that, if not precisely fixed, is commonly constructed and commonly felt, experienced and understood. All of these assumptions have since been questioned.

At the same time, however, this identity, constructed in oppression, is always the identity of the 'other', the excluded. 'We are', as the 1970 Women's Liberation Workshop Statement says, 'brought up to feel inadequate; educated to narrower horizons than men. This is our specific oppression as women' (Wandor 1990: 240). Or, as Sheila Rowbotham put it in 1973, 'We are oppressed by an overwhelming sense of not being there' (1973: 35). Women, as women rather than as glossy image and spectacle, are 'not there' in media representations,[4] and they are 'not there' in the theoretical and critical frameworks through which such representations, and the institutions that produce them, have been understood. If then, as the Statement continues, it is 'as women therefore that we are organising', this is a difficult position to occupy and from which to speak. 'As women', write the Birmingham Women's Studies Group, 'we are inevitably the subject and object of our study' (Women's Studies Group 1978: 12). As 'objects' of their study, the group members share a common experience of a cultural position, femininity, and a common embodiment as women. But finding a *subject* position from which to analyse this sense of being 'somehow, outside history, and both central to, and absent in, culture' (Brunsdon 1978: 20) seems an altogether more difficult matter. How does one speak from a position of absence? As Charlotte Brunsdon commented nearly twenty years later, 'it seemed almost impossible'. There was no theoretical framework available: 'At what level of theory could one defend a concept like "women's oppression"? What order of concept was "patriarchy"? And did we have to do it all ourselves – a double shift of intellectual work . . .?' (1996: 282). Faced with the difficulty that to really answer the question 'What about women?' it would be necessary, as the Women's Studies Group recognised, to 'think . . . differently about the whole field or object of study' (1978: 11), and thus to change it both theoretically and institutionally, it is not surprising that goals were often less ambitious. Feminist scholars sought to 'carve out' spaces within existing fields, to 'extend' current methodologies, to 'intervene in' academic discourses, and, more tentatively, to 'envision the kind of transformations we need and want'.[5] In this, the formulation 'Women and . . .' proved extremely useful. Looking at it now, however, we can note its uneasy combination of political assertiveness (women's position *must* be recognised) and intellectual uncertainty (but how . . .?).

From Woman to feminist

I noted above the striking difference in tone between Ann Kaplan's 1983 Preface to *Women and Film* and the editors' Introduction to *Feminist Media Studies* in 2001. The difference is also one of terminology. The key term, the identity from which the editors *speak*, in 2001 is that of 'feminist' not 'woman'. 'Women' as a category appear only four times in the Introduction. The identity 'feminist', however, is strongly affirmed, appearing over thirty times, though it might be crossed by differences in 'nation, race, ethnicity, class, age, physical abilities and sexual identities' (McLaughlin and Carter 2001: 6). This shift in terminology, from the 'women' of 'Women's Liberation' to the 'feminists' of 'second-wave', and more recently 'third-wave' feminism, has been noted by a number of writers.[6] The category 'woman' or 'women', as Denise Riley has pointed out, has increasingly been recognised to be an unstable one. '[H]istorically, discursively constructed, and always relatively to other categories which themselves change' (1988: 1–2), what it *means* is uncertain and shifting. To seek to speak as and on behalf of 'woman' no longer seems possible. The category is fractured within by structuring inequalities (of nation, race, class, for example), so that to claim to speak for women can seem to be an act of cultural imperialism. It is also the case that to speak as and for women is to remain bounded by a category whose characteristics – however subject to historical change they might have been – are still defined by and in relation to men. Feminism is anchored in that category: Rosalind Delmar defines it as 'a way of thinking created by, for, and on behalf of women' (1986: 27). But to speak as a feminist is to claim an agency beyond that characterisation. Feminism, as Denise Riley says, is 'the voicing of "women" from the side of "women"' (1988: 112).

The position of feminist is therefore a *critical* one, standing in a critical relation to patriarchal structures and institutions, but also to social constructions of femininity, the dominant identity position offered to women but experienced by them, in the words of Beverley Skeggs, as 'almost impossible', 'uninhabitable as a complete and coherent category' (1997: 102). It is this 'uninhabitable' quality of femininity which was described by Betty Friedan in *The Feminine Mystique*, in terms that inspired the emerging Women's Liberation Movement.[7] 'The feminine mystique', argues Friedan, insists that women 'can find fulfilment only in sexual passivity, male domination, and nurturing maternal love' (1965: 38), and she traces this 'myth of the Eternal Feminine' as it was reconstituted in the images to be found in 1950s American women's magazines, cinema stars and advertising images. Feminist media studies continued to develop this analysis of femininity, its representations and

women's complex relationships to them. As Charlotte Brunsdon writes, 'Traditional first-world femininity is made strange by feminism – it is denaturalized, and therefore the multiple sites on which it is elaborated become areas for possible investigation' (2000: 25).

Increasingly, therefore, the position of feminist is also a *theoretical* one, seeking to develop the theoretical frameworks that would move analysis past the paralysing position described by the Birmingham Women's Studies Group in 1978. Finally, as I have suggested above, the position of feminist is a *subject* position. For Betty Friedan in 1963, no such position was possible: for her, feminism was 'dead history. It ended as a vital movement in America with the winning of that final right: the vote' (1965: 88). Seven years later, however, Cellestine Ware could confidently articulate the 'demands' of 'the new feminists'. Ware's claim for a 'new feminism' which is also a 'renaissance of feminism' (1970: 7) is important not least because it is a *performative* claim. That is, in making claims to the name, the category, of feminist, a category that is anchored in, but goes beyond that of 'woman', Ware and others were making claims to a shared and politicised *identity*, and hence to a position from which to speak. It is a position, too, which claims authority from a history of its own. By the 1970s 'feminism' already had a meaning and a history. If earlier feminisms had repeatedly been pronounced dead, the 'new feminists' performed their own act of self-authorisation in proclaiming its rebirth.

Women/media/feminism

Thirty years on, I can write with the benefit of a substantial body of feminist theory and feminist media scholarship. It is a body of work through which we can trace a number of interwoven narratives or histories. One is the working through of what becomes an increasingly problematised relationship: that between 'women and media'. A second concerns the issues and debates thrown up when 'feminist' is inserted into this pairing, so that we now have three terms: women, feminism and media. A third maps the development of the subject position outlined above: that of the feminist, and specifically the feminist intellectual. Charlotte Brunsdon, in her study of the development of feminist television criticism, points out that the history she is tracing is also that of the production of a subject position. 'The feminist,' she writes, 'and more specifically the feminist intellectual, produces herself in this engagement with this popular television genre, just as she produces a text for media studies' (2000: 4). That is, to write the relationship 'women and media' *from the position of women*, is to produce and assert a subject position that was previously excluded from, even impossible within, conventional frameworks – a position which then challenges and cracks open existing frameworks.

Women and media: texts

Turning to the first of these narratives, that of the relationship between women and media, we find a number of related areas of focus. One begins from the 'packaging' of *women as images* referred to above. A polemical writer like Germaine Greer, building on Friedan's influential *The Feminine Mystique*, attacked the stereotyped images of the 'Eternal Feminine', with her 'glossy lips and matt complexion, her unfocused eyes and flawless fingers, her extraordinary hair all floating and shining, curling and gleaming', to be found in advertising, cinema, television, newspapers, 'trash magazines' and romance novels for women (Greer 1971: 60, 173). The Women's Liberation Workshop Statement of 1970 includes in its first paragraph the words, 'We are commercially exploited by advertisements, television, and the press' (Wandor 1990: 240). More scholarly analyses, such as those to be found in the 1978 American collection *Hearth and Home: Images of Women in the Mass Media*, edited by Gaye Tuchman, applied the quantitative survey methods of mainstream American mass communication research to analyse 'sex-role stereo-typing' within media images, with Tuchman arguing that such images amount to the 'symbolic annihilation' of women.

It was this work on 'images of women' or 'sex-role stereotyping' that dominated much early research. An example is the 1974 paper by the Birmingham Women's Studies Group on 'Images of Women in the Media' which, like many of these studies (Busby 1975: Janus 1977), produces a typology of media images of 'woman'. Across media forms ranging from news to advertising, such images, argue the authors, produce 'woman' 'as commodity-object and as a negative sign in a male-dominated culture' (Butcher et al. 1974: 33). Unusually for this period, however, these writers move beyond the idea that these images are distortions of women's 'reality', to focus on the ways in which they function to produce the 'modes of subjectivity available to women' in contemporary Western culture (1974: 31). As Janice Winship went on to argue in her work on advertisements and women's magazines,

> We are never just spectators who gaze at 'images' of women as though they were set apart, differentiated from the 'real' us. Within the ads are inscribed the images and subject positions of 'mother', 'housewife', 'sexually attractive woman' and so on, which, as we work to understand the ad, embroil us in the process of signification that we complete. (1980: 218)

Such work moved the textual study of woman and media away from a focus on 'images of women', and towards an exploration of the ways in which *ideologies of femininity* are produced and reproduced in media representations. These representations offer pleasures – the pleasures of self-recognition, of finding women placed centre-stage in a 'woman's genre', of participation in a shared 'women's culture' – but simultaneously act to contain women within the accepted bounds of femininity. It was an exploration which focused in turn on '*women's genres*': those popular media genres aimed at, and enjoyed by, female audiences. Soap opera and women's magazines were early subjects of this research, as we have seen, as were film melodrama and romance fiction. Later work focused on sitcom, romantic comedy, daytime television and radio, and what Charlotte Brunsdon has called 'heroine television',[8] as well as fashion and other 'body cultures'. Throughout, the emphasis has been on understanding the pleasures, complexities and contradictions of these productions. It is, in Rosalind Coward's words, to seek to understand the ways in which 'female desire is constantly lured by discourses which sustain male privilege', but simultaneously to 'listen out for the pleasures which escape, slip out between the cracks and perhaps spell the ruin of existing definitions of female desire' (1984: 16).

Women and media: production/consumption

A 1987 British collection, *Out of Focus: Writings on Women and the Media*, alerts us to another aspect of the early work on images. This book, too, declares itself to be a 'book about images of women', images produced by 'the capitalist, patriarchal scheme of things' in order 'to convince the less privileged that the oppressions and limitations of their lives are inevitable' (Davies et al. 1987: viii, 2). Here, the focus is shifting away from the images themselves, and towards the gendering of the production/ consumption process. Anna Coote and Beatrix Campbell pursue this argument further. In *Sweet Freedom: The Struggle for Women's Liberation* (1982), they write:

> Men control the means of expression – from the press and broadcasting, to advertising, film, publishing and even criticism – by occupying dominant positions within them, and by using the power this gives them to convey the ideas and values of a patriarchal order. (1982: 189)

It was an argument given substance by evidence of the overwhelming clustering of women in low status and service occupations within broadcasting institutions (Gallagher 1980, 1985; Murray Eddings 1980;

Baehr 1981; Creedon 1989; van Zoonen 1994), the historical absence of women as mainstream film directors, particularly in Hollywood (Mulvey 1979), and their absence from decision-making forums (Creedon 1989; van Zoonen 1994). In 1972, writing as one of the few women directors in television, Lis Kustow described the situation she encountered. Among the more striking evidence she gives concerns the number of jobs closed to women. These included at that point not only the positions of camera operator or videotape editor but also those of newsreader and network announcer. The then Controller of BBC2 commented on the prospect of women newsreaders in 1972:

> It seems unnatural to a lot of people to see a woman behave in that way. During the war, could you imagine any other than a male voice like John Snagge saying, 'This is London?' There is always bad news about and it is much easier for a man to deal with that kind of material. (Kustow 1972: 65)

She adds that at a meeting 'to decide the future of the fourth television channel, there was not one woman present'. Women, she writes, are assumed to be consumers not producers (1972: 69).

If women's absence as producers of media texts was an important theme of early work on 'women and media', a related but far more complex question concerned the assumptions about their female audience contained within texts aimed at women.[9] Twenty years after the event, Terry Lovell reflects on the reception given to the paper on soap opera which she, Richard Dyer and Jean McCrindle presented to the first Edinburgh Television Festival in 1977, from an audience largely composed of media professionals. Reading this paper now, what is most striking is its ambivalence towards its object. Soap opera, the authors write, is 'at present largely contemptible. Although it is for and about women it is dominated at the point of production by men and it gives us male definitions of women and how they relate to each other and to men'. At the same time, however, a soap opera like *Coronation Street* celebrates 'strong, independent women from whom much of the action is generated', and the fact that it 'validates *relationships*; it is *not* about social structures, material realists, physical strength, dramas of career or struggles for power' gives it 'radical possibilities' (Dyer et al. 1993: 37, 40). The paper, recalls Lovell, was attacked with 'ferocity' by media professionals for its perceived criticism of broadcasting attitudes. But, she adds, what was revealed in these attacks was precisely the kind of gendered contempt which the paper – ambivalently – critiques: 'the kind of contempt that they themselves [the producers] actually had for the punters and for the product' (Brunsdon 2000: 139).

Dorothy Hobson, researching the Midlands-based soap opera *Crossroads* in the 1970s, describes similar attitudes. Hobson's study was developed within the conceptual framework of the 'encoding/decoding' model developed by Stuart Hall at the Birmingham Centre for Contemporary Cultural Studies (Hall 1973). Against traditional 'mass communication' paradigms, the model asserted that each 'moment' of the communication process, those of 'encoding' (the production process), text (the programme's 'meaningful discourse') and 'decoding' (audience reception), is the site of cultural negotiation. Although unequal power structures will produce an encoded 'preferred reading' of the text, this reading will not be the only possible reading; nor will audiences, who might be situated very differently in the social formation, necessarily 'decode' the text as intended.[10] Hobson's study, in which she interviewed production staff and watched with viewers, was concerned to link an 'understanding of the production process of specific episodes or programmes with the audience reception and understanding of those same episodes or programmes' (1982: 107). Whilst for the programme's female audience, she found, soap opera viewing became a space within which to negotiate their own identities and positioning as women, for the mainly male directors and producers of *Crossroads* the programme was 'appalling', 'abysmal', 'tacky', an insult to their professionalism for which they felt only contempt (1982: 156–71). As a result, whilst Hobson continued to argue that a television programme 'is a three part development – the production process, the programme, and the understanding of that programme by the audience or consumer', for her it became the *audience* which produced the meanings of the text, and on which she concentrated her analysis (1982: 136).

Inevitably, then, the perceived gendering of the production/consumption process has meant that, whilst there has been feminist work both on women's employment in media industries (see van Zoonen 1994) and on the processes of cultural negotiation within the production process suggested by Hall's model (see particularly Julie D'Acci's work on the US police series *Cagney and Lacey*, 1987 and 1994), far more work has focused on women as *audiences*. Hobson writes of the *meanings* constructed by the female audiences of *Crossroads*, Coward writes of unruly and disruptive *pleasures*, but both are concerned to explore the ways in which women do *not* simply slip into what Skeggs calls the 'uninhabitable' position of femininity offered by media texts. It is a search that Charlotte Brunsdon has characterised as 'the search for feminine agency' (2000: 27), and it takes us into the tricky territory of what has now become a triangular relationship between women, *feminism* and media.

Women, feminism and media

Hobson's study of the production and reception of *Crossroads* concluded that the audience transforms and so produces the text. 'To try to say what *Crossroads* means to its audience is impossible,' she argues, 'for there is no single *Crossroads*, there are as many different *Crossroads* as there are viewers' (1982: 136). Such a conclusion insists on the agency of the heterogeneous women viewers of soap opera, but we can argue that it is evasive in two important respects. One is that it ignores the question of the ideological power of the text. As the work of Janice Winship and others had suggested, the constructions of femininity offered within 'women's genres' may be contradictory, but they continue to position women firmly within the conventional bounds of patriarchal relations (Winship 1980: 220). The second concerns the relationship of the feminist researcher to the women who are the subjects of her research. When Winship argued that 'women's genres' offered 'a terrain for women's struggle', the struggle she describes is one experienced by the *feminist*, who is caught between her subject positioning as 'woman' and her feminist understandings. Hobson, however, elides her own voice as researcher with those of her women viewers, ascribing to them the power to transform and produce textual meaning. In so doing, she evades the issue of the potential gap between the feminist and the 'ordinary woman' whose experiences and interpretative frameworks she both shares and contests.

It is this relationship between 'the feminist and other women' which Charlotte Brunsdon (1997: 192) sees as central within the development of feminist media studies. Within feminist audience research it has played a key, if problematic, role. If Dorothy Hobson's work insisted on the agency of 'ordinary women' as producers of textual meaning, later researchers struggled to align this search for female agency with investigations of the ideological constructions of femininity to be found within the texts of 'women's genres'. Janice Radway, for example, in her (1984) study of romantic fiction and its readers in the US, *Reading the Romance*, analyses the genre's structural and ideological features, the meanings constructed by its readers, and the context within which those readings are constructed. Her analysis concludes that whilst the fantasies offered by such texts might originate in 'the failure of patriarchal culture to satisfy its female members' (1987: 151), their narratives offer 'magical solutions' which simply reaffirm patriarchal relations. The act of reading itself, however, is accorded a different significance. It constitutes a 'declaration of independence' (1987: 7), women's carving out of 'a solitary space within an arena [the home] where their self-interest is usually identified with the interests of others and where they are defined as a public resource to be mined at will by the family' (1987: 211). It is to this act, rather than the meanings produced through it, that an oppositional agency is ascribed. Unlike Hobson, then, Radway separates the feminist, who understands the ideological power of the romance text, from the 'ordinary woman' reader, who does not. Whilst the latter is accorded agency, it is an agency always bounded by patriarchal power.

Ien Ang's study of Dutch viewers of the American prime-time soap opera *Dallas* tackles this question of agency rather differently, shifting focus from the ideological *meanings* of the text to its (feminine) *pleasures*. The reading position *Dallas* fans share, she argues, is not a shared 'knowledge of the world, but a subjective experience of the world: a "structure of feeling"'(1985: 45). This 'structure of feeling', which Ang identifies as 'the tragic', is, she writes, 'inscribed in the meaning-system of *Dallas*', in its combination of melodramatic scenario – with its focus on intensity and excess – and the lack of narrative resolution, the endless deferral and delay, of soap opera. That this tragic structure of feeling is felt as pleasurable by its women viewers is due to the 'melodramatic imagination' they share (1985: 79–82). Women's pleasure in viewing is the pleasure of recognition, recognition of an emotional structure which 'is felt as "real" and which makes sense for these viewers' (1985: 87). Whilst Ang recognises that, viewed ideologically, the *content* of the fantasies offered by *Dallas* must be judged as conservative, for her it is the fact of shared pleasures and collective fantasy that is important. It is this which is unruly, excessive, and potentially liberatory.

Both Radway and Ang struggle with the contradiction between the ideological conservatism of 'women's genres' and the liberatory or oppositional potential felt to lie in the agency of their readers/viewers. They struggle, too, to determine the precise relationship between the feminist researcher, who possesses intellectual capital and interpretive power, and the women she studies, who do not, and whose positioning as 'feminine subject' she therefore both shares and does not share. The feminist media studies researcher, that is, finds herself frequently with a sense of being both inside and distanced from the subject position 'woman', and both inside and distanced from the academy. Looking more closely at these issues, we can see that they suggest some even more fundamental questions, questions about subjectivity, identity and culture which have been raised within the broader framework of feminist theory.

The feminist subject

One such question concerns the gendering of culture itself. In 1986 Dale Spender described her introduction to the canon of English literature. 'I have no reason to suspect that my own university education was peculiarly biased or limited', she writes:

> On the contrary, it appears to have been fairly representative. Yet in the guise of presenting me with an overview of the literary heritage of the English-speaking world, my education provided me with a grossly inaccurate and distorted view of the history of letters. For my introduction to the 'greats' was (with the exception of the famous five women novelists) an introduction to the great men. (1986: 115)

Yet women, Spender later found, had written many of the early novels; it was simply that these early novelists 'had *all* "disappeared"'from the literary canon (117). Spender's resulting determination to rediscover and write the lost history of women writers was one shared by many feminist literary critics in the late 1960s and 1970s (Ellmann 1968; Moers 1976; Showalter 1977), with its outcomes labelled 'gynocritics' by Elaine Showalter (1979). In her own account of this critical 'disappearance', Showalter describes the assumptions about women's fiction inscribed within nineteenth-century criticism. Victorian male reviewers, she writes, acknowledged women's dominance in the field of fiction, but saw the 'feminine' novel as an inferior form. Women's writing was 'acknowledged to possess sentiment, refinement, tact, observation, domestic expertise, high moral tone, and knowledge of female character'. Only male writers, however, exhibited 'originality, intellectual training, abstract intelligence, humor, self-control, and knowledge of male character' (1977: 90). Women's creative production, that is, was seen as the generalised product of their femininity. It was not, in the canonical sense, 'authored'. 'High culture', like 'abstract intelligence', was decidedly gendered.

Celia Lury (1993) has traced the ways in which these repeated reaffirmations of the high-culture/low-culture divide served to confirm the masculinity of the Enlightenment concept of 'the individual' who is the source of value, judgement and authenticity, and who is embodied above all in the figure of the artist. In nineteenth-century art women were confined to the 'lesser genres' of portraiture, still life and flowers; within print culture their involvement remained confined to the low-status activities of novel and periodical writing. Once the novel in turn acquired the status of high culture, as a public, realist form whose author could claim 'creative autonomy', it too became a 'masculine' form. The high-culture/low-culture divide, she concludes, is a thoroughly gendered one, corresponding to a division between mainstream cultural activity and public professionalism on the one hand, and a critically marginalised, privatised and less 'original' form of production on the other. Lury goes further, arguing that this constituting of culture as high/low, public/

private does not merely correspond to an already existing, socially structured sexual division. The category of the feminine, of 'Woman', is also constructed *through* these cultural distinctions. Thus the 'feminisation' of 'mass' cultural forms (the romance novel, the woman's magazine), in opposition to 'authored' writing, does not simply reflect gendered social divisions. It also helps *construct* notions of 'the feminine' which align it with commodification, standardisation and passivity, and which maintain it within the sphere of the private, understood as subordinate, emotional and domestic.

That this division is intensified in discussions of twentieth-century *mass* culture, or mass media, is hardly surprising. It is not simply that mass media abound with 'women's genres'; 'mass culture' is itself seen as feminine. As Andreas Huyssen has pointed out, in thus gendering 'mass culture', male critics have positioned it as both seductive lure and as threat – the threat of 'losing oneself in dreams and delusions and of merely consuming rather than producing' (1986a: 55) Behind this threat, however, lies a more fundamental fear, the fear of woman. Here 'woman' is seen as that which is undifferentiated, unbounded and sexualised, and which threatens man's autonomy and individuality. This view has been identified by feminist philosophers and cultural theorists from Simone de Beauvoir onwards as underpinning the traditions of Western philosophy (see, for example, Grimshaw 1986; Griffiths and Whitford 1988; Whitford 1991; Battersby 1998). As both Huyssen and Tania Modleski (1986) have pointed out, it has also characterised twentieth-century descriptions of 'mass culture'. From F. R. Leavis to Jean Baudrillard, the metaphor employed has been one of seduction, the corresponding fear that of surrender to the 'spreading ooze' (Dwight Macdonald 1957), the 'irresponsible flow' (Raymond Williams 1990) which threatens to engulf: the flow of mass culture.

In such writings, an attempt is often made to distinguish a masculine difference, characterised by distance, authorship, individuality and public responsibility, from this more generalised flow. Thus 1970s 'auteurist' film criticism celebrated directors such as Douglas Sirk for the ways in which they brought an ironic and critical distance to the undifferentiated material of the 'woman's film' with which they worked (Gledhill 1987a: 7). In a similar way, writers on television have sought to distinguish 'quality' or 'serious' programmes from the 'ceaseless flux' (Potter 1984: 30) seen to characterise television in general. For John Caughie, for example, television is a feminised medium, its endless flow in essence maternal, its pleasures those of the 'ornamental, the everyday and the feminine' (2000: 215). In contrast, however, *serious* programming invites a different engagement, one that is both detached and critical.

In these accounts, serious, individualised programmes invite the attention of critically engaged but detached viewers. The 'irresponsible flow' of the merely popular, with its 'dreams and delusions', however, invites merely passive consumption. The set of identifications established here – serious/differentiated/critical/masculine versus trivial/undifferentiated/consuming/feminine – makes it particularly difficult for feminist writers to establish their own positions as critical subjects. To write *as a woman* is to run the constant risk of re-absorption into the 'ceaseless flux' that is both femininity and mass culture. To write as a critical subject implies distance from both. To insist on writing as both woman *and* feminist subject is to challenge the assumptions about subjectivity, identity and culture that underpin the history of cultural criticism.

A similar point is made by Susan Bordo, who quotes a comment made by Edward Said in 1991 about recent developments in cultural theory and criticism. 'There are certainly new critical trends', writes Said:

> We *do* know more about the way cultures operate thanks to Raymond Williams, Roland Barthes, Michel Foucault, and Stuart Hall; we know about how to examine a text in ways that Jacques Derrida, Hayden White, Fredric Jameson, and Stanley Fish have significantly expanded and altered; and thanks to feminists like Elaine Showalter, Germaine Greer, Helene Cixous, Sandra Gilbert, Susan Gubar, and Gayatri Spivak it is impossible to avoid or ignore the gender issues in the production and interpretation of art. (Said, *Musical Elaborations*, quoted in Bordo 1997: 193)

As Bordo notes, women are completely absent from the lists of cultural and textual theorists (that is, theorists of culture and texts *as a whole*), but are confined instead to the realms of 'women and . . .'. But we can also note the distinction drawn between the projects of the two groups: men stand outside their fields of study, concerned with expanding and altering public knowledge; women are entangled in theirs, fully identified with the (inevitably partial) 'issues' they raise.

It is in this light, I think, that we must read John Corner's account of the 'two rather distinct kinds of project' which he sees as characterising the field of media studies: the '*public knowledge* project' focusing on 'the politics of information and the viewer as citizen', and the '*popular culture* project', concerned with entertainment, 'the social problematics of "taste" and of pleasure' (1991: 268). It is not simply, as Liesbet van Zoonen writes, that feminist work has been 'seriously underrepresented' in the first of these projects (1994: 9). 'Low culture', the province of 'entertainment' and 'pleasure', comes, as a project, already saturated with the feminine; 'public knowledge', 'information', what John Caughie calls 'ethical seriousness' remain the province of masculinity. As Susan Bordo concludes, such frameworks constitute 'not merely an annoying bit of residual sexism but a powerful conceptual map that keeps feminist scholarship, no matter how broad its concerns, located in the region of what Simone de Beauvoir called the "Other"' (Bordo 1997: 194).

After 1990: post-feminism and its others

In a recent article, Angela McRobbie suggests that the year 1990 marks an important shift in the theoretical trajectories I have outlined above (McRobbie 2004: 256). As an example of this shift, she cites Andrea Stuart's article, 'Feminism: Dead or Alive?', in which Stuart distinguishes between what she calls 'professional Feminism' and a new 'popular feminism', its 'errant' but more attractive daughter. Whilst the former has retreated to the academy, she writes, the new popular feminism 'comes at most of us through the media': in soap operas, TV drama, advertisements, women's magazines and popular fiction (Stuart 1990: 30). It is a feminism grounded in consumption as play, it is 'knowing and ironic', and it celebrates individuality not collective action, pleasure not politics. Since 1990 terminology has changed, with 'popular feminism' becoming 'power feminism'[11] and then 'post-feminism', but Stuart's article does mark two important and interrelated shifts: a shift within popular media representations, and a shift in theoretical positionings.

Within popular media representations, there are a number of changes in the relationship 'woman and media' which we can chart. 'Women's genres' are no longer so clearly marked. The revaluation of soap opera noted by Dorothy Hobson, in which its (still male) producers now see it as 'television that speaks your language', 'a showcase', even the contemporary 'replacement . . . for *Play for Today*' (from interviews in Hobson 2003: 41, 50, 51), has been accompanied by an increasing space given to men within the genre. Hybrid dramas have appeared which cross generic boundaries – between soap opera and police or medical series, for example. Their elision of a further set of boundaries, those between public and private spheres (the worlds of work/action and home/ emotion), is repeated even more strikingly in the emergence of the 'docu-soap' and 'reality TV' forms. Here, the emphasis on public responsibility and critical distance, on knowledge, evidence and fact, which has marked the value claims of documentary (see Nichols 1991 and 1994), has been replaced by surface, spectacle and intimacy. Intimate relations, as Lois McNay has remarked, are no longer confined to a feminised domestic space, but played out in public arenas previously associated with impersonal debate and social action – as the new centrality of the intimacy-based talk show also demonstrates. What this means for the relationship 'women and media' is, however, a contested issue. On the one hand, this collapse of boundaries between a feminised private and a masculinised public sphere can be seen as potentially liberatory for women. On the other, the depoliticisation of both, which characterises these programmes, and the replacement of politics with what McNay calls a 'fetishization of the self' (2000: 71), suggest a reassertion of the idea that mass culture operates as the realm of the degraded feminine.

A similar ambivalence marks the emergence of the 'post-feminist heroine' in advertising and popular drama. Both Susan Bordo and Angela McRobbie have commented on what McRobbie calls the 'work of undoing feminism' (2004: 258) in contemporary advertising. From the knowing and self-conscious sexism of the 1990s Wonderbra ads or the Citroen TV ad featuring a naked Claudia Schiffer, all of which invite ironic amusement, to the 'Because you're/I'm worth it' L'Oréal slogan, we are offered what McRobbie calls a new 'female individualism' which invokes, only to dismiss, an 'old' feminism. A similar phenomenon can be seen within popular television drama, with the emergence of a range of popular US series like *Buffy the Vampire Slayer* (1997–2003), *Ally McBeal* (1997–2002), and *Sex and the City* (1998- 2004), all generic hybrids, all aimed primarily at a female audience, and all featuring young, independent, usually single women in an urban environment. Such series engage repeatedly with feminist issues, but in an ironic, playful, style-conscious and ambivalent way. Feminism itself is seen to belong to the past; what characterises the post-feminist woman of popular culture is individualism, sophistication and choice.

What is being invoked in these popular fictions is, however, a very different image of the 'ordinary woman' from that described by Charlotte Brunsdon as the 'other' of post–1970s feminism. Indeed, we can argue that the relationship between the two has in some ways been reversed. It is no longer the case that the 'ordinary woman', the woman who un-self-consciously *enjoys* popular cultural forms aimed at women, stands as a rather uncomfortable shadow figure to the feminist subject, a figure she both incorporates and rejects. Rather, it is now feminism which is simultaneously acknowledged and rejected, a shadow figure for the post-traditionalist, post-feminist 'ordinary woman' whom Stuart invokes (1990: 29). The feminist, as Stuart writes, is now within the academy; she is white, middle-class, and probably – despite her own sense of margin-alisation and the erosion of her discipline, Women's Studies – by now a professor. The post-feminist heroine of the new women's genres, on the other hand, offers a new point of identification: a post-conventional subject position, characterised by freedom and choice.

Stuart's article makes it clear that this figure is a heroine not only within popular culture. She also offers a powerful identificatory position for the 'post-feminist' critic and theorist. As the category 'woman' has seemed to dissolve, with the recognition that 'women' occupy subject-positions marked as much by 'race', class, sexual preference, and cultural location, as by being assigned to the category 'female', so the position of 'post-feminist' – with its paradoxical promise of closing the gap between 'feminist subject' and 'ordinary woman' – has become increasingly attractive. Ann Brooks offers a definition of just such a conception of 'post-feminism'. It represents, she writes, 'the intersection of feminism with postmodernism, post-structuralism and post-colonialism'. Both a continuation and a critique of second-wave feminism, it can, unlike its predecessor, address 'the demands of marginalized, diasporic and colonized cultures' (Brooks 1997: 4). Such definitions are, however, highly problematic. In them, 'post-feminism' becomes a conflation of 'post-modernism' and/or 'post-colonialism' and feminism, appropriating under its banner the voices of writers whose own self-identification would be as feminist. Yet in neither post-modernism nor post-colonialism does the prefix mark a simple chronology; both also signal relations of opposition, of what McRobbie calls 'undoing'. Whereas the post-colonial feminist remains a feminist, in the conflated 'post-feminism' presented by Brooks, such an identity is no longer on offer. Feminism is returned to what Bordo calls the region of the 'Other'.

'Post-feminist' critics, then, look to shifts in media forms, representations and technologies for evidence of a contemporary cultural shift towards a greater fluidity in gender relations and identities, and the renegotiation by women of 'feminism and its goals in the contemporary era' (Lotz 2001: 117). Yet the instabilities in gender representation which they identify do not necessarily signify a shift in private or public relations of power, particularly for those women (older women, working-class women, young black and Asian women) who do not feature readily as 'post-feminist' heroines. Nor, despite their promises to extend choice into the realms of the post-gendered (dis)embodiment of cyber-space, do new media technologies necessarily create 'spaces for women to play with, create, subvert and renegotiate subjectivities and identities' (Kennedy 2000: 285). With feminism no longer seen as a position from which to speak, and 'woman' no more than a 'fluctuating identity' (Riley 1988: 1), the discourse of 'post-feminism', despite the rhetoric of choice which accompanies it, may in fact function as another form of regulation and silencing. Angela McRobbie has commented on the 'regulative functions' of these 'popular discourses of choice and self-improvement'. To celebrate the promise of choice and freedom that they present may, she writes, be to miss the 'modality of constraint' within which they operate (2004: 261).

Beyond Post-feminism?

If the theoretical claims of post-feminism seem an inadequate foundation on which to build an analysis of the contemporary relationship between women, feminism and media, what more satisfactory models might be at hand? In this final section, I want to point to some of the work within feminist theory that I think can suggest more productive models for understanding what remains a complex, interwoven and often ambiguous relationship.

Writing, like Andrea Stuart, in 1990, Teresa de Lauretis states, in sharp contrast to Stuart's emphasis on a new playful and ironic popular feminism, 'I know that learning to be a feminist has grounded, or embodied, all of my learning and so en-gendered thinking and knowing itself' (1990: 263). I would wish to draw attention to a number of themes here, which contrast with the arguments of 'post-feminism' outlined above. One is her emphasis on 'embodiment': her knowledge, she writes, is 'embodied, situated' (ibid.). This emphasis on the embodied nature of what Rosi Braidotti calls 'being-a-woman' is one shared by a number of recent theorists. Sexual difference, they argue, is an embodied, and therefore a foundational difference. Being a woman means, argues Christine Battersby, a 'shared positioning vis-à-vis the founding . . . categories that inform our notions of individuality, self and "person-hood"'(1998: 16). It means living in, and with, unequal relations of power which are at once material and social, and symbolic – a matter of language and representation. As Braidotti writes, '"I, woman" am affected directly and in my everyday life by what has been made of the subject of "*Woman*"; I have paid in my very body for all the metaphors and images that our culture has deemed fit to produce of "*Woman*"' (1994: 187).

The recognition of shared embodiment as a foundational difference does not imply, however, a common identity – women's identities are marked by many other subject positions beyond that of gender – or an unchanging one. De Lauretis writes above of 'learning to be' a feminist: identity, she continues, is 'an active construction and a discursively mediated political interpretation of one's history' (1990: 263). Our identities are formed and re-formed through experience, relationships, society, culture, history and language. Our sense of self is not illusory, but neither is it unchanging: it is a matter of constant (re)interpretation, of what de Lauretis calls 'an active construction': an interpretation of ourselves in time. That de Lauretis also calls this interpretation 'political' draws attention to two more aspects of her account. One is its emphasis on agency: we may be produced within and by structures of material, social and symbolic power, but the self thus generated is also capable of agency, and agency, as Judith Butler has remarked, always 'exceeds the power by which it is enabled' (1997a: 15). This is a self which, whilst never completely free or autonomous, and never outside the structures of history and power, can nevertheless make its own meanings.

The final aspect of de Lauretis' account which I want to suggest as important is its focus on narrative. The 'interpretations of [our] history' which constitute our identities are the stories we tell of ourselves: in telling them – to others and to ourselves – we produce our sense of self. This emphasis on narrative as constitutive of identity is explored further by Italian feminist philosopher Adriana Cavarero. Cavarero's concern, like that of many of the other writers referred to above, is with the relationship of the symbolic structures – the names, the terms – which define us (that which she calls the *what* of our identities) to what she calls the *who* of our existence. *What* we are, she says, can be defined by others; it 'changes and is inevitably multiple and may be judged or reinterpreted in many ways' (2000: 73). *Who* we are, on the other hand, is an 'embodied [and therefore sexed] uniqueness' that unfolds not in history or philosophy – which define what we have in common – but in narrative. The narratives of our lives do not reveal unitary and coherent identities, and their very uniqueness is constituted out of the ways in which they are interwoven with others, but we all have what she calls 'narratable selves'.

Narrative, however, is not only internally generated. The public narratives of history and culture – endlessly circulated in media forms – offer frameworks for our self-understanding, frameworks which are externally generated but in which we may have powerful internal investments. Writing of the provisionality of his own sense of identity, Stuart Hall comments:

> Who I am – the 'real' me – was formed in relation to a whole set of other narratives. I was aware of the fact that identity is an invention from the very beginning, long before I understood any of this theoretically. Identity is formed at the unstable point where the 'unspeakable' stories of subjectivity meet the narratives of history, of a culture. (1987: 44)

The 'unspeakable' narratives of which Hall writes here, the narratives of the unconscious which are expressed, if at all, in fantasy, may find outlet through our investments in more public narratives – for example, conventional stories of femininity or masculinity – which serve to both stabilise and constrain our self-understandings. But they may equally generate a sense of unease, displacement, difference when confronted by public narratives which do not quite fit. They may produce, indeed, what Cavarero calls the 'feminist impulse to self-narration' (2000: 61) that has generated the 'active constructions' and 'political interpretations' of which de Lauretis writes.

How, then, might we apply these models to our understandings of the relationship between 'women and media'? Regarding gender as an embodied and foundational, but far from immutable, identity category allows us to examine both differences and commonalities in the experience of 'being-a-woman' which will inflect our social and cultural understandings. Seeing these identities as grounded in material and social structures which are persistent, reiterated, and lived out in the everyday (McNay 2000), gives us a framework for understanding research on women within media structures and as media audiences, accounting for the persistence of gendered understandings and pleasures, as well as their shifts and contradictions. At the same time, the emphasis on narrative as important both in our own self-constructions as coherent identities and as the 'narratives of history, of a culture' which we must all confront, allows us to see how our material existences (our lives-as-lived) connect to public forms of representation (media texts, images, structures) in ways that do not reduce one to the product of the other. Finally, the continued emphasis by these theorists on feminism as an authorising strategy which produces and empowers the subject position 'feminist' is important for two reasons. First, it counters those recent 'meta-narratives' that, in asserting a transformation in the social order which heralds a new flexibility in gender identities, would render feminism redundant and a feminist speaking position impossible. Second, in insisting on speaking as a 'female feminist subject', from a subject position grounded in 'the politics of ontological difference' (Braidotti 1994), such writers provide a powerful counter to the fantasies of 'post-feminist' choice and freedom or post-gender disembodiment which have characterised some recent writing on 'women and media'.

Women/media/feminism

In the chapters that follow, I trace the issues, questions and debates outlined above through four key topic areas. In Chapter 2, 'Fixing into Images', I return to one of the first preoccupations of feminist media analysis: the relationship between women and images. If we are really to understand how media images of women *work*, I argue, we must both understand the theoretical 'slipperiness' of the term 'image' itself, and pay precise attention to the *ways* in which women are imaged, to the texts in which these images appear, and to the ways in which readers/spectators are invited to, and do actually engage with them. Focusing first on the work that has been done in analysing images of women within painting, photography, advertising and 'post-representational' media images, I turn then to examine the kinds of questions about the nature and power of the image which such studies pose, and the theoretical issues they raise.

In Chapter 3, 'Narrating Femininity', I turn to the narratives of femininity produced within cultural texts, and the ways in which these are bound up with, and in some ways construct, our sense of ourselves as women: that is, as individuals whose embodied, subjective and social experience is fundamentally gendered. If, as a number of theorists have argued, it is through such narratives that our identities are formed and re-formed, then a further question for feminism concerns the space which might be found within these narratives 'rarely of our own making' for *agency*: that is, for a movement towards change or transformation. In this chapter I explore some of these feminist analyses, the theoretical frameworks on which they draw, and the difficulties they find in exploring possibilities for change. I then go on to examine more broadly theories of narrative and identity which suggest some of the reasons for, and possible responses to, these difficulties.

If one of the central concerns of early second-wave feminism was with the *mis*representation of women in the fantasy images circulated by the media, a second concern was with the way in which real women were actually represented – or more accurately, *not* represented. In research studies spanning the past thirty years, the over-visibility of women as sexualised *spectacle* has been contrasted with their virtual omission from those genres seen as having a privileged relation to the real world: news, documentary and 'current affairs'. Chapter 4, 'Real Women' examines the issues around the absence of women from those genres which make claims to address the viewer/reader as citizen, part of an interpretive community concerned to gain and share knowledge about the real, historical world, knowledge which will lead to action *in* the world. Secondly, it looks at those 'real women' who now increasingly *do* populate television and women's magazines, but within 'reality' genres very far from the 'sobriety' of journalism, television news and documentary. These are genres which specifically address, and construct, a 'woman's world' whose 'everyday reality' is that of the familial and emotional, not that of civic responsibility and social action.

Chapter 5, 'Technologies of Difference', examines the relationship between feminism, women and new media technologies. It considers claims that new technologies have profoundly changed not only gendered identities but embodiment itself, and the counter-argument that they represent instead a continuation of existing power relations and the re-articulation of pre-existing cultural narratives. The chapter traces a number of central, overlapping narratives in accounts of new media technologies, arguing that each of these narratives is organised around a key image, an image which in each case carries gendered connotations. Precisely because of these connotations, these images – of the network, the screen, and the cyborg – in turn become contested sites: at once sites for the repression of sexual difference and opportunities for its reassertion by feminist critics. In this way, the organising concepts of the first three chapters, the image, narrative, and the real, return to structure this account of the media as technologies of difference.

Notes

1. Kaplan herself is of course very aware of these issues and discusses them in later works. In particular, *Looking for the Other: Feminism, Film and the Imperial Gaze* (1997) picks up many of the issues, particularly that of the exclusions performed by white, Western feminism in its assumption that it could speak for all women.
2. This group was in turn responsible for the first academic work in Britain on soap opera. See Brunsdon 2000: 101–05.
3. The Women's Studies Group at Birmingham University's Centre for Contemporary Cultural Studies was a politically motivated postgraduate study group. See its *Women Take Issue* (1978) and Brunsdon 1996 and 2000. The London Women and Film Group was composed of women in white-collar and educational jobs, though many of its members were later to enter academic careers. See Brunsdon 2000.
4. See Claire Johnston 1973; and Sharon Smith 1972.
5. See Treichler and Wartella 1986; Long 1989; and Rakow 1989.
6. See, for example, Riley 1992; and Delmar 1986.
7. See Mitchell 1971 for this contemporary assessment of Friedan's influence.
8. Chiefly the sub-genre of the crime series, from *Cagney and Lacey* to *Prime Suspect* and *Silent Witness*, which offers representations of strong, active and powerful women as potential role models.
9. Dorothy Hobson quotes a Radio 1 executive who refers to the 'dreaded housewife figure' whom he envisages as his audience (Hobson 1980: 105).
10. See Hall 1973 and 1980; Morley 1980; and van Zoonen 1994.
11. In *Fire with Fire* (1993), Naomi Wolf offers the slogan of a Nike ad, 'Just do it', as her symbol for this new 'power feminism'.

2 Fixing into images

In proportion to women's exclusion from cultural participation, their image has been exploited. (Mulvey 1979: 179)

[A]ll . . . visions of woman are contaminated by male-defined notions of the truth of femininity. This is true not only of the negative cultural images of women (prostitute, demon, medusa, bluestocking, vagina dentata) but also of positive ones (woman as nature, woman as nurturing mother, or innocent virgin, or heroic amazon . . .). Woman is always a metaphor, dense with sedimented meanings. (Felski 2000: 182)

On this side of the screen of their projections . . . I can't live. I'm stuck, paralyzed by all those images, words, fantasies. *Frozen*. (Irigaray 1985: 17)

'Images of women'

Images have been a central concern of feminist media criticism since the 1960s, when Betty Friedan's *The Feminine Mystique* (1965) traced the post-war construction of America's ideal image of femininity (what Friedan called the 'happy housewife heroine') through media representations she found in women's magazines and advertising images. Studies in the 1970s mapped the 'sex-role stereotyping' within media images (Busby 1975; Janus 1977; Friedman 1977; Tuchman 1978a), the journal *Women and Film*, launched in 1972, saw its task as that of 'taking up the struggle with women's image in film' (1972: 5), and advertising images were an early target of both feminist criticism and feminist activism (Thornham 2001).

The concern in most of this work was with media images as distortions: inaccurate stereotypes that damage women's self-perceptions and limit their social roles. As a 1979 UNESCO report put it:

to the extent that television programming provides information about and mirrors real life sex roles, its depiction of women is inaccurate and distorted . . . Entertainment programmes in all types of format emphasize the dual image of woman as decorative object and as the home and marriage-oriented passive person, secondary to and dependent on men for financial, emotional and physical support. (UNESCO 1979: 26–7)

This approach has proved remarkably resilient. At the UN's Fourth World Conference on Women, held in Beijing in September 1995, we find the Beijing Platform for Action on Women and the Media formulating its strategic objectives in terms identical to those of thirty years earlier. 'The continued projection of negative and degrading images of women in media communications – electronic, print, visual and audio – must be changed', it argues. 'Print and electronic media in most countries do not provide a balanced picture of women's diverse lives and contributions to society in a changing world. In addition, violent and degrading or pornographic media products are also negatively affecting women and their participation in society.'[1]

Yet, as critics since the 1970s have pointed out, such statements lack explanatory power, whatever their political force. The studies underpinning them have been limited by their reliance on the quantitative survey methods of mainstream American mass communication research. Two methods in particular have dominated such research, especially in its early years: 'content analysis' and 'effects studies'. The first of these examines the frequency of specific categories of words and images within media texts, and it has tended, after what Jaddou and Williams (1981: 106) call 'a long and tedious process of statistical compilation', to conclude merely by confirming that women are represented in a limited and stereotypical range of roles (see, for example, Steenland 1995). The second, which seeks to trace direct behavioural or attitudinal outcomes from exposure to specific media images, has produced equally limited conclusions. One 1979 study concluded, for example, that children exposed to such stereotypes tend to have a more restricted view of appropriate sex roles than those exposed to counter-stereotypical representations (Tuchman 1979: 539). Both assume a straightforward 'solution' to the problem they identify. We need, says the Beijing declaration, to 'eliminate . . . gender-based stereotyping'. To achieve this, we need more women in positions of power in media organisations, since, as the UNESCO authors argue, the 'images of women in the media which have been documented . . . are productions of the people within the media organisations who conceive, create, produce and approve them' (UNESCO 1979: 49). Both of these goals are seen to be achievable within existing social and cultural frameworks; indeed, as Gaye Tuchman argued in 1978, they are *necessary* if national or global economies are to continue growing. Such stereotypical images, she concludes, are 'an anachronism we can ill afford' (Tuchman 1978b: 38).

In a 1979 article Tuchman herself produced a powerful critique of such 'Images of Women' research. 'Perhaps because the media associated with the "mass" were insistently differentiated from high culture and intellectual substance', she writes, researchers had approached their study not from the theoretical perspectives to be found elsewhere[2] but as 'scientists'. Simultaneously, they had 'hired themselves out as media consultants'. Armed with 'the sophisticated techniques of modern social science', they had carried out empirical studies for 'both Madison Avenue and the media conglomerates'. It was not surprising, she concludes, that research on women and the media – including her own – had become 'theoretically stalled', bound within the functionalist perspective that underlay its research methods (1979: 528). Intent on finding 'practical answers to seemingly practical questions' (1979: 528–9), it had been 'naive' in its conclusions. These she summarised as:

1. Few women hold positions of power in media organizations, and so:
2. The content of the media distorts women's status in the social world. The media do not present women who are viable role models, and therefore:
3. The media's deleterious role models, when internalized, prevent and impede female accomplishments. They also encourage both women and men to define women in terms of men (as sex objects) or in the context of the family (as wives and mothers). (1979: 531)

Such arguments, she suggests, offer neither analytic purchase nor radical critique. If we are really to understand how media images of women operate, we must have a more theoretically informed understanding of the work that images do, of their functioning within media texts and social discourses, of their relationship to 'ways of seeing the world' and of seeing ourselves, to power, and to what she calls 'the unconscious passions'. Since it seems so bound up with the notion that the media do or should 'reflect' or 'mirror' the 'real world', we might be better, Tuchman concludes, to discard the concept of 'image' altogether (1979: 541).

Thinking about images

Like other such 'slippery' terms, 'image' is not so easily discarded.[3] A 2006 internet search under the heading 'Images of Women' yields over 69 million results, but the meaning of the term across these results varies hugely. Some sites, such as 'About-Face',[4] carry on the tradition of protest against 'negative and distorted images of women' begun in the 1970s, producing posters that aim to 'get people thinking more critically about the images and messages our culture produces for and about women'. The most common reference under the heading 'Images of Women' – apart from the large number of sites advertising 'erotica' or 'free porn' – is to advertising and other 'media images'. But the results also produce references to painting ('Images of Women in Ancient Art'; 'Goya's Images of Women'), photography ('Creative Images of Women', 'The Portrayal of Women in Photography'), popular music ('Images of Women in Hip-Hop', 'Images of Women in Folk Music'), history ('Images of Women in the Past'), psychology (both 'The Psychology of Images' and 'Images of Women in Male Psychology'), medicine ('Medical Images of Women'), theology ('Images of Women in the Bible', 'Images of Woman in the Jewish and Christian Traditions'), and, most frequently ·of all, literature. Indeed, 'Images of Women in Literature' itself yields over 25 million search results.

What, then, are we to make of this slipperiness, in which 'image' can mean a literary trope (a 'mental representation', 'figure of speech' or metaphor) or a visual picture, and can be found in folklore, fiction and literature; in music, history, religion or medicine; in a painting or photograph, a star portrait, advertising or cinema representation; or in the form of the circulating commodities of mass culture? To what extent do later uses of the term incorporate the meanings of earlier ones, and do contemporary visual senses of the term incorporate the meanings of more literary or religious uses? And if they do, can such incorporations bring us closer to understanding what Annette Kuhn has called 'The Power of the Image' (1985a)? When Mary Jacobus, writing about literature, discusses the way in which 'woman or womanhood' is both 'image' and '*sign*', the silent and subordinate object that is both foundation of, and other to, masculine discourse and the male subject, and so 'becomes the site of both contradiction and repression' (1979: 13), her analysis has a cultural reach beyond that of the novels are her immediate concern. It looks, indeed, rather like the kind of analysis for which Gaye Tuchman was calling. On the other hand, when critical theorists seek to explain the workings of literary codes through the analysis of visual advertising images on the assumption that '[l]iterary realism works in much the same way' (Belsey 1980), we have to be concerned at the loss of attention to the specificity of *form*: to the *ways* in which women are so imaged, to the texts in which these images appear, and to the ways in which readers/ spectators are invited to, and do actually engage with them.[5] This chapter will explore these issues, focusing first on the work that has been done in analysing images of women within painting, photography, advertising and 'post-representational' media images. It will then examine the kinds of questions about the nature and power of the image such studies pose, and the theoretical issues they raise.

Women's images in art

In 1977 Griselda Pollock addressed the question: 'What's Wrong with Images of Women?' Like Gaye Tuchman, Pollock was concerned by the gap between the *political* interest in images of women within the women's movement and the much less developed level of theoretical analysis available to support it. The dominant assumption underpinning writing on 'images of women' is, she writes, that they merely *reflect* meanings that originate elsewhere (in the intentions of media producers, or in social structures). They can therefore be divided into 'bad' (distorted or glamorised) and 'good' images ('"realist" photographs, of women working, housewives, older women, etc'). This idea, she argues, needs to be challenged and replaced by more adequate theoretical models. Images are never direct or unmediated reflections. Her own work within art history seeks to establish such models. In it she pursues what she calls a 'double project'. Since art by women has been excluded from dominant definitions of what constitutes great art, either erased altogether from conventional art history or consigned to a special category of work by 'women artists', such art must be recovered. But this work of historical recovery cannot, she argues, simply construct an alternative and separate canon of 'great works'. What is considered art, what can or can not be represented within it, who can properly produce such representations and will be granted access to the means of production and distribution, who will evaluate them and how: all these are questions decided by the structures of power within a given society. In post-Renaissance art in particular, they have centred around the social and cultural construction of sexual difference, and this, the 'theorization and historical analysis of sexual difference', constitutes the second part of Pollock's project. This construction of sexual difference, argues Pollock, has determined 'both what and how men and women painted', excluding women from the academies which trained great artists whilst rendering them over-present as spectacle. It has also structured – and been structured by – the discourses of art history that have framed and evaluated this work (1988: 55–6). It is a history Rita Felski has summarised as 'a history of men looking at women, of female bodies being objectified, exoticized, and entombed in works of art' (2000: 177). Within it, she writes, women are deemed capable of reproduction and imitation, but they cannot achieve the 'transcendent and universal qualities of great art' (176). Since women are the *material* of art, their own work can only be a form of limited self-expression, an extension of themselves. They are, as Nietzsche proclaimed, incapable of the distance and the 'bold, insurrectionary vision' (ibid.) required of the artist:

> Would any link at all be missing in the chain of art . . . if the works of women were missing? . . . woman attains perfection in everything that is not a work: in letters, in memoirs, even in the most delicate handiwork . . . precisely because in these things she perfects herself, because she here obeys the only artistic impulse she has – she wants to *please* . . . (1968: 432–3)

As this quotation indicates, this is a view which received its most powerful expressions with the coming of modernity in the nineteenth century. The modern city brought a separation of the spaces of production – the factories and mills on its outskirts – from the public spaces of spectacle, leisure and consumption which were now at its centre. With this separation came the particular social organisation of the gaze identified with the *flâneur*. The *flâneur* was the ironic, detached observer of the modern city, strolling through its crowded public spaces – in the words of Walter Benjamin, 'botanizing on the asphalt' (Benjamin 1973: 36). Watching and browsing but not interacting, his gaze is the gaze of modernity. It is also the gaze of masculine privilege, since this freedom of access to the city's spaces of visual pleasure – its arcades, exhibitions, galleries, museums and leisure gardens – was a freedom denied to women, who were confined by the doctrine of separate spheres to the domestic. The exception, of course, was the prostitute, and though some critics have sought to see in her the *flâneur's* female equivalent, her position in relation to both city spaces and the gaze was very different. She is a street-walker whose gaze, whatever irony and detachment it might possess, marks her as commodity as well as (worker and) consumer. For Benjamin she functions as an ambiguous *image* of the city, like its arcades. '[S]aleswoman and wares in one', she is an image available to the *flâneur* for his consumption or contemplation; she is not his like (Benjamin 1986: 157).

In Benjamin's analysis the figure of the *flâneur* is embodied above all in the poet Charles Baudelaire, whose own essay 'The Painter of Modern Life' sets out a vision of woman as image very similar to that of Nietzsche quoted above. For the artist, writes Baudelaire, Woman is:

> the object of keenest admiration and curiosity that the picture of life can offer to its contemplator. She is a kind of idol, stupid perhaps, but

dazzling and bewitching . . . Everything that adorns women, everything that serves to show off her beauty, is part of herself . . . No doubt
woman is sometimes a light, a glance, an invitation to happiness,
sometimes just a word. (1995: 30–1)

This image, then, is both visual – a picture – and verbal – a word. The
product of artifice, without substance or identity, it is an image whose
dazzling surface is inseparable from that which adorns it – the two, says
Baudelaire, form 'an indivisible unity' (31). It looks back, but fleetingly,
and with the lowered eyes and half-smile which constitute a teasing
invitation. In the male subject who gazes, it evokes fantasies of sexual
pleasure but also contempt: it is an image of an inferior. It is entirely
constructed by and for that subject.

Pollock traces just these features in her analysis of the paintings of
nineteenth-century artist Dante Gabriel Rossetti. These paintings of
women, she argues, are not portraits, since the portrait 'documents an
individual's presence', and in these paintings all traces of both individuality and presence are obliterated (1988: 122). Instead, what the
paintings organise is a particular visual field, in which woman is
naturalised *as* image, a fetishised object to be looked at, a 'mask of
beauty'. In this process of construction of a gendered field of visual
pleasure, the *work* of construction is effaced. Not only is the category of
woman-as-image naturalised in this way. So, too, is what Celia Lury
calls the 'gendered technique of objectification' (1993: 181): the *ways* in
which this image is constructed for our gaze. This is seen to be quite
simply a matter of *art*, of aesthetics; the regime of sexual difference
constructed in these paintings is offered – and received – as a self-
evident aspect of art, truth and beauty. As Frank Lentricchia has
observed, the 'aesthetic moment' is also the 'manipulative moment',
in which 'the subject-audience is submitted to the productive force of
ideology' (quoted in Nichols 1991: 262).

If these paintings present what Jacqueline Rose calls a 'seamless image'
of perfection (1986: 232), however, we can also note other, more
disturbing aspects to them. First, these 'perfect' images are predicated
on a particular set of effacements or repressions: of those women whom
they *cannot* represent. These images do not represent working-class or
black women, whose bodies, when they appear at all, function to point up
the perfection of white femininity. In other words, these images in their
very blankness and white perfection bear uncomfortable traces – whether
visible or repressed – of those women who cannot be contained within
the category of woman-as-image. They thus always threaten to reveal its
constructedness. Second, that 'seamless image' of perfection, argues

Pollock, itself functions to ward off a fear: the fear of women's otherness. Again, Rossetti's paintings can serve as examples. Fetishised and blank, these images of women represent, she writes, an attempt to stabilise the structures of sexual difference for the benefit of the male viewer. In them the 'troubling act of looking at an image of woman/difference' (Pollock 1988: 128) is neutralised through the painting's organisation of a field of visual pleasure.

This protective fantasy of perfection also acquires another layer of effacement, however. Despite the over-visibility of her body as spectacle and surface, the woman as individual presence is, as we have seen, absent. What is offered instead in this encounter with the work of art is the experience of transcendence: the image, as rendered by the artist, is seen to transcend its historical moment in order to express eternal truths. In this sense we can argue that the woman's body is both all that is offered of her and itself absent, standing in for something else – not something that is in or of *her*, however, but something both in and beyond the artist himself. In this way she is both endlessly looked at and not seen at all. Whilst her image is eroticised and exoticised, the erotic/exotic is simultaneously given the alibi of sublimation – this is not *base* eroticism, but the means of accessing the sublime or transcendent. It is interesting to note that it seems to be those paintings in which the woman's individual presence is not successfully effaced but instead remains to trouble what Pollock calls the 'formalized realm of aesthetic beauty' (1988: 163) that have generated most dispute about their status as art.[6]

'The moment the look predominates, the body loses its materiality,' argues Luce Irigaray (quoted in Pollock 1988: 50). If the dematerialised, fetishised body of woman is seen to give access to a transcendent realm, it also signals the loss of that very materiality. Art thus both enshrines and kills. Stopping time, its realm of perpetual representation is associated not only with transcendence but also with death. This argument was to be used again about photography, as we shall see; here it is important to note the sense of loss which is an integral part of the aestheticisation of woman-as-object which is being described here. For Pollock, the nine-teenth-century paintings which she discusses trace the establishment of the new order of sexuality that appears with modernity. In them woman functions as the sign of 'that Other in whose mirror masculinity must define itself' (1988: 153). But it is a mirror haunted by anxiety: anxieties about absence and loss, about sameness and difference, about desire and death.

It is a mirror which is also constantly displaced. The image of the (white Western) woman captured by her own reflection in the mirror is a familiar one in Western art. It is there in the Rokeby Venus of 1649 by

Figure 2.1 *Rokeby Venus* (1649) by Velasquez

Velasquez (Figure 2.1), as it is in Rossetti's *Lady Lilith* of 1868 (Figure 2.2), which Pollock discusses. As mythical Narcissa, this image sees woman gaze in upon herself, not out beyond the painting. It is a gesture which simultaneously signals her self-absorption and renders her unable to return the spectator's gaze. It also, as we see in the Velasquez painting, serves to fragment her: both her body and her face are visible to and for us, but in dismembered form. If we examine the antecedents of this image, however, not one but two classical myths suggest themselves, and both are present here in curiously distorted form. The first and most obvious is that of Narcissus. According to Rachel Bowlby, it supplies the origins of the word 'image':

> In Ovid's version of the story . . . *imago* is the word used for the beloved reflection . . . Narcissus' tragedy is that he cannot free himself from the image with which he has fallen in love, which he wishes to grasp and possess and know (the Latin *comprendere* includes all three uses), but cannot recognize as being only a derivative reflection of his own body. He is seduced by, and wants to seduce, something which is both the same as and different from himself, something both real and unreal: there to be seen but not tangible as a substantial, other body. (1985: 29–30)

Bowlby's account here is interesting in that, when we apply it to paintings such as the Velasquez *Venus*, it seems to describe, not the

Figure 2.2 *Lady Lilith* (1868) by Rossetti

relationship of Venus to her image – this seems curiously devoid of desire[7] – but the invitation the painting makes to its male spectator. The desire to grasp, possess and know the dematerialised image of a body which is the same and different from himself: this is what the painting invokes.

The second myth, also recorded by Ovid, is that of Medusa. The darker, female equivalent of Narcissus, Medusa was raped by Poseidon and subsequently punished by the goddess Minerva, who transformed her hair into snakes and her beauty into a terrifying mask whose stare had the power to kill or turn to stone. For Freud, the Medusa's head, with its hair of writhing (phallic) snakes, served both as an image of the monstrousness of female genital difference and as its denial (1993: 212). In Ovid's version, Medusa was defeated by Perseus who used his shield as a mirror: as reflection, she could be safely viewed and her mirror-image used to destroy her. Once severed from the body, her head could serve as weapon for Perseus, now worn *on* his mirror-shield.

For Freud, writing at the turn of the twentieth century, the myth of Narcissus provided the outline of one of the stages in the development of human subjectivity, to be moved beyond as the child enters the social or symbolic order. But it is a stage girls, with their lack of access to a position within the symbolic, find more difficult to leave behind – hence their greater narcissism and enclosure within the private sphere. Reading this myth and its horrific female counterpart in the light of the art which drew upon and reinforced its meanings, however, we might draw rather different conclusions. Self-absorbed and often fragmented, these images of women offer to their spectator an idealised beauty, one whose lack of a return gaze guarantees both possession of the image and its function as mirror, reflecting back that sense of the eternal and sublime which confirms his sense of self. At the same time, they bring anxiety. As his sexual other, the imaged woman embodies the threat of sexual difference, a threat both allayed and potentially increased by her self-absorption, which excludes him. Woman is both displayed and fragmented, therefore; her threat, like that of the Medusa, dispersed across the fetishised and aestheticised surface of the image.

Taking photographs

Enjoyment of the nudes is ensured through the erasure of the threatening gaze of the woman, either through a literal beheading, aversion or covering of the eyes, as if she did not know that she was the object of your gaze . . . She is the one to be looked *at* without looking herself. The denial to look is also, by implication the denial of woman's access to the production of knowledge. (McGrath 1987: 34)

In this comment by Roberta McGrath on the photography of Edward Weston, we can see both the continuity in representational mode with the paintings discussed above, and a suggestion of difference. 'At work in all this', continues McGrath, 'is the story of the Medusa'. Weston's camera protects its owner against the threatening gaze of the woman he photographs, not only by denying her return look, but by freezing her in time, thus causing 'a sort of death' (1987: 34). Weston's own writing both confirms and disavows McGrath's analysis. For him, the 'instantaneous recording process' of the photograph sets it apart from the painting; the camera's 'penetrative vision' (1987: 30) gives it access to the 'basic reality' of the photographer's subjects, beyond that which the painter might capture. Interestingly, however, the photograph is also offered as a protection against this reality. Confirming McGrath's view of the fetishistic quality of his photographs, Weston adds that 'the beholder may find the created image more real and comprehensible than the actual object' (Weston 2003: 107).

The debate about photography's relationship with art characterised the beginnings of modernity. For Walter Benjamin, famously, the photograph's reproducibility meant the destruction of the 'aura' of the work of art, so that photography represents 'the first truly revolutionary means of reproduction' (1999: 218). But he also identifies it with commodification. If the early daguerrotypes inspired fear that those photographed could look back at *us*, 'so powerfully was everyone affected by [their] unaccustomed clarity', he writes, later photographs serve the desire for *possession* of the object-image. Nor are they neutral depictions: photography's alliance with advertising and fashion and its use of captions turns it into a meaning system, a kind of 'literature' (Benjamin 1979: 244, 250, 256). At the same time, photography has links with the unconscious, revealing 'aspects of visual worlds which . . . find their hiding place in waking dreams' (1979: 243).

All of these suggestions have been taken up by later commentators. Christian Metz identifies the 'timelessness' and 'immobility' of photography with both death and the unconscious. The photograph captures always the moment which is already past, he writes: the 'person who *has been photographed* . . .' is always dead, abstracted from the flux of life. Frozen in time in this way, the photograph also functions for each of us as both the mirror of our own ageing and its disavowal. The photograph therefore also operates as a fetish. Fixed forever by a single visual *take* but 'always active later', in memory and in the unconscious, it is both the sign of loss and a protection against that loss (Metz 2003: 140–1). Metz's description here suggests that the photograph operates as both Lacanian mirror – in which an idealised mirror image functions as a misrecognised but comforting self-image – and as fetish. The click of the shutter, he writes, 'marks the place of an irreversible absence, a place from which the look has been averted forever' (2003: 143). The photograph is therefore haunted by that which it excludes. Whereas film, he concludes, *plays on* the mechanism of fetishism, in its constant movement between presence and absence, the photograph becomes itself a fetish.

Victor Burgin makes similar connections. 'The signifying system of photography', he writes, 'like that of classical painting, at once depicts a scene *and the gaze of the spectator*, an object and a viewing subject' (original emphasis). As in the painting, the object viewed is organised for our gaze, through framing and point-of-view, 'into a coherence it actually lacks' (2003: 133). That which seems most unproblematically to reflect the real, therefore, is in fact both the product of ideology (the socially constructed 'point-of-view' which organises its gaze) and invested with desire. In the act of looking we are recruited into this point-of-view and this structuring of desire. But, adds Burgin, the photographic image is also the source of anxiety. We can never truly possess the image; as we contemplate it, it 'as it were, avoids our gaze', leaving us anxious and uneasy.

Despite their use of psychoanalytic theory, neither Metz not Burgin explicitly genders the structures of looking which they describe. Nor do they deal with two other aspects of photography suggested earlier in this section: its relationship to 'the production of knowledge' (McGrath 2002), and its status as commodity. Unlike paintings, however, photographs are often accorded the status of document or evidence. They are used in courts and public enquiries, as medical and police records, as well as in the gallery or family album (Lister 2003: 223). And they circulate as the commodities of mass culture: as advertisements, magazine features or pornography. Their status shifts, therefore, according to the social institution and the discourse which 'frames' them and which they in turn authenticate. With this shift comes another shift, too, in the 'relations of looking' which are constructed through them, though these also have a great deal in common, organised as they are according to the structures of power within which they are all positioned.

Roberta McGrath's study of medical archives explores many of these issues. Arguing that 'the modern medical gaze was forged in relation to the woman's body as spectacle, as sexual object' (2002: 1), she traces this through the medical images which have explored women's bodies, displaying their difference for the scientific male gaze. What she uncovers is a gaze which objectifies and classifies but at the same time reveals its fascination with and horror at the body of woman, especially in the 'frighteningly, viscerally visible' images of childbirth in which the woman appears as a headless, anonymous but terrifying torso (2002: 15). Like Pollock, McGrath argues that 'sexual difference . . . lies at the heart of enlightenment thought' (2002: 1). Nature, of course, is gendered feminine, and the triumph over nature which is envisaged in the new discourses of science is represented as a triumph over the feminine. McGrath quotes the first edition of *The Photographic News* of 1858 which pairs science and photography together in the simultaneous investigation, conquest and plundering of nature:

[N]o discovery can compare with this (photography), the last and greatest acquisition that the bold hand of science has snatched from the secrets of nature. And yet new mines of undiscovered wealth invite the enterprising disciples of this, as every other science. The exhaustless stores of nature are unfolded to us only as pressing wants urge on adventurous spirits to ransack her boundless reserves. (quoted in McGrath 2002: 22)

The woman's body, too, was to be subject to this exploration, as medicine's anatomical atlases made visible the invisible, 'discovering new territories, redrawing boundaries and expanding frontiers' (2002: 28). In this process, the woman's body, now pathologised, is dismembered and dissected, rendered transparent and legible.

Commenting on the most recent developments in techniques of medical visualisation, in which the growing foetus can be fully imaged, visually detached from the mother's body which simply encloses it, Rosi Braidotti calls this 'triumph of the image' a form of 'medical pornography'. She is referring to the way in which in these images 'the body becomes a visual surface of changeable parts, offered as exchange objects' (1994: 68). But, as McGrath's historical account makes clear, the boundaries between the medical/scientific and the pornographic have always been blurred. The waxen medical 'venuses' of the seventeenth and eighteenth centuries, with their sexualised pose and naked, skinned bodies, were the antecedents, she writes, of not only the anatomical but also the pornographic model. And in the museums of nineteenth-century London, 'Anatomical Showrooms' operated 'on the edge of what was legal' (McGrath 2002: 20). Later, these showrooms were to be supplemented and then replaced by the photographic studio and gallery and the filmhouse.

In Beatrix Campbell's study of the Cleveland child sexual abuse case, *Unofficial Secrets*, she too raises this question of the ambiguous status of the photographic image. In the cases of child abuse diagnosed by doctors in Cleveland in 1987, the evidence to support the doctors' diagnosis took the form of evidential photographs of the bodies of children. These photographs of sexual anatomies, however, were uncomfortable to view, crossing as they did 'the boundaries between "evidence" and "pornography"' (Campbell 1988: 80). Placed in the position of viewing subject, asked to view these images of 'anuses and vulvas, prone, open, available', yet denied the viewing position they would adopt if these were images of women, the male officers of Cleveland's police force found the position intolerable, and the photographs were destroyed.

These points are taken up by Annette Kuhn, in her essay 'Lawless

Seeing' (1985). Pornographic images, she writes, are like other forms of photography in their project of 'privileging the visible, of equating visibility with truth' (1985b: 40). In the case of pornography, the truth that is sought is the 'truth' of femininity, which it equates with the physical markers of sexual difference. Her account of these images points up their similarities to the medical images analysed by Roberta McGrath. The image, she writes,

> addresses the spectator as desiring – desiring specifically to penetrate this mystery, to come to terms with it, to know it – and says that knowledge is to be secured through looking. If the desire to understand implies that the spectator is in some sense set apart from the object of his look, then the pornographic image constructs the woman's sex as other, as *object* of a masculine gaze . . . (Kuhn 1985b: 40)

Thus, she concludes, the 'subject-object split proposed by positivist science puts in an unexpected appearance in pornography . . . porn places the masculine on the side of the subject, the feminine on the side of the object, of enquiry' (1985b: 40).

In this process, as in the paintings analysed by Griselda Pollock, the masculine position is 'taken for granted as the place from which the spectator looks', and thus reinforced as the position of 'knowledge, pleasure, closure' (Kuhn 1985b: 34). The face of the woman is typically turned away or angled – she does not return the gaze – but her body is open and available. Yet as before, the anonymity of this display is simultaneously a source of anxiety: it remains a display of *difference*, and one whose own desire remains unfathomable. Kuhn suggests two defences which the pornographic image may deploy to counteract this anxiety. The first is the 'come-on' expression often found on the model's face. Here, as in Baudelaire's description of the Parisian *fille publique* quoted above, the offer of pleasure is attributed to the woman herself. In thus seeming to *put herself* on display, her image both disavows the relationship of possession/power which the photograph constructs, and suggests a comforting reciprocity to the spectator's desire. The second, more extreme response which Kuhn discusses is to be found in sado-masochistic pornography. In these images, the relationship between sexuality and power is made explicit – and explicitly pleasurable – so that the threat represented by the 'otherness' of femininity is allayed through a process in which 'investigation [turns] to torture, the final affirmation of the objecthood of the other' (1985b: 46). In the soft-core 'lads' magazines which have become so numerous over the past few years, we might note a third response. In the overcrowded pages of these magazines, as in the tabloid newspaper pages which they imitate, the repetitive anonymity of the poses adopted by the models is simultaneously denied by the accompanying captions. These, we are assured, are indeed 'real girls', the authenticity of their invitational display confirmed by a name and designation ('Law graduate Lucy', 'eighteen year-old Vikki', 'Jamie-Lee from East Sussex'), a history, and an attribution of agency and desire ('I love my body and don't hide it', 'My eyes and my bum are my sexiest features', 'Sex scenes are fine . . .').[8] Photographs, as Kuhn notes, 'are evidence', but a photograph 'can conceal, even as it purports to reveal, what it is evidence of' (1995: 13). Such ambiguity must be denied, again and again, by captions which purport to speak in the voice of the women displayed.

Image as commodity: advertising and women's magazines

As we have seen, the power of photography was from the start bound up with the emergence of mass circulation and the production of the photographic image as commodity. Walter Benjamin associates the two, writing of the 'desire of contemporary masses to bring things "closer" spatially and humanly, which is just as ardent as their bent towards overcoming the uniqueness of every reality by accepting its reproduction'. This desire is characterised, he continues, by 'the urge . . . to get hold of an object at very close range by way of its likeness, its reproduction' (1999: 217). As we saw, however, this 'urge' to possession through commodification is complicated in the case of women by their status *as* image, *as* commodity. Yet, as Rachel Bowlby argues, in the late nineteenth-century Paris of which Benjamin writes, the 'new commerce' which characterised modernity made its appeal above all *to* women,

> urging and inviting them to procure its luxurious benefits and purchase sexually attractive images for themselves. They were to become in a sense like prostitutes in their active, commodified self-display, and also to take on the role almost never theirs in actual prostitution: that of consumer. (1985: 11)

What distinguishes the commodified images of advertising, therefore, is their combination of the simultaneous invitation and display which we saw in painting and pornography, with an appeal to an imagined *female* consumer.

Once again, we can see both continuity with and differences from the images discussed so far in this chapter. We must also note a blurring of boundaries around what constitutes the advertising image. There is a continuity between the shop window, 'the *glass* which reflects an idealized image of the woman . . . who stands before it, in the form of the model she could buy and become' (Bowlby 1985: 32), and the fashion pages of a magazine (both themselves forms of advertising), as there is between the shop window and mirror. There is continuity between all of these and the commodity images which we usually think of as advertising images, whether in magazines, on billboards, or as television or cinema advertisements. What links them all is the triangular positioning of the woman: as seducer/saleswoman, as commodity, and as consumer.

For Griselda Pollock, it is the continuity between the structures of looking constructed in contemporary advertising and those constructed by the Rossetti paintings which she analyses that is the most striking. Like the Rossetti paintings, she writes, these contemporary images are not portraits, but fantasy. As in the paintings, traces of the woman's individual presence have been effaced, so that her image functions as a 'screen across which masculine fantasies of knowledge, power and possession can be enjoyed in a ceaseless play on the visible obviousness of woman and the puzzling enigmas reassuringly disguised behind that mask of beauty' (1988: 123). She is thus at the same time both utterly transparent and eternally mysterious, both reassuring and a source of anxiety. In addition, as John Berger pointed out in 1972, contemporary advertising images reproduce not only the facial and bodily expressions but also the specific poses of the images of women found in Western art (see Figure 2.3). Thus we find as a frequent advertising trope the image of woman with mirror, self-absorbed but available for our gaze. Yet what differentiates the advertising image is the frequency with which this idealised mirrored image is explicitly positioned as the mirror image of the assumed female spectator, and it this aspect of the advertising image which has

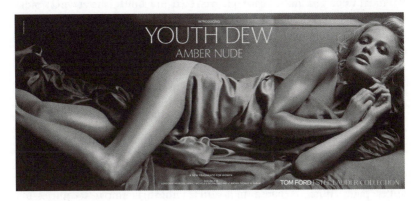

Figure 2.3 Estée Lauder Youth Dew

preoccupied other critics. How, then, should we think of the relationship between this image and its assumed spectator: me?

Perhaps the first point to note is the sheer *familiarity* of this relationship. Women have always been spectators of images of women, however marginalised their gaze.[9] With their entry into the public arena of the shopping arcade and department store, however, their gaze as consumers was actively solicited, with both spectacle and commodities on display for their consumption. Yet, as Bowlby points out, as the public space of the shop window replaced the domestic setting of the mirror for the modern woman, the image reflected back became that of herself as commodity. We are now used to seeing ourselves in this way. Similarly, Janice Winship argues that advertising images are powerful precisely because of their familiarity. We do not, she argues,

> come 'naked' to the ads or to any ideological representation and simply take on those representations. We already have both a knowledge of images of women from other discourses and an acquaintance with 'real' women in our everyday lives. The signification of an ad only has meaning in relation to this 'outside' knowledge of the ideology of femininity. (1980: 218)

The second point we might note is the commonality of mode of address across the different forms of advertising image noted here. It is a mode of address characterised by Hilary Radner as an ' "imaging" [of] the moment of interpellation' within 'a process of scattering' (1995: 131–3). She is referring here to two specific features of organisation. The first, shared by the woman's magazine and the department store or shopping arcade, is its lack of *narrative* structure – its 'process of scattering'. The magazine, writes Radner, 'has numbered pages, hence a certain order, but it is architectured rather than narrativized – a house that readers walk through at will rather than a movie in front of which viewers sit captive' (1995: 133). Its assumed reader, as Bowlby comments, is constructed on the model of a particular kind of shopper: her 'distractable attention, as she flips from one page to another, is of the same type as that of the impulse buyer drifting round the shop' (1987: 190). Yet within this structure, the magazine's fragmented sections each work to produce an intensity of imaging which interpellates the consumer in terms of a series of ideal images: images of 'the woman to whom the readers [are assumed to] aspire' (Radner 1995: 131, parenthesis added). This can take the form of a star feature, an interview with a style/beauty creator, a fashion spread, a make-over feature, a full-page advertisement, or the magazine's cover page. What is common to all of these is the intensity of the relationship with the image which is assumed. It is a relationship, as Mary

Ann Doane has observed, of excessive closeness, but not the closeness identified by Walter Benjamin: that of the desire for possession. Rather, it is a closeness which implies, in Doane's words, 'passivity, overinvolvement and overidentification' (1987: 2). Invited to produce herself in the image of the magazine's 'cover star' or fashion pages through careful application of a range of specified products, the woman who browses through the contents of the magazine (or store) is asked to construct herself as image through the work of consumption. As Radner comments in relation to *Vogue* magazine, 'the issue of display remains a primary imperative, and the ability to function within a regime that privileges display is underlined as crucial to the constitution of the *Vogue* subject – the subject position that it offers its readers' (1995: 137).

If we examine the process outlined above, we might be led to make a third point about the relationship between these images and their assumed spectator. As Janice Winship and John Berger have both pointed out, the structures of possession described by Benjamin are not entirely absent from this relationship. Berger's words are now well known:

> Men look at women. Women watch themselves being looked at. This determines not only most relations between men and women but also the relation of women to themselves. The surveyor of woman in herself is male: the surveyed female. Thus she turns herself into an object – and most particularly an object of vision: a sight. (1972: 47)

As women, adds Winship, our pleasures in cultural forms such as the women's magazine are constructed always within the terms of *masculine* fantasy and desire. Sometimes the advertising image makes this explicit (see Figure 2.4). More often, however, it is implicit. We have only, argues Winship, to look at the magazine's cover image – the coy, smiling, often anonymous female face – to see that 'what appears to be *central* to the magazine and its appeal, the relation of women to women, 'is simultaneously defined in relation to absent men/masculinity'. It is his gaze that is important; this woman, in her perfection, 'is a *man's* woman' (1978: 133–4).

A fourth point to be made, touched on above, concerns the *work* that is involved in this process. An influential early articulation of this argument was Judith Williamson's 1978 *Decoding Advertisements*. Williamson employs semiotics, Althusserian definitions of ideology, and Lacanian psychoanalysis to offer an analysis of how advertisements operate as semiotic and ideological structures. Ideology, she argues, creates subjects, and advertisements work by creating us 'not only as subjects, but as particular kinds of subjects' (1978: 45). They assume 'an "alreadyness" of "facts" about ourselves as individuals: that we are consumers, that we

Figure 2.4 Special K cereal 2003

have certain values, that we will freely buy things, consume, on the basis of those values, and so on' (1978: 42). On the basis of this, they present us with signs (Catherine Deneuve/Chanel No. 5; the VW Polo/the independent woman) between which *we* make the connections, the meanings. We become, then, both the 'space' in which meaning is made and the active makers of that meaning. We 'step into' the subject position offered by the ad:

> You have to exchange yourself with the person 'spoken to', the spectator the ad creates for itself. Every ad necessarily assumes a particular spectator: it projects into the space in front of it an imaginary person composed in terms of the relationship between the elements within the ad. You move into this space as you look at the ad, and in doing so 'become' the spectator . . . (1978: 50–1)

Above all, she argues, the ad offers us, as object of desire, ourselves as coherent and unified subject. It thus acts, like Lacan's mirror-image, as ideal ego, offering to bind our 'fragmented' selves into unity via the product – and Williamson notes the sheer number of magazine advertisements that offer their female spectator an image which is presented precisely as her mirrored self.

A similar argument is made by Jackie Stacey, in her (1994) study of female fans' memories of Hollywood stars in 1940s and 1950s Britain, *Star Gazing*. Stacey's argument begins from the idea of the 'impossibility of femininity' within a culture which defines it as 'an unattainable visual image of desirability' (1994: 65–6). Like other writers, she argues that the 'work of femininity' requires consumption – of both commodities and images – so that women are both subjects and objects of exchange, their sense of identity bound up with a sense of 'woman as image', forever unattainable, always invoking a sense of lack. For Stacey, however, this process involves rather more freedom of movement than has been so far suggested. She argues that this 'work' also involves the 'active negotiation and transformation of identities which are not simply reducible to objectification' (1994: 208). Identities, she argues, are partial, provisional and constantly 'in process', but they are also fixed – however unsuccessfully, temporarily or contradictorily – by particular discourses. The idealised images of Hollywood female stars, like the images found in magazines, function as one such discourse, and her examination of spectators' memories of such stars suggests the way in which this relationship involves a 'complex negotiation of self and other, image and ideal, and subject and object' (1994: 227).

The ambiguity of this process and its power relationships is described by Hilary Radner, who gives less emphasis than Stacey to women's freedom to negotiate within it. 'The woman as subject', Radner writes, 'is invited to take control of the process whereby she represents herself. At the same time, she is constantly reminded that she must submit to a regime that externalizes figurability through product usage.' She is thus split, both actively engaged in the processes of construction and 'complicit in the system of consumerism that constitutes her as a subject' (1995: 178). Anne Cronin's study of magazine advertisements explores these issues further. From her initial analysis of a range of ads from 1987 to 1995, she divided the sample into 'reflexive' and 'unreflexive' ads. The first of these she defines as that growing number of ads which employ ironic or self-conscious forms of address, thus explicitly signalling their constructed nature and the *activity* expected of the 'knowing' reader in producing meaning. The second group assumes 'a static or literal location of meaning generated purely within and through the text' (2000: 57): they offer 'self-actualisation' through identification with an image. Unsurprisingly, the first group she found to be targeted at men, the second group at women. Whilst male viewers are discursively positioned to mobilise a form of play, through ads which draw attention to their own visual codes and extra-textual references (see Figure 2.5), women are typically offered images of 'Woman' as icon: 'repetitive images of conventional, or socially established, images of female beauty, self-control (through diet, exercise, etc.) and self-management (through make-up, clothes, etc.)' (2000: 63). For the male viewers targeted by reflexive ads, she continues, this constitutes a mode of viewing which incorporates irony: a mode

Figure 2.5 Snickers, in *FHM*, April 2006 (SNICKERS is a registered trademark. Masterfoods 2006)

characterised by a movement back and forth between different planes of engagement, and between connection/immersion and distance/detachment. No such mode is offered to female viewers.

Cronin is careful not to equate this gendered difference with the possibility or impossibility of critical distance from the message of the ad. 'Reflexive' ads, she points out, incorporate into their structure strategies 'aimed at eliciting a complicity between the viewer and the advertisement' (2000: 64). Viewers of these ads, that is, are interpellated precisely *as* knowing consumers of popular culture; their possible modes of interpretation are incorporated into the ad's structure, thus reducing the potential for critical distance. Not is it true that there are *no* reflexive ads aimed at women: the 1994 'Hello Boys' Wonderbra ad might be cited as one such example (see Winship 2001), though, as the continuing series of these ads suggests, we might also argue that their target audience is hardly exclusively women. We might also wish to argue that these ads, which knowingly play on stereotypical images of women for ironic effect, nevertheless return us constantly *to* those images as positions that solicit our identification. Nevertheless, Cronin's analysis prompts the question of how, if she is correct, women can find or construct a position of distance which might allow them to negotiate with these images in the way that Jackie Stacey, for example, suggests they do.

For her answer, Cronin draws on the work of film theorists. She points to the argument made by Teresa de Lauretis that 'women are both inside and outside gender, at once within and outside representation' (de Lauretis 1989: 10). We have seen already that women have always been viewers of images of woman, however marginalised their position might have been. We have seen too how the viewing structures constructed within modernity have positioned women simultaneously as consumers of images and as images to be consumed. Yet the two are never the same, as de Lauretis points out: the one is 'women as historical beings, subjects of "real relations" '; the other 'Woman as representation, as the object and the very condition of representation' (ibid.). As historical beings, we cannot be *outside* representation: we are constructed by and in relation to its images and discourses. Language and culture, as Rita Felski writes, 'go all the way down, shaping our most intimate sense of self' (2000: 181). Nor, however, can we be entirely contained by it: those fetishised 'masks of beauty' described by Griselda Pollock, with their obliteration of all traces of individuality and presence, leave us outside as well as shaped in part by them. In the words of B. Ruby Rich, therefore, the woman spectator is an exile, and as such the 'ultimate dialectician', living the tension of these two positions (Citron et al. 1978: 87). Applying this argument to her analysis of advertising images, Cronin takes up de Lauretis' ideas to argue that it is this 'doubled vision' produced by her historical and cultural positioning, not any reflexive structure in the ads themselves, that permits the female spectator a distance from them. Since her image is always standing in for something else – Woman as 'the real', as 'beauty', as 'the eternal' or 'the sublime' – a distance will always be created, however unreflexive the identificatory position she is offered. As a position, the femininity offered by woman-as-image *cannot* be occupied or lived; it can only be worn or performed.

Image as simulation

If we look at some recent advertising images, we can see a further development in this process. These images of women often appear *only* to be masks or mannequins; there seems to be no longer any attempt to reference (or seem to reference) 'the real'. It is a process which resonates with the writings of contemporary 'postmodern' philosophers, in which advertising and 'the feminine' come together in a concept of 'simulation' in which the image is seen to lose all grounding in reality. For Jean Baudrillard in particular, the all-embracing network of simulation which is contemporary Western society means that advertising has absorbed all other cultural forms. Advertising 'is no longer . . . a means of communication or information'; it 'has become its own commodity' (1994: 90). Its images and signs are what is being sold, not the commodities which they are supposed to reference. Its 'saturated and empty form' has thus effaced reality, so that 'advertising is not what brightens or decorates the walls, it is what effaces the walls, effaces the streets, the facades, and all the architecture, effaces any support and any depth'. In Baudrillard's chronology of the image, its four phases take it from having been 'the reflection of a profound reality', through phases in which it 'masks and denatures a profound reality', and then 'masks the *absence* of a basic reality', and finally to the point of having 'no relation to any reality whatsoever: it is its own pure simulacrum' (1994: 6). This 'immense field of the mockery of signs' is then consumed '*for* their mockery and the collective spectacle of their game without stakes' (1994: 91–2).

Baudrillard's account has some similarities with Cronin's analysis of the reflexivity of contemporary advertising, though it is of course much more sweeping in its generalisations. What it also does is identify both the empty simulation and the seductive invitation of this depthless world of images with femininity. In the feminine, writes Baudrillard, 'the very distinction between authenticity and artifice is without foundation', a proposition, he adds, which aligns femininity with simulation. Baudrillard, then, opposes the power of production (masculine) to the power of *seduction* (feminine). Woman 'is but appearance. And it is the feminine as appearance that thwarts masculine depth' (1990: 10–11). Her power comes from 'never having acceded to truth or meaning, and of having remained absolute master of the realm of appearances'. It is the power of seduction, the capacity 'to deny things their truth and turn it into a game, the pure play of appearances' (1990: 8). When the woman looks, her gaze is emptied of meaning: 'Eyes that seduce have no meaning, their meaning being exhausted in the gaze, as a face with makeup is exhausted in its appearance'. Her attraction is the 'attraction of the void': the 'beautiful woman absorbed by the cares that her beauty demands is immediately infectious because, in her narcissistic excess, she is removed from herself, and because all that is removed from the self is plunged into secrecy and absorbs its surroundings' (1990: 76–7).

Two things are apparent here. First, Baudrillard's nostalgia for a lost world in which the image was once 'the reflection of a profound reality' is itself an empty nostalgia. The image, as we have seen, was always metaphoric, always haunted by a sense of loss and by the anxieties provoked by the insufficiency of its relation to 'the real'. The 'fullness' of the image to which Baudrillard harks back in his chronology is the 'fullness' and sufficiency of an imaginary masculinity, reflected back by a 'truthful' image. The second point to make is that Baudrillard's elegiac account has remarkably similar antecedents in the writings of modernity. His view that women's power could never lie in their capacity as subjects, because the feminine can never *be* a subject position, but that it lies instead in the capacity to seduce and thus undo masculinity, echoes the views of Baudelaire and Nietzsche, as does his view that this is a position which is itself devoid of desire. Catherine Constable comments that this

> construction of the seductress as excessive, more false than false, . . . breaks the traditional dichotomy of truth versus falsehood . . . [since] the seductress' foregrounding of her status as illusion can be seen to construct her as a pure play of appearances that is not deceptive, but rather possesses a particular authenticity. (2005: 143)

Yet whether her power is seen to be that of truth or falsehood (or the truth of falsehood), this power attributed to femininity is one which is wholly the construction of masculine fantasy, and one which is very familiar. Baudrillard's 'beautiful woman absorbed by the cares that her beauty demands' rearticulates – and is parasitic on – the image of the woman in front of her mirror familiar from painting, photography and advertising. As in those images, its construction of both her beauty and her self-absorption functions to deny her the status of subject.

Unfixing the image

How, then, might we think about this persistent 'fixing into images' of Woman in a way which does not, as in Baudrillard's account, merely return us to its original terms? One starting point might be to focus on the *power* so consistently attributed to these images, and the fear which accompanies this sense of their power. Ann Kibbey writes of the 'long-held fears of the power of images to overwhelm the viewer, to bypass the conscious mind, to render the viewer helpless and unable to think – even to imagine . . . that the image was somehow alive' (2005: 35), a fear she traces through from the writings of the sixteenth-century iconoclast Jean Calvin to the ideas of Lacan, Barthes and Baudrillard. Victor Burgin, too, writes of our attribution to the image of 'a full identity, a *being*'. It is, he argues, 'a projection, a refusal of an impoverished reality in favour of an imaginary plenitude' (2003: 133). To identify *Woman* so thoroughly with the image, therefore, could be seen to produce the paradoxical effect of endowing her image with this power, a power at once sacred and horrifying. Baudrillard refers to this when he writes of the 'murderous power of images, murderers of the real' (1994: 5). But the image thus animated threatens not only the real which it usurps but also the power of its creator, who becomes vulnerable before his creation. Yet this image also conceals; its very effacement of the individuality and presence of its model makes it unreadable. It is at once, as Anne Cronin suggests, both 'utterly knowable' because repetitively constructed, and simultaneously opaque and mysterious (2000: 86). The 'flattening out' of women's images to produce the pleasures of a constructed visual field, therefore, a process which should act to contain woman's troubling difference, can produce the reverse effect. She remains opaque, mysterious, deceptive; *her* desire, which should be effaced, becomes merely veiled and unreadable (Doane 1991).

If this analysis suggests reasons for the obsessive production and re-production of images of women, and for the simultaneous attraction and fear which they have induced in the male spectator, it does not explain how they function in relation to their female spectators. Anne Cronin's account of how advertising images work to constitute subjects is helpful here. Advertising does not, she argues, work in the way that much writing on 'images of women' suggests, by producing an 'image-pool' from which we draw in constructing and expressing our sense of self. Rather, we are produced *performatively* as subjects in the moment of our engagement with these images, just as we are through the speech acts which authorise us as subjects at the moment we engage in them (Butler 1997b). The act of viewing/interpreting these visual signs, that is, produces not only knowledge and pleasure, but also the sense of ourselves as knowing and desiring subjects. The advertisements in turn, through their textual strategies, authorise certain forms of understanding and pleasure, certain modes of subjecthood. Thus the male-targeted reflexive ads which she describes work to produce not only an authoritative subject (one who 'gets' the joke and can occupy the position of privilege it offers) but also a flexible one (one who can engage in the playful use of signifiers). The 'unreflexive', female-targeted ad, on the other hand, offers a less flexible position, one which seeks to produce its viewing subject within a limited range of subordinate positions.

Yet, as we have seen, women's 'doubled' position as both inside and outside representation works to produce a more complex viewing position than that which the ads apparently offer. For some (more privileged) groups of women, argues Cronin, this 'enables a "trying on" of different femininities and of different modes of performing/ interpreting which access self-consciousness and reflexivity in a way which runs counter to the notion of "literal" advertisements as unre-flexive' (2000: 129). For others, however, these iconic images of female beauty may simply represent an impossible position. As Beverley Skeggs' study of working-class women and femininity suggests, for groups of women like this, such 'trying on' is desperately serious, the product of 'a desire not to be shamed but to be legitimated' (1997: 87). For these women, to 'perform' an ironic or 'excessive' femininity would be to place themselves on the side of the vulgar, the tarty, the pathological and the valueless (1997: 115). Femininity may be a matter of commodification and performance, but for women without access to other modes of self-empowerment – other forms of 'cultural capital' – it also confers legitimacy. Indeed, women's magazines themselves – and increasingly the advertisements within them – often oscillate, as Hilary Radner (1995) points out, between these two positions, so that the images they present are offered simultaneously as the stuff of knowing performance and play, and as an ideal to be approximated through the *work* of self-regulation and self-management.

The work of Michèle le Doeuff, and its application to visual images by Catherine Constable, also suggests a way in which the repetitive images of women described in this chapter can function in a more ambiguous and destabilising way than is often suggested. Le Doeuff's concern is with the way in which images – defined by her in the sense of extended metaphors or linguistic tropes – function within the discourse of philosophy. Philosophy, she argues, secures its status *as* philosophy through 'a break with myth, fable, the poetic, the domain of the image' (2002: 1). As rational, logical thinking, it presents itself as employing images only as illustrations, to make its difficult material more accessible to its less rational audience. What le Doeuff demonstrates, however, is its *dependence* on images; images, that is, perform the work that secures the philosophical argument. In particular, she points to the work that images of woman do in securing the position of the rational male philosopher. Woman is constructed as the 'outside' or 'other' of philosophy, that against which its status is defined, but her image permeates it. Philosophy's 'imaginary portrait of "woman"' is, she writes, that of

> a power of disorder, a being of night, a twilight beauty, a dark continent, a sphinx of dissolution, an abyss of the unintelligible, a voice of underworld gods, an inner enemy who alters and perverts without visible sign of combat, a place where all forms dissolve. (2000: 113)

The portrait is familiar, as its obverse: the passive, virtuous woman who is man's (and the philosopher's) willing subordinate.

For le Doeuff, then, images both sustain and *undo* the philosophical system. They undo it because they reveal its dependence on its opposite: the irrational but culturally sanctioned body of images that circulate between discourses and that it is philosophy's defining task to explain. Catherine Constable extends this argument to take in visual images, pointing out, for example, the dependence of psychoanalytic concepts of female narcissism on the visual images of the self-absorbed woman which we have seen to be so common in Western painting. For Constable, what is important in le Doeuff's formulation is the idea that images *cannot* be fully absorbed by the system that deploys them. They always bear traces of the wider discourses in which they circulate; they are always outside rational argument; they can always be mobilised in other, potentially contradictory ways. Put slightly differently, we might want to argue that images cannot fix desire in the service of the discourse which reproduces and employs them, however much they might seek to do so.

Strategies of contestation?

How, then, to undo the work of 'fixing'? Le Doeuff herself merely comments that 'women (real women) have no reason to be concerned' by the image of the feminine she describes: 'we are constantly being *confronted* with that image, but we do not have to recognize ourselves in it' (2002: 116). Elsewhere, she provides some expansion of this statement. She herself was able to analyse this 'icon of the feminine in philosophical texts', she argues, because 'my personal trajectory has also taken me through places in society where another image of the feminine is proposed for, or imposed upon, women's self-identification', and she reminds us that 'culture is something which circulates *between* different groups, fields, practices and knowledges' (2002: 4). Three possible ideas seem to be suggested by this rather enigmatic group of statements. The first is that in the contradictions between different images of femininity – however constructed and imposed from elsewhere they might be – women can find the space for analysis and understanding, and hence for constructing alternative discourses and self-understandings.

The second idea which is suggested would align le Doeuff more closely with other feminist thinkers. Here, it is not so much the contradiction between different images which creates the space for contestation, but the contradiction between image and women's lived experience. If women, that is, cannot live *outside* the images available for their self-identification, nor do we live entirely inside them. We operate with the 'twofold pull, . . . that division, that doubled vision' of which de Lauretis writes (1989: 10). This enables us to unpick those images, and in the process to reveal the dominant discourse which deploys them to be not a 'pure' knowledge (as philosophy claims) but a partial and 'situated' knowledge (Haraway 1991a), however powerful. Both images and discourse then become available for re-articulation from other, differently situated positions.

A third idea suggested by le Doeuff's statement is that her own freedom to contest philosophy's dominant image of woman comes from her exposure to alternative, perhaps oppositional images. Here her argument might be aligned with that of Griselda Pollock, whose exploration of the work of women artists explores the ways in which they might be seen to shift the image-spectator relationship. This is not a matter simply of arguing that when women are given the power to be producers they will produce 'truer' images of women. Rather, it is to explore the ways in which women, who have always, no less than men, worked from a position within dominant cultural assumptions, have nevertheless found ways to shift the relationship between seeing and power 'so that it ceases to function primarily as the space of sight for a mastering gaze' (1988: 87). It is also to explore the ways in which contemporary feminist artists have sought more consciously to dislocate and disrupt these relationships.

Yet such feminist art, as Pollock says, 'cannot speak to women in easily consumed terms' (1988: 198). And to see analytic practice as itself a form of strategic political intervention (Kuhn 1985a), whilst undoubtedly accurate, is likely to be equally limited in its effectiveness. Such a strategy is in constant danger of setting up an implicit opposition between the (politically aware and oppositional) feminist analyst or artist and the (complicit and duped) ordinary woman. Other strategies also pose problems. Valerie Walkerdine, for example, writing about photographs of herself as a child, speaks of the 'terrible rage' that can lie concealed behind the manifest content which is the surface of the image. She argues for retrieving this rage, because with it comes power and strength, and the exposure of the fear of women which lies behind men's reduction of them to 'a fantasy of what is desired' (1991: 45). But this, like Luce Irigaray's strategy of 'pushing through to the other side' of the 'looking glass' of representation (1985), is not only difficult to envisage; if achieved, it risks leaving women once again positioned on the side of the inarticulate, the irrational, the unintelligible.

Such strategies also risk underestimating what Rita Felski calls the weight of 'sedimented meanings' which give conventional images of women their power. Susan Bordo writes of the 'homogenizing' and 'normalizing' power of such images, arguing for their implication in a whole range of contemporary body practices, from dieting through to cosmetic surgery and eating disorders such as anorexia nervosa. Such practices, through which 'female bodies become docile bodies' in conformity to 'an ever-changing, homogenizing, elusive ideal of femininity', constitute, she writes, 'an amazingly durable and flexible strategy of social control':

> Through the exacting and normalizing disciplines of diet, makeup and dress – central organizing principles of time and space in the day of many women – we are rendered less socially oriented and more centripetally focused on self-modification. Through these disciplines, we continue to memorize on our bodies the feel and conviction of lack, of insufficiency, of never being good enough. At their furthest extremes, the practices of femininity may lead us to utter demoralization, debilitation, and death. (1993: 166)

Looking at these images, then, we might view them in distracted fashion, often in the form of magazines which may be flicked through, their contents fragmented or re-ordered, the images lingered on or passed over. This does not mean, however, that the moment of vision, of exposure to the image, is any the less constitutive of our sense of self. As Anne Cronin argues, the act of vision stretches both forwards and back. Stretching back, it is simultaneously an act of interpretation which draws, however unconsciously, on other images, the images of memory and the Unconscious. If, as Annette Kuhn suggests, the 'language of memory does seem to be above all a language of images', so that it shares with dreams and fantasies the ability to condense and displace our desires and fears into powerful images (1995: 160),[10] then the power of the mass circulation images which offer themselves often precisely as mirrors of our (idealised) selves will lie in their capacity to evoke these other, buried images. Stretching forward, it offers to stabilise momentarily our sense of self through the act of identification, a sense of self which can then be projected forwards into our daily living. At the same time, however, these images are social constructions produced within relations of power. They therefore seek to bind us into specific, socially sanctioned senses of ourselves, not only through the gendered self-images they offer, but also through the *ways* in which they invite us to engage with them. As critics from Pollock to Cronin have argued, whilst male spectators are more often offered a sense of unique, coherent selfhood through mastery over, or ironic play with, that which is imaged, for female spectators the invitation is more likely to be towards an over-involvement with an idealised image-as-object.

Two things, however, seem to me to point effectively to the limitations of this power. The first is the *slipperiness* of the image. Images, as le Doeuff and others have suggested, sustain and 'authenticate' discourses, seeming to ground them in a visible and self-evident truth, as in, for example, the medical images discussed by Roberta McGrath or the construction of the female nude as icon of beauty in Western painting. But they also slip between discourses, the very intensity of our engagement with them serving to dislocate them from their textual positioning. If images seem to 'fix' discourses, then, they can also be dislodged and made to serve the purposes of other, very different narratives. As John Berger argues, 'only that which narrates can make us understand', and images 'in themselves do not narrate' (1991: 55). The second is the incommensurability of Woman and women (de Lauretis). If women, as Rita Felski observes, are constantly being translated into metaphor, then they always in some sense *remain elsewhere*. The notion of femininity as performance, which has been articulated so strongly in feminist thought (Doane 1991; Irigaray 1985; Butler 1990, 1997a), must, as Beverley Skeggs (1997) reminds us, be approached with caution as a possible tool of resistance: performative play with images of femininity is a strategy only for the privileged. Nevertheless, the persistent sense of disjunction which women experience in relation to Woman-as-image creates the possibility of a 'space between'. In some instances this may be productive only of a sense of unease – an unease which may, as Bordo suggests, be disabling as well as empowering. In others, however, it may instead produce a distance capable of generating other images, other discourses, other narratives.

Notes

1. See the United Nations, Beijing Declaration and Platform for Action at www.un.org/womenwatch/daw/beijing/official.htm
2. Tuchman cites examples from anthropology, sociology, historical studies and cultural theory.

3. See, for example, John Corner (1992) on uses of the term 'realism'.
4. See www.about-face.org/
5. Addressing the issue of the 'sheer diversity' of the list of things which can be called 'images', W. J. T. Mitchell (1986: 10) constructs a 'family tree' of these uses, in which each subset corresponds to its use in a particular academic discipline:

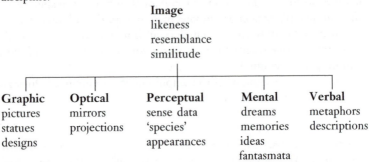

Image
likeness
resemblance
similitude

Graphic	**Optical**	**Perceptual**	**Mental**	**Verbal**
pictures	mirrors	sense data	dreams	metaphors
statues	projections	'species'	memories	descriptions
designs		appearances	ideas	
			fantasmata	

6. See the debates about Titian's *Venus of Urbino* (1538) in David Freedberg's *The Power of Images: Studies in the History and Theory of Response* (Chicago: University of Chicago Press: 1989), for example, or those about Manet's *Olympia* (1863).
7. In this context, Patricia Mellencamp (1992: 281) suggests that the 'narcissistic self-other calibration is different for men and women'. In addition to the 'double vision' described by John Berger ('seeing ourselves being seen'), she writes, women are also caught in an 'envious gaze', in which 'I can see myself only comparatively, through you, often another women'. There is thus, in Mellencamp's view, no narcissistic gaze for women which does not 'negatively rebound' to produce anxiety.
8. These are all from *Nuts* magazine of 27 January – 2 Febuary 2006
9. Griselda Pollock discusses the scandal created by the exhibition of Manet's *Olympia* (1863), with its rendering of the nude image-of-woman explicitly as prostitute. She reminds us that one of the reasons for the sense of outrage was the assumed presence of 'bourgeois ladies' at the exhibition, that is, 'in that part of the public realm where ladies do go' (1988: 54)
10. Freud compares dreams to painting in their reliance on images, a reliance which leads to an incapacity to express logical, verbal connections. See *The Interpretation of Dreams* (1976: 422).

3 Narrating femininity

Identity is formed at the unstable point where the 'unspeakable' stories of subjectivity meet the narratives of history, of a culture. (Hall 1987: 44)

[I]t is through narrativity that we come to know, understand, and make sense of the social world . . . [A]ll of us come to be who we are (however ephemeral, multiple and changing) by locating ourselves (usually unconsciously) in social narratives *rarely of our own making.* (Somers and Gibson 1994: 58–9, original emphasis)

A central concern within feminist media studies has been the narratives of femininity produced within cultural texts, and the ways in which these are bound up with, and in some ways construct, our sense of ourselves as women: that is, as individuals whose embodied, subjective and social experience is fundamentally gendered. If, as Hall and Somers and Gibson suggest above, it is through such narratives that our identities are formed and re-formed, then a further question for feminism concerns the space which might be found within these narratives 'rarely of our own making' for *agency*: that is, for a movement towards change or transformation. In this chapter I shall explore some of these feminist analyses, the theoretical frameworks on which they draw, and the difficulties they find in exploring possibilities for change. I shall then go on to examine more broadly theories of narrative and identity which suggest some of the reasons for, and possible responses to, these difficulties.

Romance and the feminine

Feminist work on mainstream narratives which claim to speak to and about women, to inhabit a 'women's world', and to offer positions of identification for their female consumers has ranged across a number of media forms. Throughout this work, however, we can discern a recurrent problematic and an attempt to establish how, given the nature of this problematic, we can find space for female agency and/or social transformation. The problematic is summarised by Rosalind Coward in her 1984 collection of essays, *Female Desire*. Female desire, she writes, 'is constantly lured by discourses which sustain male privilege' (1984: 16). This process works, she continues, through narrative: if fantasy is the space where desire, in all its unruly excess, can subvert conventional gender positionings, then the publicly sanctioned fantasies which constitute the narratives of popular media forms work to contain this excess. 'Publicly sanctioned fantasies', writes Coward, 'confirm men's power, women's subordination' (1984: 203) even when aimed at women. The fantasy embodied in romantic fiction, for example, works to secure 'women's desire *for* a form of heterosexual domination and *against* active sexual identity' (1984: 196). If this is the case, however, what are we to make of the pleasures which women find in these narratives – pleasures of self-recognition, of finding women placed centre-stage in a 'woman's genre', of participation in a shared 'women's culture'? Are there perhaps elements in these pleasures which evade their structuring within dominant narrative forms and suggest possibilities for transformation – for, in Coward's words, 'the ruin of existing definitions of female desire'? (1984: 16) These are questions which have preoccupied feminist analysts of popular narrative forms aimed at women.

Janice Radway's *Reading the Romance*, a study of mass-market Harlequin Romances and their readers in the US, is one such analysis. Radway's study looks at 'the institutional matrix' of romance fiction publishing, at the underpinning narrative structure of what readers see as 'the ideal romance', at the 'unconscious needs' which that structure both expresses and regulates, and finally at the meanings attributed to romance reading by a 'community' of women romance readers in an American Midwestern town. Reading her conclusions, we find at their heart a tension arising directly from the questions posed above. In terms of narrative structure, she argues, the romance performs a quite specific function. Through its formulaic patterning, which Radway sets out as a series of thirteen narrative moves or 'functions', we find mapped the heroine's journey from an initial state of isolation and loss (the loss of her relationship with her mother) towards 'the promise of a mature, fulfilled, female identity' through her relationship with the hero (Radway 1987: 135). Initially 'a man incapable of expressing emotions or of admitting dependence' but powerful in the public sphere, the hero is transformed in the course of the story, via the heroine's 'womanly sensuality and mothering capacities', into a figure possessing both 'masculine power and prestige' and a quasi-maternal sensitivity to the heroine's emotional needs (1987: 127). This transformation, however, involves, not *change* in the hero so much as, first, the flowering of a tenderness already present in his 'true character' but repressed as a result of a previous (female inflicted) hurt, and second, the education of the *heroine* who, in order to nurture this development, must learn to reinterpret his initial coldness. She must learn, in other words, '*how to read* a man properly' (1987: 148, original emphasis). In making *his* transformation *her* responsibility, this narrative structure thus manages to leave existing gendered arrangements intact. For Radway, then, whilst the romance's initial scenario of unfulfilled heroine and emotionally repressed hero speaks to women's dissatisfaction with gendered relationships as currently structured within patriarchy, its 'magical solution' reaffirms those very structures and their constructions of male and female identity:

> Because the romance finally leaves unchallenged the male right to the public spheres of work, politics, and power, because it refurbishes the institution of marriage by suggesting how it might be viewed continuously as a courtship, because it represents real female needs within the story and then depicts their satisfaction by traditional heterosexual relations, the romance avoids questioning the institutionalized basis of patriarchal control over women even as it serves as a locus of protest against some of its emotional consequences. (1987: 217)

In terms of its narrative structure, Radway concludes that romance fiction functions as 'an active agent in the maintenance of the ideological status quo because it ultimately reconciles women to patriarchal society and reintegrates them with its institutions' (1987: 217). Yet this is not how its readers see it, and Radway must somehow reconcile her structural analysis with their sense that romance reading is an empowering event, an act of 'private pleasure' (1987: 211) in which their self-confidence and sense of independence are strengthened by identification with just such qualities in a heroine whose triumph the novel celebrates. Radway's solution is to 'distinguish *analytically* between the meaning of the act [of reading] and the meaning of the text as read' (1987: 210, original emphasis). Whilst the former originates in an oppositional and utopian impulse, the latter works to recuperate and disarm this impulse. In this opposition between structure and agency, the (ideologically conservative) force of structure is equated with text and narrative, whilst agency is identified with (the act of) reading. What this formulation does, however, is effectively to separate the reader from her desire, which in Radway's analysis is always already recuperated in the narrative, of whose unconscious functioning the reader is unaware. *Consciously*, romance readers see themselves as agents, their reading an act of rebellion; unconsciously, however, 'they act on cultural assumptions and corollaries not consciously available to them precisely because those givens constitute the very foundation of their social selves, the very possibility of their social action' (1987: 210).[1] These assumptions are carried in the romance narrative, which therefore acts both to manage desire and to limit agency.

Radway's model of female identity development is based on Nancy Chodorow's object relations theory.[2] For Chodorow, the female self as constructed under patriarchy is a 'self-in-relation' (unlike the 'autonomous' male self); hence the desire around which the romance narrative is structured is, for Radway, the desire of the heroine (and reader) for an emotionally fulfilling heterosexual relationship which will satisfy this mature female self. The narrative's ideological sleight of hand consists in the pretence that this desire can be fulfilled within a patriarchal culture which constructs masculinity in terms of distance, separation and control. Other feminist critics, however, have suggested a less benign relationship between desire and the structure of romance. For Hilary Radner, Radway's decision to frame her account of the heroine's development in terms of Chodorow's more 'optimistic' reworking of Freud causes her to misread the true functioning of the romance narrative, which is not to fulfil a female fantasy of 'the nurturing feminine man'. Rather, 'the romance as a genre is built upon a silencing of the feminine voice – a transformation of the feminine into a voice that speaks not for itself but for its "master" as a subjected voice'. The principal object of the romance, she concludes, 'might be best summarized as the transformation of this loss of "voice" into a dream of love and happiness' (1995: 67–8). It is therefore Freud's, not Chodorow's, version of the female journey to maturity which these stories enact: a journey from a 'masculine' predilection for activity and speech (the heroine begins as an independent young woman, often a 'tom-boy' and always characterised by her determination to 'talk back') to a 'feminine' passivity and silence. The 'Ur-narrative of romance', suggests Radner, is therefore 'not the Cinderella story at all, but a taming of the shrew, the shadow text that in our reclaiming of the romance we would rather forget' (1995: 13).

The underlying fantasy which structures these public narratives of femininity is therefore for women a profoundly masochistic one. To be 'singled out as heroine' the protagonist 'must be positioned as silent, a silenced shrew' (1995: 69), and the romance narrative functions to legitimate this silencing. The climactic moment of the Harlequin (or Mills and Boon) romance is a moment at which the heroine is rendered speechless as she succumbs to the hero's overwhelming passion – as in this typical encounter between the heroine, here an independent television producer, and the hero, from Patricia Wilson's *Jungle Enchantment* (1991):

'Let me go! I'm going to get my photographs and go back to the hotel and I'm never coming back here to this bug-infested place again. And as for you . . .'

His hand came to circle her throat and he tilted her head back, his eyes looking deeply into hers for a minute before his lips closed firmly over her own.

For a second she resisted him, anger still inside her, but his lips held hers drowsily, coaxing and gentle, seducing her senses, ensnaring her until she sighed against his mouth and opened her lips, inviting him to take whatever he wanted, her head pressed back against his shoulder. (1991: 108–9)

Invited to position herself within this fantasy, the reader, argues Radner, is similarly silenced, although for her this 'fantasy of misreading' is also accompanied by a quite different pleasure. For the reader, who knows the plot in advance because she has read it many times, the repetition inherent in the romance formula also provides illusory fantasies of control – perhaps the feeling Radway's readers sought when they turned repeatedly to romances they had already read, or expressed in their 'disappointment and outrage' when the formula was varied (Radway 1987: 63). For Radner even more than for Radway, then, the narrative structure of romance is part of the operation of patriarchal law. Just as in social terms the law produces social coherence in exchange for the repression of desire, so the 'narrative apparatus of the text (the rules of meaning and story)' (1987: 21) functions to reproduce the social order and regulate (female) desire.

Soap opera and pleasure

If the narrative closure of romance has inspired largely negative readings, in the soap opera feminist scholars found a narrative form which did *not* conform to the usual rules of narrative, with its structure of order/disorder/restoration of order. Unlike 'traditionally end-oriented fiction and drama', the soap opera narrative, as Dennis Porter has pointed out, seems to offer 'process without progression, not a climax and a resolution, but mini-climaxes and provisional denouements' which lead only to further difficulties and complications (1977: 788). As such, and as a female-centred genre, it might perhaps, in Tania Modleski's words, 'provide a unique narrative pleasure' which could provide an alternative to the pleasures of dominant male-centred narrative structures (Modleski 1984: 87). Modleski highlights three key points of difference. The first is the soap opera's endless deferral of narrative closure which refuses the promise of a 'happy ending', presenting desire instead as 'unrealizable' (1984: 92). The second is its structure of 'multiple identification' which refuses the fantasy of power that comes from identification with a single, narratively successful protagonist, producing instead a diffused, at times contradictory, structure of empathy with a range of characters. The third, with which we are familiar from the discussion of romance fiction, is its preference for dialogue and emotional complexity over action and resolution. Like the romance reader, the soap opera viewer is invited to learn to *read* situations and characters.

Modleski is uncertain, however, about the conclusions to be drawn from these differences. The subversive potential of the soap opera narrative lies, for her, in its frustration or negation of conventional narrative structures, with their identification with patriarchal law. However, what the soap opera substitutes for this repression of female desire is its investment in a fantasy of family and community in which the viewer is still constituted within the terms of a Freudian femininity, as 'a sort of ideal mother' whose own desire is repressed in favour of sympathy with 'the conflicting claims of her family (she identifies with them all), and who has no demands or claims of her own' (1984: 92). Like Radway, then, Modleski concludes that this 'women's genre', whilst it may allay real anxieties and satisfy real needs, does so in 'distorted' form, so that it must be the task of feminism to find 'more creative, honest, and interesting' alternatives (1984: 108–9).

Other feminist discussions of soap opera have been more unequivocally positive about the pleasures it offers, though in very varying ways. For Mary Ellen Brown, soap opera is undoubtedly a hegemonic form, its pleasures designed to reinforce 'dominant conceptualizations of women' by positioning them as 'consumers for their households' (1994: 4, 8), but it is nevertheless a 'leaky' form which creates 'gaps' through which women can contest that position. This contestation is achieved primarily through the way in which women *use* soap operas. Picking up the notion that women constitute 'a silenced majority' in culture, she argues:

> It can be said that soap operas in some ways give women their voice. The constant, active, playful discussions about soap operas open up possibilities for us to understand how social groups can take a somewhat ambiguous television text and incorporate it into existing gossip networks that provide outlets for a kind of politics in which subordinated groups can be validated and heard. (1994: 2)

Soap opera, then, provides space for the creation and expression of a specific 'women's culture', constructed in the spaces between, but also in opposition to, dominant or official culture. Brown is drawing here both on Pierre Bourdieu's concept of 'cultural capital' and on the idea that 'mass' or 'low' culture has been persistently equated with a 'feminised' culture (Huyssen 1986a; Modleski 1986). Soap opera's cultural positioning, she writes, 'marks its audience as having low social status' (Brown 1994: 114). Like romance fiction it is regarded as *trash* by the dominant value system. Its fans, however, choose it – in defiance of these values – as their cultural capital, and in so doing constitute themselves as a site of opposition to dominant or official culture, operating a 'symbolic inversion' between high and low culture (1994: 150). This inversion is a site of pleasure and of play for women, argues Brown, offering 'carnivalesque' laughter and parodic pleasure.[3] In offering a challenge from a marginalised group to 'the hierarchy of sites of discourse' (1994: 151), it also constitutes a potential site of political transformation. Paradoxically, then, 'the very devaluation of soap opera in dominant culture can protect the boundaries of women's culture' and provide 'important points of contact for women and women's politics' (1994: 109, 176).

If soap opera is seen as oppositional by Brown largely because of the narratives which (communities of) women viewers create *from* it, however, this is partly also, she argues, because of the genre's own narrative form and conventions. Soap opera, writes Brown, owes its form less to traditional literary narratives, with their emphasis on linear development and narrative resolution, than to the sprawling oral narratives of women's culture. It is this which gives soap operas their episodic quality, their open-endedness, their reliance on the viewer's memory of past events, their narrative redundancy and their emphasis on dialogue rather than action. Soap operas, writes Brown, 'more than most other forms of fictional television programming, parallel and replicate women's oral traditions' (1994: 65). At this point Brown's argument seems ambiguous. On the one hand, she argues that the very devaluation of the soap opera form – its *trashiness* – generates its subversive potential, since this makes it available for women's strategic re-appropriation. On the other, she seeks to revalue the form itself, seeing in its orally-derived narrative structures a reflection of a specifically female pleasure, fantasy and desire. Desire, however, is a little used concept in Brown's work; she professes herself unhappy with the psychoanalytic definition which links it to fantasy and sexuality: unruly and insatiable and identified with the unconscious (see Grosz 1990: 61–6). She prefers instead to write of 'feminine pleasures', which, as the product of a subordinate group and its discourses, are inevitably 'resistive' (though undefined), whether or not they are consciously political (Brown 1994: 173). This recuperation of the soap opera form as expression of an alternative female structure of desire and fantasy, which is at times – though far more tentatively – suggested by Tania Modleski, is here claimed as an important tool for thinking 'in oppositional ways' (1994: 182). To claim this, however, is to simplify the relationship between desire and narrative structure, and to essentialise gendered difference. For women, in this view, desire and pleasure operate differently: in the words of John Fiske, who draws on Brown's work, 'feminine sexuality and narrative emphasise the process over the end product, whereas the masculine gives the product priority over the process' (1987: 215), so that the soap opera form becomes the direct expression of female sexuality. This is surely a dangerous move to make. To equate soap opera's narrative openness (in which the story is 'never-ending') with a differently structured sexuality is to ignore the ways in which female desire and fantasy can be mobilised in the service of what are often deeply conservative gendered structures. To claim, too, that soap opera is the direct expression of women's pleasure whilst at the same time arguing that both language and 'classical . . . narrative' function as expressions of patriarchal Law (Brown 1994: 19) is to place both soap opera and women somehow outside both narrative and language. From such a position, it is difficult to see how we could ever move from 'resistive readings' to social change.

Watching Dallas (1985), Ien Ang's study of the 1980s prime-time soap opera *Dallas* and its women viewers in Holland, places a similar emphasis on the *pleasures* of soap opera, but to far more ambivalent effect. The framework for Ang's analysis is twofold: how the narrative structures of *Dallas* work to produce pleasures for (some of) its viewers, and, then, the nature of those pleasures. A third and related question, as for Brown, concerns the 'political and cultural meaning of the specific forms of pleasure which women find attractive' and the potential relationship of those pleasures to a feminist political project (1985: 131). Drawing on the responses of a small sample of viewers who answered her advertisement in a women's magazine asking readers to write with explanations of why they liked or disliked the serial, Ang uses these both to interrogate dominant evaluations of soap opera (as 'bad mass culture') and to support her own theoretical claims.

Ang uses the viewers' responses to establish two key theoretical principles. The first is the opposition between what she calls 'the ideology of mass culture', the denigration of popular cultural forms found within 'official' discourses, and its opposite, 'the popular aesthetic', which is grounded in the recognition and valuing of pleasure. Ang's definitions, like those of Mary Ellen Brown, draw upon the work of Pierre Bourdieu whose *Distinction* (1979) is concerned to identify patterns of cultural 'taste' with class positioning. The dominant class is distinguished, argues Bourdieu, by its taste for what he terms the 'legitimate consumption of legitimate works' (1986: 182), a 'high culture' aesthetic which is marked by critical distance and an emphasis on form. In stark contrast are the 'more direct, more immediate satisfactions' of popular culture, with its emphasis on spectacular delights – 'fabulous decors, glittering costumes, exciting music, lively action, enthusiastic actors' (1986: 178). Like Brown, however, Ang appropriates Bourdieu's class-based analysis for a gendered opposition. Those respondents who reported disliking *Dallas*, she writes, take their discursive stance from the dominant 'ideology of mass culture' in which ' "female" forms of "mass culture" such as soap opera and popular romances are the lowest of the low' (Ang 1985: 119). In contrast, viewers who countered this dominant perspective with an emphasis on the *pleasures* of *Dallas* are positioned, Ang argues, within Bourdieu's 'popular aesthetic', a feminised mass culture in which 'what matters . . . is the recognition of pleasure' (1985: 116). And pleasure is a matter of emotion, of a 'structure of feeling'.

Ang's second theoretical principle concerns this 'structure of feeling'. Again this is a borrowed concept, this time from Raymond Williams, for whom an era's 'structure of feeling' represented the expression of its 'meanings and values as they are actively lived and felt' (Williams 1977: 132), an experience often felt as 'a certain kind of disturbance or unease, a particular type of tension' (Williams 1979: 168) because of its distance from official ideologies. Ang's use of the term, however, identifies it with a particular constituency of viewers, women, and a particular kind of 'structure of feeling', the tragic. Allied to this concept is a second defining feature of the pleasures of *Dallas*, that of 'the melodramatic imagination', in which an 'excess of events and intensity of emotion are inextricably intertwined' (Ang 1990: 80).

Both of these concepts are ambiguously positioned. In the description of 'the melodramatic imagination' above, an 'excess of events' can only be a property of the text and its narrative, whilst 'an intensity of emotion' seems to describe the viewer's response. In a similar way, the *structure* in the 'tragic structure of feeling' is provided by the text – 'organized (concretized, made material) in the narrative structure of the serial' (Ang 1985: 87). But as a 'subjective experience of the world', a 'rather passive, fatalistic and individualistic reaction to a vague feeling of powerlessness and unease' (1985: 45, 82), it is clearly an attribute of the viewer. Like Brown, then, Ang focuses her revaluation of soap opera on the pleasures of its viewers, but at the same time wants to reclaim the form itself for a 'women's culture', since the alternative would be to deny these pleasures any transformative potential. Yet her analysis of the pleasures themselves is far less sanguine than Brown's very generalised account. The melodramatic imagination, she writes, is characterised by 'the sense that life is marked by eternal contradiction, by unsolvable emotional and moral conflicts, by the ultimate impossibility, as it were, of reconciling desire and reality'. Soap opera's lack of narrative resolution makes it 'fundamentally anti-utopian': the characters with whom its viewers identify are 'ultimately . . . constructed as victims of forces that lie outside their control' (Ang 1990: 80–1). In the end, then, the pleasures of its viewers are masochistic pleasures.

Ang is acutely aware of the difficulties this conclusion poses for a feminist analysis. Her solution is to turn to theories of fantasy. Fantasy, she writes, is 'a dimension of subjectivity which is a source of pleasure *because* it puts "reality" in parentheses' (1985: 135). It is 'the place of excess, where the unimaginable can be imagined' (Ang 1988: 187). In fantasy women within patriarchy can indulge 'with impunity' feelings of pessimism, sentimentality or despair, feelings 'which we can scarcely allow ourselves in the battlefield of actual social, political and personal struggles' (1985: 134). But this is an uneasy solution. It is only by divorcing 'the fact of fantasizing itself' from its content that Ang can maintain this positive view of the pleasures of *Dallas*. 'In terms of *content*', she concludes, 'the fantasy positions and solutions brought about by the tragic structure of feeling and the melodramatic imagination' are far from liberatory, serving instead to re-inscribe the 'patriarchal status quo' (1985: 134–5, 123). And yet fantasy narratives and social reality are not so easily divorced, as Ang herself recognises. If, as she accepts, feminism itself is 'sustained' and 'motivated' by fantasies of social transformation expressed in narrative terms (1985: 121), then it is difficult to see how the fantasies inscribed in the soap opera, in which 'the lack of a prospect of a happy ending . . . makes any solution . . . inconceivable', can function other than to reconcile women (however unhappily) to the 'traditional destiny imposed . . . by patriarchy' (1985: 123).

Melodrama and desire

For much of her account of 'the melodramatic imagination' Ang draws on the work on melodrama produced within feminist film theory. It is in these accounts that we find the most sustained attempts to theorise the relationship between narrative structure and female desire. Melodrama became of interest to film theorists as a result of the critique of realism which was made in the 1970s. If realism is regarded as inevitably complicit with dominant ideology, since it works always to 'naturalise' ideologically motivated representations,[4] melodrama, with its emotional extravagance and discontinuities of plot and characterisation, could be seen as providing an anti-realist excess which exposes the contradictions that realism works so hard to repress. Unlike realism, which assumes a world capable of explanation, melodrama, as Christine Gledhill writes, 'attests to forces, desires, fears which . . . appear to operate in human life independently of rational explanation'. It thus 'draws into a public arena desires, fears, values and identities which lie beneath the surface of the publicly acknowledged world' (Gledhill 1987a: 31, 33). In addition, its persistent identification with pathos, suffering and 'the point of view of the victim' (Elsaesser 1987: 64) served to designate it as a 'feminine' form. The melodrama, writes Thomas Elsaesser, is characterised by an emphasis on 'the *rhythm* of experience' rather than its moral or intellectual value, by characters who exist as types rather than psychologically rounded individuals, and by an engagement with the private and the emotional rather than the social and political. Meaning is conveyed less through what the characters *say* than through an 'orchestration' of visual and musical effects, manifest in music, decor and *mise-en-scène*. Linear action is replaced by a focus on moments of intensity, and plots, particularly in the domestic melodrama, become circular. A recurrent feature of melodrama is 'desire focusing on the unobtainable object' but this desire is represented, as in dreams, by 'a displaced emphasis, by substitute acts, by parallel situations and metaphoric connections'. Finally, in the claustrophobic settings of melodrama, externally focused violence is replaced by 'an inner violence', a self-destructive masochism (Elsaesser 1987: 44–65).

Unattainable desire, fantasy, masochism and absence of linearity: all of this is familiar territory and explains why, in Christine Gledhill's words, feminism 'claim[ed] a stake' in the 'critical reappropriation' of melodrama (1987b: 1), and particularly of that 'sub-set' of melodrama called the 'woman's film'. Analysing this 'woman orientated strand' of melodrama in 1977, Laura Mulvey drew attention to its subversive potential for women viewers:

> The workings of patriarchy, and the mould of feminine unconscious it produces, have left women largely without a voice, gagged and deprived of outlets . . . In the absence of any coherent culture of oppression, a simple fact of recognition has aesthetic and political importance. There is a dizzying satisfaction in witnessing the way that sexual difference under patriarchy is fraught, explosive, and erupts dramatically into violence within its own private stamping-ground, the family. (1989b: 39)

At the same time, however, she argues that through its narrative structures melodrama acts to recuperate that potential, functioning less as a disruption of than as a 'safety-valve' *for* patriarchy. On the one hand, she argues, 'it is as though the fact of having a female point of view dominating the narrative produces an excess which precludes satisfaction', so that 'Hollywood films made with a female audience in mind tell a story of contradiction, not of reconciliation'. On the other, the 'fantasy escape' and momentary fulfilment which melodrama offers to women is clearly marked *as* fantasy – 'closer to a day-dream than to fairy story' – and its final message is stark: 'Even if a heroine resists society's overt pressures, its unconscious laws catch up with her in the end' (1989b: 43).

The work of Mary Ann Doane on the 'woman's film' of the 1940s developed these ideas further. She begins from the sheer difficulty of representing the 'woman's story' in mainstream cinema: 'For the figure of the woman is aligned with spectacle, space or the image, often in opposition to the linear flow of the plot' (1987: 5). Women, that is, are 'to-be-looked-at' (Mulvey 1989a: 25), and as such can only be objects not subjects of the gaze, of the narrative, and of that which drives narrative: desire. Yet the narratives of the 'woman's film', self-consciously addressed as they are to a female audience, must at least claim to place female subjectivity, desire and agency at their centre. The result of this contradiction, which is both internal to the structures of cinema and a function of wider cultural constructions of masculinity and femininity, is an instability and incoherence in the structures of both narrative and looking in the 'woman's film'. 'Ways of looking', argues Doane, are linked not only to what Laura Mulvey calls 'sexual objectification' (Mulvey 1989a: 20) but also to 'ways of speculating, of theorizing' (Doane 1987: 37). 'Seeing' functions for us as a metaphor for understanding, so that the detective-hero 'looks' for clues and finally 'sees' the truth. To position the woman as subject of the gaze – so that as spectators we share her point of view – is therefore not only to attribute to her desire and narrative centrality, but also to place her as potential point of knowledge or understanding. The incompatibility of this with dominant gendered assumptions produces, Doane writes, 'gaps and incoherences which the films can barely contain' (1984: 69). Examples are the inability of these films to sustain the female protagonist's voice-over, the collapse or undercutting of point-of-view shots or flashbacks identified with her, or the tendency, during the course of the narrative, to replace her point of view with that of an authoritative masculine discourse. This discourse, most frequently the medical discourse, diagnoses the female protagonist's 'symptoms', by subjecting her to the 'medical gaze', and then proceeds to restore her to normality/passivity by 'curing' her (1984: 74). When she does act as investigator, in films such as *Gaslight* (1944), *Rebecca* (1940) or *Suspicion* (1941), what she investigates is usually her own potential status as victim. In such films the woman's investigation, like her narrative journey in the romance genre, is a matter of learning to 'read' the hero: the question most often posed is whether he is, or is not, planning to murder her (in *Gaslight* he is; in *Suspicion* he is not). In consequence, writes Doane, the woman's exercise of the investigative function is often 'simultaneous with her own victimization' (1987: 136), and the fantasy which is explored in these films is one of persecution or paranoia. Once again, then, we are presented with a 'women's genre' whose pleasures – intense, excessive, contradictory – are narratively structured around a masochistic fantasy.

Comedy and excess

In situation comedy, another 'feminised' genre, we find a far more ritualised playing out of the tension between narrative structure and female desire, 'containment'[5] and excess. From its earliest television incarnations the sitcom, as Patricia Mellencamp has written, was constituted as a space in which women's rebellion against the 1950s stereotype of the 'happy housewife heroine' (Friedan 1965) could be explored, but, she argues, it was able to perform this function precisely because its episodic narrative format, which returned its characters each week to the status quo,[6] served to contain this rebellion. Mellencamp's (1986) analysis of the US sitcoms *The George Burns and Gracie Allen Show* (1950–8) and *I Love Lucy* (1951–7) demonstrates how these shows gave space to the 'unruliness' and desires for independence and escape of their female stars. At the same time the shows returned them each week, via the repetitive structure of the sitcom form, to domestic subordination. In these series humour became the means by which conventional 'meanings' could be 'unmade' and patriarchal assumptions overturned by female leads who were the physical and verbal centres of their shows. Yet humour – together with the sitcom form which returns each episode to the point at which it began – is simultaneously the means through which these reversals can be rendered 'unserious', and hence both pleasurable and 'contained'.

In the case of more recent sitcoms centring on women, feminist critics have tended to focus more on their disruptive potential than on the strategies of containment mobilised by the sitcom form. Kathleen Rowe, writing about the US series *Roseanne* (1988–97), for example, emphasises Roseanne's inheritance of the role of 'unruly' domestic woman from earlier figures like Gracie Allen and Lucille Ball. But she argues that in Roseanne this 'semiotics of the unruly' is employed to produce a total critique of domesticity. *Roseanne*, then, is a domestic sitcom, but one whose star's unruly and *spectacular* excesses violate all the norms of domestic and erotic femininity, drawing attention to the impossibility – and absurdity – of such norms. Referring back to the arguments of Laura Mulvey, Rowe argues that such '*making visible* and *laughable*' of the norms of femininity disrupts conventional gendered power relations and begins to construct another possible position for the female subject, one which can lay claim to desire – however 'excessive' – rather than represent desirability: 'By returning the male gaze, we might expose (make a spectacle of) the gazer. And by utilizing the power already invested in us as image, we might begin to negate our own "invisibility" in the public sphere' (Rowe 1997: 77). Yet, as Jane Feuer has argued, the extent to which we regard a sitcom such as *Roseanne* or *Absolutely Fabulous* (1992–6 and 2001) as radical or subversive will depend on the power which we attribute to its 'narrative architecture' (Feuer 2001: 68). The power of these 'unruly' or 'excessive' women to disrupt assumptions about the 'naturalness' of feminine norms is always tempered by a narrative structure which refuses them agency in effecting change.

Woman as hero

The final narrative form I want to consider here is one which women have entered in some sense illegitimately. If popular genres, in John Tulloch's words, divide 'the social totality across differentiated bundles' (1990: 72), assigning some (the police series, the thriller, the legal or political drama) to the public sphere of masculinity, and others (the soap opera, the costume drama, the domestic comedy-drama) to the private sphere of femininity, then women's intrusion *as protagonists* into the first of these groups creates immediate problems for both the narrative and the ideological structure of these genres. The crime genre, for example, is concerned with issues of the public social world; its central characters are both confident actors in that world and uncoverers of truth, empowered with the investigative (and conventionally also the erotic) gaze. Traditionally these investigators are men, often in a buddy or father-son relationship, and the investigation first threatens their integrity and even identity, and then reaffirms it through the linked modes of action and knowledge. Women are marginal figures, either symbolic of the domestic world from which the detective's mission excludes him but which it is his task to preserve, or – as 'bad woman' – duplicitous, tempting the detective away from his investigative path. Finally, unlike the traditionally 'feminine' genres of soap opera or sitcom, the concern of the crime series with the public world of action rather than emotion has identified it with a 'realism' which brings it nearer to a 'masculine' high culture. Thus, for a female character to become the *hero* of such a series she must appropriate agency, action, command, the occupation of public space, discursive authority and the control of the investigative gaze. All of these, of course, run counter to the norms of femininity.

With the 1980s series *Cagney and Lacey*, however, women entered the police series not as marginal or 'softening' figures[7] but as narratively central 'buddies'. As Danae Clark writes, the result is a series which disrupts the assumptions of the male-centred police series in a number of ways. One is through its narrative structure: the series combines the 'closed' structure of the police series, in which each episode closes with the resolution of a case, with the open-ended structure of soap opera, in which the personal lives of the protagonists are foregrounded and discussion is more important than action. Moreover, the police-centred stories of the characters' professional lives parallel and interact with the issues confronting their private selves, disturbing the public-private hierarchy which underpins the police series. Second, in featuring *two* women rather than a single 'heroine', *Cagney and Lacey* both places the relationship *between* women at its centre and enables the series to explore the differences between women. The two women, and those they encounter in their professional lives, are constructed across multiple differences − of class, ethnicity, marriage and motherhood − as well as similarity, and these differences must be negotiated. Third, in foregrounding women as active decision-makers and uncoverers of 'truth', the series makes the voices of women, not men, the bearers of discursive authority. Finally, argues Clark, the series challenges patriarchal discourse through its 'economy of vision'. These women are subjects, not objects of the gaze. Traditional gendered relations of viewing are subverted in a number of ways: by de-naturalising traditional gendered roles; by giving the investigating gaze and point of view to women; and by refusing the sexual objectification of female characters (Clark 1990: 128–32).

Yet such usurpations are not without their own narrative effects. Ann Kaplan has argued that when women step into 'male' narrative roles in this way, they 'nearly always lose [their] traditionally feminine characteristics in so doing − not those of attractiveness, but rather of kindness, humaneness, motherliness'. These women become 'cold, driving, ambitious, manipulating, just like the men whose position [they have] usurped' (1983: 29). In appropriating the 'male gaze', the female 'hero' has stepped into the 'masculine' position, and for this she will be punished, both narratively and by the loss of 'feminine' characteristics. We can point, for example, to the descent into alcoholism and loneliness of the ambitious and unmarried Christine Cagney in the later series of *Cagney and Lacey*, the childlessness and family alienation of Jane Tennison in the ITV series *Prime Suspect* (1991–), or the increasing social and sexual loneliness of Sam Ryan in BBC's *Silent Witness* (1996–),[8] which accompanies her growing professional success. Yet we can also argue that, excessive or difficult though they may be, the centrality of these women protagonists within the narratives in which they feature can create more empowering fantasies for their female audiences than those, for example, of Ien Ang's 'melodramatic imagination'. All of these female investigators are, after all, narratively *impossible* within the genre which they have appropriated. As women who are at the same time heroes of the narratives in which they appear, their excess *cannot* ultimately be contained.

Theorising narrative and desire

How, then, might we theorise the relationship between narrative and female desire as it is enacted in the narratives of femininity outlined above? We can profitably begin by examining the model of narrative outlined by Teresa de Lauretis in 'Desire in Narrative' (1984). De Lauretis begins from a criticism of the kind of structural analysis of narrative which Janice Radway offers in *Reading the Romance*. Like other theorists of narrative (Ricoeur 1991a: 104), de Lauretis points out that the problem with such approaches is that, in identifying the structural patterns, horizontal and vertical, from which the text is constructed, they underplay narrative's crucial elements of process or temporality, as manifest in plot, and its driving force, desire. A story, she writes, 'is always a question of desire' (1984: 112). It is through narrative that fantasy, the individual expression of desire, is worked through in culturally sanctioned public stories. As Cora Kaplan, expressing a very similar idea, puts it: 'fantasy, with its aggrandizing narrative appetite, appropriates and incorporates social meaning and, structuring its public narrative, forms the historically specific stories and subjectivities available' (1986: 153).

In such an understanding of narrative we can recognise the language of psychoanalytic theory. For Freud, the origins of desire and of fantasy are indistinguishable, and fantasy is always narrativised (Laplanche and Pontalis 1986). Further, the process by which these personal narratives of desire are translated into publicly acceptable forms can be seen to describe both the generation of the 'historically specific stories' to which Kaplan refers and the process of psychoanalysis itself. The process of analysis, as Paul Ricoeur points out, is the process by which the analysand constructs out of their personal fantasies 'a story that is both more intelligible and more bearable', one which can be effective as (self) explanation in the public world (1991b: 435). It is a process which Freud's own writing repeated constantly: in his case study narratives, stories of individual development, and in his historical and theoretical accounts. As Roy Shafer has commented, psychoanalysis is 'an interpretive discipline' organised around normative narrative structures (1981: 25).

Kaplan's account refers to the construction through public narrative not only of stories but also of 'subjectivities'. Both she and de Lauretis argue further, then, that we, as individual subjects, in turn engage with these public narratives, finding in them at once expression of our own fantasised desires and a structuring or regulation of these desires, through the social meanings with which they have now been imbued. Only certain 'positionalities of meaning and desire', in other words, are available to us, those inscribed within the public narratives of our culture (de Lauretis 1984: 106). And the paradigmatic public narrative of Western culture, argues de Lauretis, is 'the Oedipus story' (1984: 112). Such narratives, she argues, drawing on the work of Soviet semiotician Jurij Lotman, divide their characters into two types: those 'who are mobile, who enjoy freedom with regard to plot-space' and 'those who are immobile, who represent, in fact, a function of this space'. The division, she argues, is fundamentally gendered. The first type is embodied in the figure of 'the hero, the mythical subject'. He it is who 'crosses the boundary and penetrates the other space', and in so doing establishes his identity as 'human being and as male; he is the active principle of culture, the establisher of distinction, the creator of differences'. His archetype is Oedipus. Female, on the other hand, 'is what is not susceptible to transformation, to life or death; she (it) is an element of plot-space, a topos, a resistance, matrix and matter' (1984: 118–9). In the Freudian version of this story, the Oedipal narrative describes the boy's journey to maturity, during which he must sacrifice his desire for the mother, whom he now recognises as 'castrated', in return for access to the authority invested in the father. For the girl, however, the equivalent journey is one to passivity, in which she must relinquish not only her desire for the mother but desire itself, in return for becoming the potential object of male desire. It is significant, suggests de Lauretis, that Freud could never answer the question he obsessively posed: 'What does a woman *want?*' He could not, that is, attribute desire to woman – could not envisage a narrative of which she was the subject. Instead, within the Oedipal paradigm, 'each reader – male or female – is constrained and defined within the two positions of a sexual difference thus conceived: male-hero-human, on the side of the subject; and female-obstacle-boundary-space, on the other' (1984: 121). Insofar as we are desiring subjects, women too will be caught up in identification with the active 'male' position within narrative; insofar as we are visually and narratively positioned by our gender, we will also be constrained to identify with Laura Mulvey calls the 'to-be-looked-at-ness' of woman as passive image.

This account of narrative is useful in a number of ways. It separates desire, the mainspring of all narrative, from the culturally sanctioned public forms through which it is expressed. It explains how women, as readers or spectators, can be 'seduced' into complicity with public narratives which position them as sexual object, monster or obstacle: as readers we are caught up in the movement of desire which drives the narrative, even as it works towards a closure which places us – visually and narratively – as object of (or obstacle to) that desire. What this account does not do, however, is offer an explanation of how this dominant narrative construction can be contested. De Lauretis is clear about the task: 'the story', she writes, must 'be told differently' (1984: 156). *Female* desire and fantasy must be enacted through narrative so that women as social subjects might find new possibilities of identification, engagement and agency. Yet if, as she argues, 'story demands sadism, depends on making something happen' (1984: 132), and if the paradigmatic version of this story is that of Oedipus, so that 'the work of narrative . . . is a mapping of differences, and specifically, first and foremost, of sexual difference into each text; and hence, by a sort of accumulation, into the universe of meaning' (1984: 121), it is difficult to see just how, within this theoretical framework, such a re-telling might occur.[9]

Yet, as has been pointed out (Lara 1998), de Lauretis is herself the producer of a powerful explanatory narrative which has made an interpretive intervention into the public sphere. Such narratives *do* occur. In her later work de Lauretis develops an account of identity and its relationship to fantasy, desire and narrative which goes rather further towards explaining how such agency might be possible. Fantasy, she had argued, grounds both subjectivity and public narratives through the ways in which it is structured within culturally dominant representations. As individuals, we construct our identities in relation to those representations. Now, however, she sees this as a more active process. Identity, she argues, is a process of appropriation, interpretation and re-telling. We appropriate public narratives and rework them through fantasy, returning them to the public world 'resignified, rearticulated discursively and/or performatively' (1994: 308). It may be the case, then, that the Oedipal narrative has structured Western representations, but this is a historical phenomenon which can permanently constrain neither the capacity of fantasy nor its narrative expressions. Our identities are in a constant process of active construction and interpretation. If the material on which we draw comprises normative fictions, it is reworked by desire in relation to (embodied, gendered) experience, and reinterpreted in the light of changing discursive configurations. Stories, in this account, can be re-told or re-interpreted so as to represent what was 'previously invisible, untold, unspoken (and so unthinkable, unimaginable, "impossible")' (de Lauretis 1986: 11).

Narrative identity

Writing in 1990, de Lauretis defines feminist theory as

> a developing theory of the female-sexed or female-embodied social subject, whose constitution and whose modes of social and subjective existence include most obviously sex and gender, but also race, class, and any other significant sociocultural divisions and representations; a developing theory of the female-embodied social subject that is based on its specific, emergent, and conflictual history. (1990: 267)

The definition of female identity which is offered here – that of a 'female-embodied social subject [with a] specific, emergent, and conflictual history' – brings us very close to the notion that identity itself has a narrative structure, an idea which has been developed elsewhere in recent feminist theory. The accounts which explore this idea differ in a number of ways, but they all draw on Paul Ricoeur's concept of *narrative identity*. In elaborating them here, I shall be concerned with the insights they can offer into the relationship between women, feminism and media rather than in drawing out differences between them.

For Ricoeur, human existence can be defined as 'an activity and a desire in search of a narrative' (1991b: 437). Identity, that is, is best understood as neither a fixed essence nor a juxtaposition of fragmented, fractured and discordant elements, but as dynamic unity through time. It comes into being as a story which demands expression – which we *must* constantly tell and re-tell if we are to construct a concept of self through which to act in the world. And just as our narrative interpretations serve to make sense of our past actions, so they also provide the basis for future acts which will in turn be narrativised. In Margaret Somers' and Gloria Gibson's interpretation, this constitutes '*ontological* narrativity', the narrativity of becoming, of being in the world (1994: 38). *Public* narratives, on the other hand, are constructed by and in social power structures; they constitute the culturally available repertoire of narratives within which we are invited to locate ourselves and through which we structure our own stories of identity. A final narrative level, argue Somers and Gibson, is that of *meta*-narrative, the master narratives (of progress, Enlightenment, civilisation, and so on) which they argue provide the underlying structure for, and authoritative reinforcement of, the public narratives which organise our cultural experience. Further, they argue that these meta-narratives have also underpinned – though in covert and unacknowledged ways – the conceptual schema which have structured the developing human and social sciences.

This is a useful account in a number of ways. First, it can suggest why, for Teresa de Lauretis in 1984, despite the evidence of the many narratives produced by women, it could seem that narrative itself 'is the production of Oedipus' (1984: 121). For the story of the emergence of the heroic individual, the 'mythical subject', who creates himself as 'the active principle of culture, the establisher of distinction, the creator of differences' (1984: 119), is also the meta-narrative of progress, reason and the Enlightenment. Endlessly reiterated through the multiplicity of popular narratives traced by de Lauretis and others, the Oedipal narrative continues to ground its authority in the powerful meta-narrative of Western modernity. Second, the account offered by Somers and Gibson can, through its concept of an underpinning meta-narrative, offer us a way of understanding the persistent 'feminising' of mass culture which critics like Tania Modleski have pointed to as such a dominant feature of twentieth-century cultural commentary. Denise Riley has described the way in which the emerging human sciences of the nineteenth century – sociology, demography, economics, neurology, psychiatry, psychology – produced a progressive reordering of understandings of gender. Whereas man, in the formulation 'man in society' was, she writes, seen to *face* society, to be separate, individualised, his relationship to society potentially problematic, the categories 'women' and 'society' formed a continuum. Women, that is, were seen to be immersed in the social, so that 'society' (as opposed to politics, or the individual) was seen as always 'already permeated by the feminine' (Riley 1988: 15).

This 'feminisation' of the social had its counterpart in the gendering of the high/low culture divide, as Celia Lury (1993) has argued. 'High culture' was aligned with the figure of 'the individual', the source of value, judgement and authenticity, and as such was the province of the masculine, whilst 'low culture' – the 'mass' cultural forms of the romance novel, the woman's magazine or the decorative arts – was seen to be saturated with the (undifferentiated) feminine. Underlying all of these analytic categories and explanatory schemes we can discern once more the shape of the heroic meta-narrative outlined by de Lauretis – here operating at what Somers and Gibson call 'a presuppositional level' (1994: 63) and with its narrative basis obscured or denied, but immensely powerful nonetheless.

The account offered by Somers and Gibson and by others (Lara 1998; McNay 2000) is suggestive in other ways too. For Lois McNay it can account for the entrenched power of certain narratives of femininity – those of romance fiction, for example – even though they no longer reflect either our personal experience or contemporary forms of social organisation. These narratives remain powerful not simply because of their 'historical embeddedness' but because they remain 'foundational' in constructing our sense of a coherent identity. As such, we continue to invest in them not simply discursively – through the stories we tell of ourselves – but ontologically, in the way we live our lives. 'The coherence and durability of patterns of gendered behaviour', argues McNay, 'are not just imposed from without but also emerge from investments made by the individual in certain narratives' (2000: 93–4). We cannot, then, simply make and re-make such narratives at will. Both the public narratives which we find in media forms and the identities which we construct through them are 'constrained and overdetermined by culturally sanctioned meta-narratives that form the parameters of self-understanding' (2000: 93).

The entrenched nature of these public narratives of gender and their underpinning meta-narratives is something also acknowledged by those feminist writers who *have* sought to advance their own very different explanatory narratives of culture. Carolyn Steedman's *Landscape for a Good Woman* (1986) is one such account, an autobiographical narrative which is at the same time a cultural narrative of femininity literally untellable within the dominant narratives of gender or class. *Landscape for a Good Woman* is about the lives of Steedman and her working-class mother, and is a story grounded in desire, her mother's desire for another kind of life, expressed in fantasy and fairytale as much as through historical narrative. As such, however, it is a story which cannot be told within the dominant narratives of history or culture. Women, writes Steedman, cannot be 'heroines of the conventional narratives of escape' because these are men's stories (1986: 15); but neither are their lives explained by these dominant narratives in which women figure, as in de Lauretis' account, as points along the (hero's) journey. Hers is, Steedman writes, one of the 'marginal stories'; she cannot claim for it the 'massive authority' – the territory, the 'truth' – of 'history: the central story'. Stories like hers must exist 'in tension with' these other, dominant narratives (1986: 21–2). Yet it is also a story which *is* told, though its telling, Steedman reminds us, is accomplished both by means of and 'in the cracks in between' those other, more 'central' narratives (Steedman 1992: 46).

Steedman employs here a complex rhetorical strategy. She insists that her own narrative cannot carry explanatory authority because it is not grounded in the dominant meta-narrative of established history. At the same time, however, her own desire, and that of her mother, works relentlessly through and around the available dominant narratives, transforming and thus contesting their interpretative claims. Finally in this section, then, I want to draw out the implications of this complex and apparently ambiguous argument. For Lois McNay the concept of narrative identity provides a firmer framework for envisaging the possibilities for female agency than do feminist accounts primarily grounded in, for example, psychoanalytic theory or Foucauldian concepts of power/discourse. Concepts of the narrative construction of identity offer an account of the self as constructed in time, constantly configuring and refiguring its sense of identity within lived experience. The model of identity they offer is thus always caught up in dynamic and interpretative processes – and hence always capable of agency (2000: 113). But if Steedman's 'story of two lives' seems to both endorse and embody McNay's argument, it also suggests two points of caution as we seek to understand how narratives of femininity work and might be transformed. The first is one of which McNay is well aware. It cannot be enough to suggest that the emergence into the public sphere of *women's* stories will in itself contest and reorder existing dominant understandings and conceptual frameworks, as, in their very different ways, do Mary Ellen Brown and the feminist philosopher Maria Pia Lara, for example. Such a view ignores the extent to which all of our stories are grounded in the existing repertoire of public narratives – even when, like Steedman's, they work through the 'cracks in between' them – and it ignores too the fact that this repertoire is in turn underpinned by the power and social authority of dominant meta-narratives. We cannot, that is, simply tell new stories which arise direct from women's experience, since that experience is never unmediated by existing narrative understandings.[10] Lara's account of the force of women's 'emancipatory narratives' (1998: 5) forgets, too, the extent to which we may, like Radway's readers or Ang's viewers, powerfully invest in traditional narratives of femininity, since their very cultural embeddedness seems to offer stability and coherence to an identity that might otherwise seem fractured and unstable.

The second point of caution suggested by Steedman's account is one to which McNay would be rather less sympathetic, and concerns the workings of desire and fantasy in relation to narrative. McNay's own account of the structuring of desire within subjectivity substitutes for the psychoanalytic concept of the unconscious – that fundamentally disruptive core of the psyche which will always disturb identity and order through desire – the concept of the 'radical imaginary' advanced by Cornelius Castoriades. For Castoriades, writes McNay, the unconscious is not the perverse and resistant pulse of desire envisaged by Freud or Lacan but rather an 'originary capacity for figuration', a sort of constant drive towards representation (2000: 118, 138). This makes of the 'radical imaginary' a far more straightforwardly creative force than the unconscious of traditional psychoanalytic theory, and makes a concept of agency as the product of this force correspondingly easy to advance. As we have seen, however, desire and fantasy work through narrative in far more ambiguous ways, appropriating and transforming, but also repeating and investing in narratives in which traditional gendered structures are reaffirmed. Fantasy, argues de Lauretis, always 'exceeds its historically contingent configurations' (1994: 308), but to say this is not to say that fantasy is necessarily liberatory. Desire for Steedman's mother, for example, relentless and excessive as it was, was embodied in the conventional – and arguably oppressive – feminine fantasies of 'a full skirt that took twenty yards of cloth' and the romance fairytale of a 'prince who did not come' (1986: 47).

Post-feminist narratives

A 'full skirt that took twenty yards of cloth' and 'to marry a prince': ironically, these signifiers of the relentless impossibility of Steedman's mother's desire have become the very stuff of the 'post-feminist' narrative. In such narratives, as Rita Felski writes, 'women are placed at the heart of a postmodern era of consumption, pleasure, and spectacle' (2000: 102): their desires celebrated, their fantasies fulfilled. Identity itself, unfixed from traditional notions of unity or coherence, becomes, as Charlotte Brunsdon writes, a matter of 'performance, style and desire' (1997: 85), so that traditional narratives can be re-worked (re-styled) and re-authored through a process of self-conscious performance and play. In such a story, Steedman's mother's desires could be celebrated, but they would at the same time be stripped of their context and meaning. In the final section of this chapter I want to explore this notion of the 'postfeminist' narrative further, with particular reference to one such text, *Sex and the City*.

'Post-feminism' is of course a concept fraught with contradictions. Emerging as a term within popular journalism in the 1980s, its assumed periodisation of feminism has been seen by critics like Susan Faludi as unambiguously a product of an anti-feminist backlash. 'Just when record numbers of younger women were supporting feminist goals in the mid-1980s', she writes, 'and a majority of all women were calling themselves feminists, the media declared that feminism was the flavour of the seventies and that "post-feminism" was the new story – complete with a younger generation who supposedly reviled the women's movement' (Faludi 1992: 14). Tania Modleski makes a similar attack on the term's translation into academic discourse, where it can be claimed by men as well as women. Such critics, she argues, whilst 'proclaiming or assuming the advent of postfeminism are actually engaged in negating the critiques and undermining the goals of feminism' (1991: 3). More recent writing, however, has often been less hostile, suggesting either that the term is useful in describing a cultural shift in both discourse and popular representations (Brunsdon 1997), or that its 'post-ness' is not a rejection but an incorporation and a broadening of feminism's goals (Braithwaite 2002; Lotz 2001). For Ann Braithwaite, for example, post-feminism *is* feminism today, complete with all its difficult debates and animosities, its conflicts and contradictions, its pleasures and desires' (2002: 341).

As cultural moment, then, post-feminism signals a shift towards women's public success and economic emancipation, an un-fixing of traditional gender roles, and a corresponding increase in individual 'lifestyle choice' (McRobbie 2004). As a theoretical position, it is claimed as both a continuation and a critique of 'second-wave' feminism, incorporating feminism's goals whilst adopting post-structuralist definitions of the subject, and focusing on the (multiply positioned) individual rather than on social groups. Finally, the popular media texts to which the term is attached feature characters, and narratives, which play out these notions of what Angela McRobbie (2004) calls 'female individualisation' in the context of the pleasures of performance, play, consumption, style and excess, within a range of hybridised media genres.

Sex and the City (HBO 1998–2004) is one such text. Its post-feminist cityscape reworks the New York of 1980s feminist hero(in)es Cagney and Lacey, for whom New York was characterised by encounters with racial and class difference, and by the difficult relationship between the personal (the feminine/feminist world of the home and the 'women's room') and the public (the patriarchal/professional world outside). In *Sex and the City*, however, the streets of New York have, as Jane Arthurs comments, 'lost the danger of a sadistic or reproving masculine gaze. Instead of intimating the dark dangers that kept respectable women off the streets, New York is shown to be a place of freedom and safety' (2003: 93). The series' protagonists appropriate public as well as private space for a women's discourse, the primacy of women's friendship, and a shared 'economy of vision'.[11] Focusing on the series' concluding episodes, I want to examine briefly here this resignification of the city by post-feminism, and the accompanying claims to agency and authorship made by the series, specifically to the re-authoring and re-possession of the romance narrative.

In the penultimate episode of *Sex and the City*, the series' elusive hero 'Mr Big' attempts, unsuccessfully, to resume his relationship with protagonist Carrie. Carrie is on her way to her farewell dinner before leaving New York for Paris with her lover, Aleksandr Petrovsky. When she turns down Big's repeated invitations and refuses to allow him to speak, his comment, 'I'm starting to feel like a chick', signals the start of his redemption. The 'feminisation' of Big which is marked by his rueful comment, offered as an instance of Carrie's equality and power, is in fact, as Janice Radway has shown, a staple of the concluding stages of the romance narrative. His recognition of emotional dependency is traditionally the male side of the romance bargain, ensuring that when, as a redeemed Prince Charming, he is sent on his mission to rescue Carrie (by friends Miranda, Samantha and Charlotte) he will in turn be redeemed by her. No longer simply a figure of 'spectacularly masculine phallic power' – handsome, strong, experienced, wealthy – his transformation into acceptable hero of romance is accomplished, as in Janice Radway's formulation, through discovery of the nurturant, essentially 'feminine' qualities which will complete him (1987: 155). Big's 'feminisation' is, then, expected, his early designation as 'Prince Charming'[12] part of the series' knowing claim to a 're-authoring' of the fairytale as signifier of female pleasure and desire.

The series' final two episodes move Carrie's romance narrative to Paris, so that Carrie herself comes to stand in for the post-feminist freedoms and pleasures identified with New York. As her romance with the European Alex founders, it seems that it is Paris/Europe that is the problem. Its jaded and cynical women no longer believe in romance; they are sophisticated but cold, and lacking in spontaneity. Its streets are dirty, its children sullen and unpleasant. Carrie's identity, symbolised by the cheap but irreplaceable 'Carrie' signature necklace, is lost, its substitute a diamond-studded gift from Alex. Finally however, her signature necklace recovered, Carrie makes a stand, declaring:

> It's time to be clear about who *I* am. I am someone who is looking for love – real love – ridiculous, inconvenient, consuming, can't-live-without-each-other love. And I don't think that love is here, in this expensive suite, in this lovely hotel, in Paris.

If this looks like familiar pre-feminist romantic terrain, however, the post-feminist woman, as Charlotte Brunsdon comments, 'also has ideas about her life and being in control which clearly come from feminism . . . She wants it all' (1997: 86). 'Alex tells me you were a writer in New York,' says his ex-wife, making conversation. 'I *am* a writer,' responds Carrie. In the New York of *Sex and the City*, Carrie could have not only the fairytale, but also 'a job, . . . friends' and *authorship*. In identifying all of these losses – of 'real love', work, friendship, her identity as image and as author – with the loss of New York, Carrie's words serve not only to mask their incompatibilities (love is to be all-consuming but permit the primacy of friendship and work; identity is to be subsumed in love but asserted through writing), but also to suggest that these are losses which can be recouped. Carrie *can* have it all – in New York. For Big, 'feeling like a chick' meant experiencing emotional 'neediness', passivity and power-lessness; and the contradiction at the heart of the romance ending is of course that, with the hero restored to the position of rescuer and protector, it is precisely this position which is offered to its female reader as *triumph*. *Sex and the City* works to invest the fairytale ending with a rather different meaning, rewriting it as post-feminist narcissism and choice. With Carrie's rescue effected and her identity as writer restored, her final voice-over lists all the forms of relationship possible to the series' protagonists. 'But the most exciting, challenging and significant relationship of all', the voice-over concludes, 'is the one you have with yourself'. The 'ridiculous, inconvenient, consuming, can't-live-without-each-other love' which was earlier asserted as central to the romance narrative is now redefined as the quest for a Prince Charming who will confirm this central relationship: 'And if', Carrie adds, 'you find someone to love the you *you* love – well, that's just fabulous.'

Such a rewriting is not achieved without considerable discomfort: displacements and disavowals abound in these final episodes. Above all, Samantha, Miranda and Charlotte, who remain in New York, function as uncomfortable reminders of that which is repressed in Carrie's conclud-ing affirmation of narcissism and choice. Samantha's body is restored to its sexual functioning, but her post-cancer sexual re-awakening is to fulfilment within a monogamous relationship, not to her previous promiscuity. Miranda is now fully domesticated as wife and mother, her selfless bathing of her newly stroke-disabled mother-in-law observed by the maternal figure of Magda, who pronounces with all the authority of traditional femininity: 'What you did, *that* is love. *You love*.' Charlotte's desire for a baby becomes all-consuming. In all of these sequences what we seem to have is not post-feminist choice so much as a reversion to notions of the natural and the authentic. It is there in the metaphor of seasonal renewal which accompanies Samantha's sexual healing and discovery of monogamy. It is there, more tentatively, in Charlotte's recognition that her social position will not buy her a baby (at least, not an American one), though that is what she wants above all. And it is there most of all in Miranda's substitution of 'real' (that is, self-abnegating and silent) love for her habitual irony. These do not seem to be examples of *choice*, as Carrie's final voice-over suggests, so much as instances of what Angela McRobbie (2004: 257) has called the 'active, sustained and repetitive repudiation' of feminism which is inherent in post-feminism's attempt to reclaim romance. Implicitly, they also suggest something of the loss and violence which underlie these repudiations.

Reading this resolution in terms of the narrative theory outlined earlier, we can see that, unlike Carolyn Steedman's autobiographical narrative, with its careful acknowledgement of the difficulties for women in claiming authority/authorship, *Sex and the City*'s closing assertion that for the post-feminist woman both of these can be/have been achieved in fact masks the series' embeddedness in more traditional narratives of femininity. Re-authoring, as McNay has pointed out, is not such a simple matter. What she calls 'the detraditionalizing forces' at work in contemporary society may well be 'breaking down fixed gender narratives and exposing women in particular to the individualized biographies of the market subject' expressed in notions of 'lifestyle choice' (2000: 112), but the results are not straightforwardly liberatory. Neither the public narratives which result nor the individual identities which we construct at least in part through these narratives are free from the stabilising pull of more conventional narratives of femininity. To assume otherwise is to ignore the historical and ideological power of public narratives and their underpinning meta-narratives, and to risk celebrating as a product of individual lifestyle choice a narrative outcome whose satisfying sense of coherence in fact relies on the very narrative structures which it claims to supersede. Finally, then, if popular media have become the arena in which competing narratives jostle for legitimacy, it is important to remember that the public narratives which result are themselves contested spaces, in which claims to newness must always be evaluated in the light of the far older (meta-) narratives which may lie just below the surface.

Notes

1. This formulation by Radway brings her close to Pierre Bourdieu's concept of *habitus*, which expresses the idea that dominant social norms are not simply experienced as external regulation, but lived through the body as a series of dispositions and inclinations which, whilst generative and therefore productive of agency, function always to circumscribe the limits of this agency. For Radway, however, these (patriarchal) norms are also reinforced through the narrative structure of the romance text.
2. For Chodorow, the Oedipal structures which Freud describes are indeed accurate descriptions, but they are not, as psychoanalysis assumes, the result

of universal psychic processes. They are rather the result of a particular social organisation which produces a division between the 'private, domestic world of women and the public, social world of men' (1978: 174). Because it is women who mother, the first role identification for children of both genders is with their mothers. For girls, therefore, maturity means a continuity of identification. The girl's identification with her mother is established through the mother's *presence* and is unbroken, which means that 'women's sense of self is continuous with others' (1978: 207). A boy's identity, however, is established through separation and difference, and his identification with the father is based on the father's *absence*. None of this, however, is, according to Chodorow, immutable. It is rather the product of 'social structurally induced psychological processes' (1978: 7).

3. Brown is drawing here on Mikhail Bakhtin's concept of popular carnival as a space outside everyday power structures, in which social hierarchies are temporarily overturned in an atmosphere of laughter and play to produce 'a world inside out' (Bakhtin 1965: 11).

4. For a widely influential statement of this position, see MacCabe 1981.

5. In Mellencamp's chapter on *The George Burns and Gracie Allen Show* and *I Love Lucy*, she draws explicit parallels between US political and military strategies which aimed at 'containment' of both external and internal 'enemies' and the domestic ideological strategies aimed at women: ' "Containment" was not only a defensive, military strategy developed as U.S. foreign policy in the 1950s; it was practiced on the domestic front as well, and it was aimed at excluding women from the work force and keeping them in the home' (1986: 81).

6. David Marc has described this structure as 'episode = familiar status quo → ritual error made → ritual lesson learned → familiar status quo' (Marc 1989: 190–1).

7. Earlier series, like *The Gentle Touch* (1980–4) and *Juliet Bravo* (1980–5) in Britain, had used a female central character to bring a 'feminine' touch to the police series.

8. See Alcock and Robson (1990) for this reading of *Cagney and Lacey*, and Thornham (1994) on *Prime Suspect*. For an analysis of Sam Ryan in *Silent Witness*, see Thornham 2002.

9. This criticism, that an overemphasis on the regulatory power of narrative in de Lauretis' account leaves little space for a conception of female agency, is one which has also been made of the work of Judith Butler, with whose notion of the 'performativity' of gender it has aspects in common. For Butler, 'performativity requires a power to effect or enact what one names' (1995: 203). It is the process of naming gender which brings it into being, and its constant reiteration both produces and regulates the norms of sexual difference. As subjects thus produced, gender becomes for all of us 'a kind of doing, an incessant activity' performed as a 'practice of improvisation within a scene of constraint' (2004: 1). Butler's discussion of the performance of gender here is framed in terms of narrative. As subjects brought into being

by a power of naming which assigns us our gender, we are in some sense narrated; even as we attempt to be authors of our own story, the terms of that story, and our own genesis, are outside our capacity to narrate (1997: 11). For Butler, as for de Lauretis, the problem of agency is often posed as the problem of authorship. Both agency and authorship are possible, she writes, since once called into being we are not fixed, and to some extent the power that produces us can also be assumed by us. The limits of both, however, are highly circumscribed; '[i]f I have any agency,' she writes, 'it is opened up by a social world I never chose'. As such, though not impossible, agency is limited and 'riven with paradox' (2004: 3).

10. Bridget Byrne, for example, in her exploration of narratives of the self produced in interviews with a number of women, reports that when women were able to produce interpretative narratives of their lives it was because they had available to them existing narrative patterns through which to realise their stories. As a result, they were able to claim agency. When available narratives could not be made to 'fit', however, her subjects were not able to construct a coherent story of the self. See Byrne 2003.

11. See Danae Clark (1990).

12. At a number of points, particularly in the early series, 'Big' is explicitly referred to as 'Prince Charming', for example in 'I Heart New York', 4.18.

4 Real women

Once an oppressed group becomes aware of its cultural as well as political oppression, and identifies oppressive myths and stereotypes – and in the case of women, female images that simply express male fantasies – it becomes the concern of that group to expose the oppression of such images and replace their falsity, lies and escapist illusions with reality and the truth. (Gledhill 1984: 20–1)

Women – 52 per cent of the world's population – are barely present in the faces seen, the voices heard, the opinions represented in the news. The 'mirror' of the world provided by the news is like a circus mirror. It distorts reality, inflating the importance of certain groups, while pushing others to the margins. (Gallagher, *Who Makes the News? Global Media Monitoring Project 2005*, www.whomakesthenews.org)

'Real' women are as socially constructed, as much the product of discursive practices, as the sign 'woman' in the visual image. (Rakow and Kranich 1996: 664)

Women and 'the real'

The notion of 'the real' is of course as problematic as that of its presumed opposite, 'the image', discussed in Chapter 2. Yet it, too, has been crucial in the formation of a feminist media studies and in any exploration of the relationship of women to the mass media. The two, indeed, are often found together, as in this plea from Julienne Dickey in her chapter on advertising images: 'where are the alternative images of real women with which we might identify?' (1987: 75). Thus, if one of the central concerns of early second-wave feminism was with the *mis*representation of women in the fantasy images circulated by the media, a second was with the way in which real women were actually represented – or more accurately, *not represented*. In research studies spanning the past thirty years, the over-visibility of women as sexualised *spectacle* has been contrasted with their virtual omission from those genres seen as having a privileged relation to the real world: news, documentary and 'current affairs'. For Gaye Tuchman in 1978, this amounted to 'symbolic annihilation'. 'Consider the symbolic representation of women in the mass media', she writes:

Relatively few women are portrayed there, although women are 51 per cent of the population and are well over 40 per cent of the labor force. Those working women who are portrayed are condemned. Others are trivialized: they are symbolized as child-like adornments who need to be protected or they are dismissed to the protective confines of the home. In sum, they are subject to *symbolic annihilation*. (1978b: 8)

This chapter examines the issues around the 'symbolic annihilation' of women from those genres whose 'discourses of sobriety' (Nichols 1994) make claims to address the viewer/reader as citizen, part of an interpretive community concerned to gain and share knowledge about the real, historical world, knowledge which will lead to action *in* the world. It will also examine the causes of this absence. Secondly, it looks at those 'real women' who now increasingly *do* populate television and women's magazines, but within discourses very far from the 'sobriety' of journalism, television news and documentary, and in genres which specifically address, and construct, a 'woman's world' whose 'everyday reality' is that of the familial and emotional, not that of civic responsibility and social action.

Women and news

'The news', writes Margaret Morse, 'is a privileged discourse, invested with a special relation to the Real' (1986: 55). Like documentary, its claim is to offer us not *a* world, however realistically constructed, but access to *the* world. As Bill Nichols writes of documentary, in these genres 'we look out from a dimly lit room, hearing and seeing what occurs in the world around us . . . Our attention is immediately directed outward toward the historical world, past or through the text, and into the realm where action and response are always possible' (1991: 112). It is this role as provider of direct and independent information about the public world beyond the private realm of experience which has given news its status as guarantor both of the social responsibility of the mass media and of the healthy workings of a democratic society. News, as Morse writes, is seen not as representation but as 'an act in reality itself' (1986: 61). Its 'realism' operates on a different epistemological level to that of other, fictional genres. It is, in John Corner's words, a realism of *reference*, one which relies on notions of *veracity*, not – as with fictional genres – a realism of verisimilitude, which relies on notions of *plausibility* (1992: 98).

The news, then, is presented to us, in the words of Margaret Gallagher quoted above, as a 'mirror on the world' – accurate, objective, balanced, complete and fair. 'The news', as Morse comments, has become a singular rather than plural notion: 'there is only one *news*' (1986: 56). As an outraged *Radio Times* reader, protesting about the intrusion of 'viewers' opinions' into 'what should be serious news programmes', puts it (*RT*, 8 April 2006, 160), 'Here's what I'd like to see on the news: the news. You know, what's happened in the world today . . . Just the facts, please'. Yet the news we get is the product of institutional pressures and structures, and of processes of both selection and construction. From the work of Galtung and Ruge (1965) onwards, analysis of 'news values' has suggested that whilst 'objectivity' and 'impartiality' might define the *working practices* of news journalists, the events of news, far from being 'just the facts', are always, in Hall et al.'s words, ' "mapped" . . . into frameworks of meaning and interpretation':

> If the world is not to be represented as a jumble of random and chaotic events, then they must be identified (i.e. named, defined, related to other events known to the audience), and assigned to a social context (i.e. placed within a frame of meanings familiar to the audience) . . . An event only 'makes sense' if it can be located within a range of known social and cultural identifications. (1978: 54–5)

If events are not self-evidently meaningful as news, but have to be 'made to mean', then, as Stuart Hall argues elsewhere, 'it matters profoundly what and who gets represented, *what* and *who* regularly and routinely gets left out; and *how* things, people, events, relationships are represented. What we know of society depends on how things are represented to us and that knowledge in turn informs what we do and what policies we are prepared to accept' (1986: 9). And, as the 2005 *Global Media Monitoring Project* concludes, 'The world we see in the news is a world in which women are virtually invisible' (Gallagher 2006: 17).

The 2005 project was the third such project to be undertaken, and the largest: groups in seventy-six countries submitted data that were analysed and compared; in total 12,893 news stories were monitored on television, radio and in newspapers. Its findings are common to research of this nature (Gallagher 2001; Rakow and Kranich 1996; Bridge 1995; van Zoonen 1988) and so worth summarising briefly here. Women, the project found, are dramatically under-represented in the news: only 21 per cent of those heard and seen in the news are women – though this represents an increase on the 17 per cent of 1995. In stories on politics and government only 14 per cent of news subjects are women; and in economic and business news only 20 per cent (in stories about family relations the figure is 41 per cent). Even in stories about sexual or domestic violence, it is the male voice (64 per cent of news subjects) that predominates. As experts or authorities women rarely appear: men are 83 per cent of experts, and 86 per cent of spokespersons. Where women do appear, it is usually as celebrities (42 per cent), or as 'ordinary people' – eye witnesses (30 per cent), contributors of personal views (31 per cent) or the voice of popular opinion (34 per cent) – women are 42 per cent of those news subjects who are assigned 'no stated occupation'. Above all, they appear as victims. As victims of war, disaster or crime they outnumber men two to one (19 per cent of female news subjects, compared with 8 per cent of male subjects), and women are much more likely than men to appear in photographs of such scenes. But issues that specifically involve women – sexual or domestic violence, for example – are given little coverage. From a study of news reports over a two-month period in 1993–4, Cynthia Carter similarly concludes that 'violence in the domestic sphere is somehow seen to be "ordinary"'. 'Real violence' is equated with the public sphere (1998: 221–2). Where women *are* central in news stories, it is in stories that are at the periphery of the news, and even here they are likely to appear only if they are young: 72 per cent of female news subjects are under fifty (Gallagher 2006: 17–19).

Such findings are both devastating and, perhaps, surprising: things *seem* to have been getting better. This might be because the number of women *delivering* the news *has* been increasing: from 28 per cent in 1995, to 31 per cent in 2000, and 37 per cent in 2005, and this has been particularly marked in radio and television, where over 40 per cent of all items were presented by women in 2005. Yet female reporters predominate in only two areas – weather reports on television and radio (52 per cent) and stories on poverty, housing and welfare (51 per cent). In stories on politics and government women report only 32 per cent of stories, in contrast to celebrity news, where they contribute 50 per cent of reporting, or arts and entertainment, where 48 per cent of reporting is by women. And as presenters no less than news subjects, women are required to be young: up to the age of thirty-four women are in the majority as both news presenters and reporters; by the age of fifty, only 17 per cent of reporters and 7 per cent of presenters are female. Finally, it is worth noting that whilst there are more female news subjects in stories reported by female journalists than in those reported by their male counterparts, the difference is small: 25 per cent compared with 20 per cent.

An early evening news bulletin on ITV1 of 16 March 2006 can serve as illustration. The half-hour bulletin is presented by paired newscasters, male and female. Both dressed in suits, they speak alternately and introduce reports in turn. He is older, much taller (they both stand), more authoritative: his ITV News biography lists a distinguished reporting career going back to 1976 and includes a spell reporting the first Gulf war. She is younger, glamorous; her ITV News biography begins in 1996 with a traineeship at Border Television. Of the reporters they introduce, all are men apart from the health correspondent; she presents a report on hospitals, in which all the experts are men, as is the representative of 'ordinary people'. The only woman featured in the bulletin is the grandmother of a newly convicted serial killer, Daniel Gonzalez, who is pictured giving an emotional speech about the failure of Britain's psychiatric services to provide proper medical help for her grandson. Her words, however, are immediately countered by those of the police chief inspector responsible for the case, whose speech direct to camera, calm and unemotional, insists that Gonzalez was not mentally ill, simply 'clever and manipulative'. The most interesting news item for the purpose of this analysis is a report on internet pornography. Introduced by a female presenter, Nina Hossain, the item nevertheless fails to mention the gendered nature of pornography. All the experts interviewed are men, the reporter is male, and the focus is entirely procedural: police and internet experts detail how consumers of internet pornography can now be caught. The closing comments are from a male psychologist: the message, he tells us, is that '*people* have to understand that they'll get caught' (my italics).

So why should this be the case? The common-sense answer would be that, since the news offers a 'mirror on the world', it is simply a reflection of reality, however regrettable. A glance at the news bulletin described above, however, tells us that this is not the case. In the UK, women now comprise 25 per cent of hospital consultants and 38 per cent of general practitioners (*British Medical Journal*, 10 September 2005), yet they do not feature at all in the item on hospitals; none of the 'experts' on pornography featured is female, despite the amount of feminist scholarship on the subject; women are under-represented even as the voice of 'ordinary people'. *The Global Media Monitoring Project* finds similar discrepancies. In New Zealand, with 32 per cent female politicians and a female Prime Minister, only 18 per cent of political news subjects are women. Other gaps are equally wide – only 18 per cent of lawyers featured in the news are women (in the UK, the proportion of women lawyers is 32 per cent, with the majority of new entrants to the profession being women); only 12 per cent of business people, and 17 per cent of government employees.

A second explanation is developed by Lana F. Rakow and Kimberlie Kranich. They draw on John Fiske's argument that news is best described as 'masculine soap opera', since it shares with soap opera the textual characteristics of lack of final closure, multiplicity of plots and characters, repetition and familiarity (Fiske 1987: 308), but plays out its narratives not in the feminised domestic sphere, but in the public sphere which 'our society deems to be masculine' (1987: 284). Rakow and Kranich argue that any understanding of news must begin with 'its essential gendered nature as a masculine narrative, in which women function not as speaking subjects but as signs' (1996: 664). The idea that women function as signs within a masculine discourse is one which has been largely developed within feminist film and visual theory. For Rakow and Kranich, however, it is as true of news as it is of Hollywood cinema. But whereas in the latter women are sexualised, their 'to-be-looked-at-ness' functioning to play out male fantasies and obsessions (Mulvey 1989a), in news they are more often used to illustrate the private consequences of public events and actions. Just as in cinema the woman '[i]n herself . . . has not the slightest importance' (Boetticher, quoted in Mulvey 1989a: 19), despite her excessive presence as spectacle, in news, too, she acts as silent 'bearer, not maker, of meaning' (1989a: 15). As victims or witnesses, argue Rakow and Kranich, women are mute evidence of a public narrative whose (male) central agents operate in the public world of politics, policy and authority. As spokespersons or newscasters, they 'function as women but do not speak as them' (1996: 671), decorating and softening the discourses of power whose origins lie elsewhere. When they do speak *as women*, they appear unruly and disruptive.

The story of three news images can illustrate this argument. The first, which appeared on 10 April 2003, was widely published around the world. In *The Guardian*'s words, it was seen to 'define the fall of Baghdad'. In it, the statue of Saddam Hussein is pictured being pulled down by the (male) citizens of Iraq, who rejoice in its demolition, thus symbolising (or so it appeared) the replacement of tyranny by an incipient democracy. The second photograph, also published in *The Guardian* in April 2003, is an image which the photographer thought might become an equally powerful symbol of the 'liberation' of Iraq. It is a photograph of a young woman who has just given birth, discovered with her baby in an out-building by some American soldiers. It is an image of private vulner-ability produced as a metaphor for a public moment, an image which is rendered public not by the woman herself but by the presence of the soldiers who 'discover' and frame her. They mediate for us both her private-ness and her otherness; displaying her, they will also be her protectors. It is an image with deep cultural resonances (the stable at Bethlehem, the bringing of peace) for the Western photographer and his readers, but one in the construction of whose meanings the woman at its centre plays no part. But the image did not achieve the wide symbolic currency envisaged by the photographer, for two reasons. First, this baby, potential symbol of a reborn Iraq, in fact died. According to its father, the gift the soldiers brought, of dried milk, made it ill and weak. And second, its mother, who had no part in the construction of this image, was photographed again some months later, and she *did* play an important part in the meanings of this second image. In it she faces the camera, foregrounded, no longer an image of passive femininity or 'pure' motherhood but angry, thrusting her baby's death certificate at the photographer. She is now, in Rakow and Kranich's terms, both unruly and disruptive. Neither this image nor its predecessor received wide publication; neither could be successfully incorporated into the 'masculine narrative' of the invasion of Iraq, despite the apparent promise of the first of the two images. It was the photograph of the toppling of Saddam's statue which instead came to symbolise these early weeks in Iraq.

A 'fiction unlike any other'

The story of these three news photographs both illustrates Rakow and Kranich's argument and suggests its limitations. For if news no less than fictional genres imposes order and interpretation on its material by means of narrative, so that it matters profoundly *whose* story we are hearing, who speaks and who is merely spoken for, news is also, to borrow Bill Nichols' words, 'a fiction unlike any other'.[1] It is the real, historical world, the world of power, dominance and control which forms its material. Narrative control therefore both matters more – in the sense that there is more at stake – and is more precarious. The real is always unruly and contingent, as we saw in the example above. That the baby born to the woman in the photograph died was an event in the real world that disturbed a potential narrative order. It could, of course, have become the material of a very different narrative, one which would have positioned the woman as discursive subject, not silent visual object, and would have contested not maintained the dominant meanings given to the Iraqi invasion. As it was, these alternative meanings remain as unassimilated, resistant traces in the early news narratives of the event.

Myra Macdonald extends this argument in her analysis of women's voices in British television documentaries. She argues that, of the three available modes of presenting women's accounts of their own lives – the confessional, the case study and testimony – only the third allows the 'movement between the woman's subjectivity and social or political circumstances' to become textually visible in a way that can challenge existing assumptions (1998: 114). The confessional mode, she writes, offers us personal emotion as spectacle, inviting 'voyeuristic consumption' rather than understanding of underlying political or social issues.

The case study allows women to speak in their own voices, but as examples, framed within an authoritative discourse originating elsewhere. Only in 'testimony', she writes, can the shift from experience to analysis, the personal to the political, take place. Through a range of techniques, the personal and experiential can in these cases cease to be merely individual, instead challenging existing political explanations and insisting on the link between women's personal experiences and the public circumstances that have helped to construct them. In such cases, the 'impossibility of accurately recollecting or representing the unrepresentable leaves the contradictions of the experience lying rawly open, and prevents any comforting closure for the viewer' (1998: 118).

Central to Macdonald's argument is a critique of the division between the public and the private sphere which underpins the claims to a privileged access to 'the real' made for news and documentary. What Bill Nichols calls the 'sobriety' of these discourses, or John Corner the 'public project of documentary' (1995: 91), relies on a privileging of the objective over the subjective, the 'independent integrity of the topic' (1995: 91) over access for the personal voice. As Corner argues, it is important for 'the public integrity of the form' that the former is not subordinated to the latter. In Nichols' terms, it is the 'objectivity' of its gaze that protects documentary against the charge of voyeurism (1991: 244). The fact that these defining concepts – objective/subjective, public/personal, sober/trivial – are also profoundly gendered lies at the heart both of why news remains so persistently, in Rakow and Kranich's words, 'a masculine narrative', and of why the claims for the *importance* of news and documentary are also always simultaneously a claim to the essential *masculinity* of these genres.

Constructing the public sphere

Any move to incorporate elements of the private into the public sphere, argues Liesbet van Zoonen, is 'likely to result in concerned discourses about the devaluation of the public sphere', and in the case of news, even the threat of its 'discursive expulsion from the public sphere' (1991: 227–8). We can see this clearly in the *Radio Times* reader's letter quoted earlier in this chapter, which ends with the charge that the intrusion into news of 'viewers' opinions' is 'another sign of the death of serious current affairs' marked by the 'turning of news into entertainment' (*RT*, 8 April 2006). Evidently making a popular case, this 'Letter of the Week' was accompanied by a black and white photograph of a 1950s BBC male newsreader at his microphone, accompanied by the caption 'Times have changed . . . too much, perhaps?'

The idea that news and documentary genres have an important function in the public sphere which is vital to the successful working of democracy, is central to our political culture. John Corner defines news as 'part of general citizenship rights', its function 'to provide knowledge and understanding about circumstances of consequence to readers, listeners and viewers, to contribute not only to their understanding but also to their capacities for judgement and action' (1995: 55). It is an idea whose origins lie in the European Enlightenment, with its replacement of the authority of the Church with a belief in universal reason, progress and freedom. Central to this were five key notions: the primacy of *reason* and rationality as ways of organising knowledge; belief in *scientific empiricism* as the way of testing and expanding knowledge; belief in *the individual* as the starting point for knowledge and action; belief in *progress* as a result of the application of reason and science; and belief in *freedom* and *toleration* as the way in which social, moral and economic life should be organised (Hamilton 1992). These beliefs were manifested in the crucial institutional transformations which characterised modernity: the development of the nation-state; the emergence of a capitalist economic order based on private property; the growth of large-scale systems of social organisation and regulation separate from king and court; and the formal separation of the 'public' from the 'private' (Hall et al. 1992: 3).

It is the last of these, the development of an autonomous 'public sphere', which has been centrally linked to the rise of critical news media. Jürgen Habermas defines the public sphere as

> first of all a realm of our social life in which something approaching public opinion can be formed. Access is guaranteed to all citizens. A portion of the public sphere comes into being in every conversation in which private individuals assemble to form a public body. (1984: 49)

Habermas argues that modern social life is composed of four realms, divided along two axes: public/private, and system-integrated/socially-integrated. The economy and the state are both system-integrated, their function being material reproduction, but the economy belongs to the private and the state to the public domain. The two corresponding socially-integrated realms, whose function is symbolic reproduction (the reproduction of values), are the two institutions of the 'life-world': the family and the public sphere. Linking economy and family are the roles of worker and consumer; linking state and public sphere are the roles of citizen and client (Fraser 1989; Livingstone and Lunt 1994).

The ideal of the public sphere as described by Habermas[2] is that of 'private individuals who came together to debate among themselves the regulation of civil society and the conduct of the state' (Thompson 1995: 70). It is an institutionalised site for debate, a space for the production and circulation of discourses which can be critical of the state. Its two key characteristics are its quality of rational-critical discourse, and the principle of universal access on which it is based. It is, in other words, the quality of the argument which is decisive here, not the status of the participant. This is a more precise usage of the term 'public sphere' than we often find. It has been more usual, particularly among feminist critics, to include the state, the official economy of paid employment *and* arenas for the circulation of public discourses within definitions of the public, in an adaptation of Marxist analyses of the division between production and reproduction, the state/industry and the family (Fraser 1992). Part of the feminist argument has been to insist that 'the personal is political': that the privatised sphere of the family and personal relationships is as suffused with power relations as the public world of industry and state politics. The use of 'public sphere' to designate a realm of *discursive* activity, however, 'brackets out' issues of power, since all who speak in this realm are assumed to do so as equals. In doing this, it allows us to see both the idealised nature of this realm – and its function *as* an ideal for its advocates – and its dependence on the notion of a free and independent news media.

It was with the emergence of the periodical press in the eighteenth century, argues Habermas, that the public sphere as he defines it was able to develop. These journals often began as publications devoted to literary and cultural criticism, but, helped by the ending of censorship in Britain in 1695, journals such as the *Tatler* (1709) or the *Spectator* (1711) became increasingly concerned with social and political issues, supplementing news with critical articles. With the expansion in these journals, argues Habermas, 'the press was for the first time established as a genuinely critical organ of a public engaged in critical debate: as the fourth estate' (1989: 60). Read and debated in the coffee houses which flourished in Europe's capital cities, they provided the means by which members of an educated, propertied elite could engage in informed and rational debate over the issues of the day. According to Habermas, this new development produced 'the critical judgement of a public making use of its reason' (1989: 24). Through it, modern states were made more accountable, their processes increasingly open to scrutiny and the force of public opinion. 'From now on,' writes Habermas, 'the degree of the public sphere's development was measured by the state of the confrontation between government and press' (1989: 60).

There have been a number of important criticisms of the Habermasian conception of the public sphere. The notion that a rational-critical discourse can be constructed which circulates outside structures of social and cultural power is highly problematic. As Stuart Allan points out, 'precisely what counts as "rational" or "reasoned", or even "critical" for that matter, is always a question of definitional power: whose discourse, we need to ask, is so defined and why?' (1997: 303). Despite its ideal of free and open participation, the bourgeois public sphere described by Habermas was in fact highly restrictive, the preserve of educated and propertied elite men. Of the various exclusions which this implies, that of women, as feminist critics have pointed out, is the most important, since it is actually *constitutive* of the concept of the public sphere. In Habermas's account, the public sphere is composed of economically independent individuals who can move freely between the private and the public realms, developing and sustaining their self-knowledge and sense of the 'human' in the former, articulating this sense through rational ethical and political debate in the latter (Habermas 1989: 50–2). Clearly, then, this rational public sphere depends for its existence and status on its binary other: the warm, intimate, *irrational* and feminised realm of the private. Equally, the social and spatial mobility, the 'capacities for consent and speech, the ability to participate on a par with others in dialogue' which characterise its participants are 'capacities that are connected with masculinity in male-dominated, classical capitalism; they are capacities that are in myriad ways denied to women and deemed at odds with femininity' (Fraser 1989: 126). Not only were women denied property rights, they 'lost and still routinely lose their proper name in marriage, and [their] signature – not merely their voice – has not been worth the paper it was written on' (Miller 1990: 118). Moreover, as Joan Landes has shown in relation to republican France, the new public sphere was constructed precisely in opposition to the 'feminised' salon culture which it replaced. The 'new category of the "public man" and his "virtue" was established via a series of oppositions to "femininity"'(Eley 1992: 309): masculinity was constructed as a social and political identity, in opposition to a femininity identified with pleasure, play, eroticism and artifice. When in 1871, then, American feminists Victoria Woodhull and Tennessee Claflin used their own newly launched newspaper, *Woodhull and Claflin's Weekly*,[3] to protest about the differential meanings of the terms 'free' and 'virtuous' when applied to men and women, they were challenging both the terms and the reality of this gendered construction of the public sphere. As 'applied to *man*', they write, '*virtue* . . . means moral goodness, or a general conformity of the whole life to high moral ideas and purposes', but 'applied to *woman*, it means . . . that woman has never been approached in a special way by man, and nothing but that', so that 'the woman may have all the nobler qualities of her sex – be a pattern of generosity, inspiration, religious emotionality even – and yet she is not virtuous, and never can become so' (Woodhull and Claflin 1972: 147). Their proposed solution, that women should *reclaim* these terms to force new definitions, would become popular as a tactic 100 years later. In the case of Woodhull and Claflin, it led to their imprisonment for obscenity and slander.

Difference and the public sphere

Michael Warner draws attention to a further aspect of the gendered distinction between public and private spheres. The principle of universality which is central to the ideal of the public sphere as site of rational-critical debate is also a principle of 'self-abstraction' or disembodiment. Implicit in it is 'a utopian universality which would allow people to transcend the given realities of their bodies and their status' (1992: 382). Yet such a denial of the body is only possible to those whose bodies are 'unmarked' by difference or an 'excess' of embodiment – those whose bodies are white and male. Women in particular cannot speak from a position of 'disembodiment' without transgressing norms of femininity. As Warner comments, 'Self-abstraction from male bodies confirms masculinity. Self-abstraction from female bodies denies femininity' (1992: 383).[4] The principle of universal self-abstraction thus acts as a powerful exclusionary device. Under this principle, the personal *cannot* become political in the way that Myra Macdonald, for example, advocates in her concept of 'testimony', since whilst bodies can be spoken *about*, they cannot be permitted to speak unless this voice is framed within the rational-critical discourse of objectivity. Yet, as Seyla Benhabib points out:

> All struggles against oppression in the modern world begin by redefining what had previously been considered private, non-public, and non-political issues as matters of public concern, as issues of justice, as sites of power that need discursive legitimation . . . There is little room in the liberal model of neutrality for thinking about the logic of such struggles. (1992: 84)

It is from the private sphere – the sphere of personal identity, everyday culture and embodied difference – that many of the most important contemporary movements for political and social justice have arisen. What has characterised these forms of 'identity politics' has been an insistence on, not a 'bracketing out' of, difference and power inequalities. A model of 'neutrality' which excludes these voices simply masks the power structures that sustain it.

In fact, of course, as Nancy Fraser has shown, gender permeates all the roles and relationships which Habermas describes as characterising his public and private realms. The roles of worker and consumer which he sees as linking economy and family are gendered roles. It is not that women cannot be workers, or men consumers, but these roles are conceived in gendered terms, so that men occupy the role of consumer 'with conceptual strain and cognitive dissonance, much as women occupy the role of worker' (Fraser 1989: 125). In a similar way, the role of citizen which links state and public sphere is an implicitly masculine role; it is identified with power and activity in the public world. The role of client in contrast, with its assumption of passivity, is gendered feminine.

Nevertheless, it is the assumed neutrality of public sphere discourse, its ideal of objectivity and rational-critical debate, which has been carried forward into our conception of news,[5] as we can see from John Corner's definition of it as 'part of general citizenship rights', which should 'provide knowledge and understanding' about the public world which will contribute to the citizen's 'capacities for judgement and action'. This, too, however, depends on a very partial history. Histories of the press in Britain suggest a far more diverse picture than is painted in the Habermasian account. As well as the *Spectator* and the *Tatler*, the eighteenth century saw the emergence of a multiplicity of titles such as the *Lover, Nocturnal News*, or the *Weekly Pacquet*; scandal sheets, used to print 'puffs' or suppress damaging gossip, were common (Williams 1998: 23–5); and the first woman's magazine, the *Ladies Mercury*, appeared in 1693.[6] If the scurrilous and sensational, scandal and the body were a large part of this early landscape of the press, however, it is the ideal of Swift's *Examiner* (1710) and Defoe's *Review* (1704), discussed 'in clubs and coffee houses, at home and in the streets' (Habermas 1989: 59), that for Habermas constitute the beginnings of a critical public sphere.

It is this ideal, too, which is carried forward into contemporary defences of news and current affairs genres, and their principles of 'objectivity' and 'impartiality', particularly where these are found within public service broadcasting, with its Reithian ideal of 'universality' (Morgan 1986: 30). In this argument, it is the 'powerful and arresting vision of the role of media in a democratic society' offered by the Habermasian model, not its historical accuracy, that is important (Curran 1991: 83). Nicholas Garnham makes precisely such a defence of the BBC, which, he argues, 'made a noble effort to address [its] listeners as rational human beings rather than as consumers' (1995: 245). His focus in this claim is and must be, he argues, on news, documentaries and current affairs genres, because it is here that rational public debate is pursued. In an argument which echoes Habermas' account of the relationship between the private and the public spheres, Garnham continues that whilst it is in our interactions with 'nonrationalist . . . forms of popular entertainment' that we develop self-understandings and a sense of identity, we develop as *citizens* only through our ability to 'arrive at more overtly rational and political opinions and actions' (1995: 374). Elsewhere, his debt to the Habermasian ideal is more explicit, and more clearly gendered. Political communication, he writes, should be about 'real issues and choices', not 'people's dreams and fantasies'. Recalling the Habernasian ideal of coffee house discussion, he asks us to 'think of the profound political difference between reading a newspaper in one's place of work or in a café and discussing it with those who share that concrete set of social relations on the one hand, and watching TV within the family circle or listening to radio or watching a video-cassette on an individual domestic basis on the other' (1995: 247–8). He is equally concerned to reject political movements arising from 'identity politics' as any form of rational political action. Instead they are identified with the (irrational) feminine and the ephemeral (fashion, consumerism). The 'current fashion for movement politics, CND, the women's movement, and so on', he writes, is born of a 'consumerist ideology' and 'in no way provides an alternative to the political party . . . You cannot develop a realistic and realizable movement towards disarmament or women's rights unless it is integrated . . . into some . . . *universal* programme of political priorities' (1995: 249, my italics).

Women and news discourse

To return to the analysis of news with which this chapter began, then, it is not surprising that women fit so uneasily within its discourse. To include the voices of women speaking *as women* would be to challenge both the principle of 'universal self-abstraction' (Warner) which underpins it, and the particular form of rationalist discourse which characterises it. To borrow Nancy Fraser's terms, women can occupy the role of news subject only 'with conceptual strain and cognitive dissonance'. How, then, should we understand the increasing presence of women as news *presenters?* In a study of the first women news presenters to appear regularly on British television, Angela Rippon (from 1975) and Anna Ford (from 1978), Patricia Holland points to the fact that the press saw them initially as 'an opportunity for jokes, pictures and suggestive comments'. 'Women', she comments, 'are about sexuality, the news is not'. Their presence was seen to 'trivialise' the serious business of news (1987: 134–5). Thus, whilst the head and shoulders shot of the male news presenter is familiar to us as an image of assurance and power, so that he seems to speak as the authoritative voice *of* the news, the same shot of the female presenter carries no such authority. Women are more usually represented in terms of their bodies, not their words, within the private not the public sphere, and their faces are more often employed to express emotion not neutrality. Women therefore represent 'the very antithesis of news values. They are the very sign of dissent and disruption' (1987: 148). To speak with authority, then, they must be seen to *perform* a discourse which they do not originate. They cannot speak *as* or *for* women, and their appearance must be carefully constructed so that it 'stresses their femininity yet defers to the seriousness of the news, . . . complements that of the man, yet takes care not to impinge on the male preserve' (1987: 148). Their growing presence as news presenters, she argues, is a consequence of the shifting address of television news, which must be seen to speak to a more varied and plural audience than in the days of the BBC's 'universal' and disembodied address, but their presence as 'decorative performers' merely masks women's actual exclusion from news discourse.

It is the move towards a greater intimacy in news address that Liesbet van Zoonen takes up in her study of women as news presenters on Dutch television. Women presenters, she writes, are increasingly used to establish 'an intimate and personal relationship' with their audience (1991: 225), mediating between the public world of news and the domestic conditions of its reception through their 'woman's touch'. Rather than blurring the boundaries of a gendered public-private division, therefore, their presence in fact 'assumes and reconstructs' it (1991: 227). In the UK, a glance at the web profiles of BBC news presenters is suggestive in this respect. As a presenter, we learn, Fiona Bruce is 'cool, calm and collected under pressure', an appearance, however, which belies 'her secret wild side'. In her first job, she confesses, she was so unhappy that 'I used to cry in the loos at lunchtime', but after a 'shaky start' as a news presenter during which she suffered from 'nervous tension', she has now found the ideal role, because her position as 'number two' presenter on the ten o'clock news 'fits in perfectly with her other job – raising two small children, Sam, five and Mia, one'. The BBC's 'number one' ten o'clock news presenter, Huw Edwards (married with five children), on the other hand, joined the BBC because it was 'an institution of huge respect'. As a political correspondent, he had 'covered most of this century's major political stories', enjoying the role because 'you were there when something important was happening', and despite his move to presenting, his 'passion for politics remains as strong as ever'. He remains, he says, 'hungry and ambitious' (http://news.bbc.co.uk). The BBC's female news presenters are far more likely also to present light entertainment shows – Natasha Kaplinsky, for example, has followed her predecessor Angela Rippon by presenting *Strictly Come Dancing* – whilst their male counterparts host current affairs discussion programmes. It is their distinguished history as reporters and political correspondents which is stressed in the case of the male presenters – as if this is their *real* identity. It is the need to balance the personal and the professional which dominates in the women's profiles (Natasha Kaplinsky has to 'make sure she looks good – and also that she's well briefed'), since this is an essential part of their 'feminine' identity. As van Zoonen points out, however, this attempt both to include women as news presenters and simultaneously to suggest that their *primary* identification is with the personal and domestic produces a precarious balance. Too much 'intimization' generates concerns that viewers are no longer being addressed as citizens, concerned to understand the serious issues of public life.[7] The intimacy of address associated with the feminine is quickly felt to be eroding rational-critical debate.

Public and private bodies

In an essay which discusses American television news coverage of the O. J. Simpson murder trial in 1994, Lisa McLaughlin details some of the shifts that have taken place in TV news reporting over the past twenty years. The live coverage of the trial, with its attendant commercial spin-offs in the form of talk shows, magazine coverage and sales of merchandise such as T-shirts and banners, was far from the 'sobriety' traditionally associated with news discourse. The CNN anchor described it on air as 'a blur of news, entertainment, and tabloid-like reporting in a surrounding of circus-like atmosphere' (McLaughlin 1998: 72). Rather than taking place in the public sphere as Habermas envisaged it, then, the trial seemed to occupy a very different public space which McLaughlin calls 'media event space', a space which comes into being *only* through media representation.

From a Habermasian perspective, such a development would seem to confirm the argument made in *The Structural Transformation of the Public Sphere* that the rise of the commercial mass media over the last two centuries has produced a shift from 'a culture-debating to a culture-consuming public', and with it the effective destruction of the public sphere (Habermas 1989: 159). 'The world fashioned by the mass media', argues Habermas, 'is a public sphere in appearance only' (1989: 171). Citizens have become consumers, individuated and fragmented, seduced by media spectacle and manipulated by media techniques. Privatised reception has replaced dialogical exchange. Instead of 'doing justice to reality, [news media have] a tendency to present a substitute more palatable for consumption and more likely to give rise to an impersonal indulgence in stimulating relaxation than to a public use of reason' (1989: 170). The public sphere has thus been 'refeudalized', as the image creation and opinion management of a growing public relations industry wipes out rational-critical debate, just as it did in the staged publicity of medieval courts. Instead of a separation between public and private, in which an 'inner life [is] oriented toward a public audience' and articulated in debate, the domain of the private is 'dragged into the open' by the forces of publicity. As a result, the separation of public and private so crucial to the workings of democracy is blurred: 'the sphere generated by the mass media has taken on the traits of a secondary realm of intimacy' (1989: 172).

For McLaughlin, as for other critics, however, this does not adequately account for the kind of media event that the O. J. Simpson trial became. In explaining this new form of 'mediated publicness', John B. Thompson distinguishes between the definition of 'public' as 'the domain of institutionalized power' and its meaning as 'open', 'visible' or 'available to the public' (1995: 121–3). The emphasis placed by Habermas on the dialogical quality of the public sphere, he suggests, obscures this second sense; a public event was always a *visible* event, even if in its eighteenth-century manifestations it would always have involved a co-present audience able to engage and respond. Electronically-based media have heightened this relation between publicness and visibility and have, as Habermas suggests, produced the 'management of visibility' so characteristic of contemporary political power. But the terrain of the publicly visible, argues Thompson, cannot be fully controlled and is never uncontested, as the frequency of political leaks and scandals suggests.

Thompson therefore contests the Habermasian narrative of the degeneration of the public sphere, but he also contests the very different account of the relationship between power and visibility developed by Michel Foucault. Like Habermas, Foucault characterises pre-modern societies as 'societies of spectacle', in which the few were made visible to the many and power was exercised through its public manifestation. In the modern world, however, he argues that these were replaced by societies characterised by discipline and surveillance, in which institutions like the army, the prison, the school and the hospital exercise power through disciplinary training and the normalising power of the gaze. In these modern societies, argues Foucault, the many are made visible to the few, and surveillance – and increasingly *self*-surveillance – is the means by which regulatory control is exercised (Thompson 1995: 132–4). For

Thompson, both accounts are faulty. Whilst the development of communication technologies undoubtedly permits surveillance of the many
by the few, he argues, what is far more characteristic of modern societies
is, as Habermas suggests, the hugely extended visibility of the few. But
whilst politicians and PR agents seek to 'manage' this visibility, this new
space of 'mediated visibility' constitutes the crucial arena not only for the
manipulation but also for the contestation of social power. Moreover, this
mediated space comprises not only news but all the forms of mediated
conversation condemned by Habermas – talk shows, reality television,
mass circulation magazines. It is non-localised and non-dialogical, but it
is also open-ended, because it can never be fully delimited or controlled.
Thus the intrusion of the private into the public, which Habermas sees as
a sign of the degeneration of the public sphere, can instead mean that the
'media can *politicize the everyday* by making it visible and observable in
ways that previously were not possible, thereby turning everyday events
into a catalyst for action that spills well beyond the immediate locales in
which these events occurred' (Thompson 1995: 248).

The O. J. Simpson trial described by McLaughlin is clearly one such
event. She describes the way in which, as a media event, it *both* opened 'a
forum for the public discussion of formerly "private" concerns, such as
domestic violence' *and* at the same time allowed 'the spectacular
representation of celebrity power . . . to act as a shield and substitute
for public debate of the issues' (1998: 81). In this space of 'mediated
visibility', then, competing interests struggle for representational power,
and the boundaries between a culture-debating and a culture-consuming
public become blurred. But McLaughlin also draws attention to another
aspect of the Simpson case coverage which is not considered within
Thompson's arguments, and which raises questions about his thesis that
the space of 'mediated visibility' constitutes the crucial contemporary
arena for the display and contestation of social power. In the media
representations of the Simpson case, McLaughlin argues, *bodies* were
everywhere: 'bodies and cultural differences . . . were irrepressible,
bursting through the seams of the objectivist epistemology that informs
the languages of law and journalism' (1998: 74). This is a powerfully
physical image, and one which McLaughlin repeats, and it takes us back
to Warner's critique of the 'disembodied' nature of the Habermasian
public sphere. In drawing our attention to this crucial difference between
the newer 'mediated public visibility' and its 'disembodied' predecessor,
however, it also alerts us to some of the difficulties in trying to think
through the gendered significance of this change. For, if *women* are
conspicuously present in the public world of television talk shows and
'reality TV' into which news now spills, their visibility as *bodies* does not

necessarily signal the politicising of the personal which some critics would suggest.

Body politics

As I have suggested elsewhere (Thornham 2001), what separated much feminist analysis of the 1970s and 1980s from male-centred work in media and cultural studies was its 'body politics'. Arguing that in the discourses of modernity, corporeality has been, in Elizabeth Grosz's phrase, 'coded feminine', so that '[p]atriarchal oppression . . . justifies itself, at least in part, by connecting women much more closely than men to the body and, through this identification, restricting women's social and economic roles' (Grosz 1994: 14), feminists have analysed the ways in which cultural structures have functioned both to confine women *to* their objectified and passive bodies and to estrange them *from* their bodies. In later studies, the work of Michel Foucault has been used to argue that women's bodies are subject to very specific disciplinary controls through cultural images and norms. What these studies of the 'disciplining' of women's bodies have in common is a focus on the ways in which discursive practices intersect with social, economic, medical, legal and political structures to produce meanings about the female body which are embodied both in representations and in cultural practices. Thus Susan Bordo, for example, writes that 'the body that we experience and conceptualize is always *mediated* by constructs, associations, images of a cultural nature' (1993: 35). This construction of femininity functions as a homogenizing and normalizing discipline, 'erasing racial, class, and other differences and insisting that all women aspire to a coercive, standardized ideal' (Bordo 1989: 16). But it is through 'the practices and bodily habits of everyday life' that these bodily disciplines are enacted: for women, 'culture's grip on the body is a constant, intimate fact of everyday life' (Bordo 1993: 17).

Extending this analysis, Hilary Radner (1995) argues that what characterises manifestations of these disciplinary practices in the 1980s onwards is the way in which this 'feminine body' has become a 'public body'. As women have moved increasingly from their position within the private domestic realm and into the public sphere of work, she argues, so the disciplinary practices which have regulated and produced their bodies have become correspondingly organised as a form of 'public discipline'. Radner's focus in this essay is on the 'aerobics craze' in the US of the 1980s, and specifically on the *Jane Fonda's Workout* books and exercise videos, which promise women self-empowerment through submission to a regime of public visibility. But in the Fonda emphasis on self-empowerment through self-mastery, in her confession to a struggle with anorexia but commitment to achieving a 'healthy body', in her emphasis on a self-transformation to be accomplished by work (and plastic surgery) but manifested in appearance, and in the centrality of public visibility to these processes, we can see the paradigm which is currently played out in a multitude of talk shows and makeover programmes. The politics of this new public visibility, writes Radner, are at best ambiguous.

A new public sphere?

For some critics, the blurring of public-private boundaries which characterises these new hybrid genres signals a positive transformation of the public sphere. Ib Bondebjerg, for example, argues that it could be seen as 'a result of the democratic impact of visual media on public discourse through a new *integration* of forms of public and private interaction which used to be clearly separated'. What we may be witnessing, therefore, is the 'democratization of an old public service discourse ... and the creation of a new mixed public sphere, where common knowledge and everyday experience play a much larger role' (1996: 29). In a similar way, Sonia Livingstone and Peter Lunt argue that 'in the audience discussion programme, experts and lay people are put together, setting an agenda of social issues and offering both established elites and ordinary people the opportunity at least to discuss the lived experience of current-affairs issues in relation to expert solutions'. In this process, both the Habermasian 'life-world' and his 'system world' experience the collapse of public-private distinctions (1994: 132, 180). Talk shows, argues Laura Grindstaff, challenge 'conventional boundaries separating public from private, reason from emotion, news from entertainment, fact from fiction, and expert knowledge from common opinion' (1997: 165). Other critics have pointed to the potential feminist implications of this boundary-blurring. Jane Shattuc, asking whether the audience of daytime talk shows might be 'the newest incarnation of the public sphere' (1997: 87), emphasises the debt which they owe to the 'feminist movement':

> Their principal aim has been to build up women's self-esteem, confidence, and identity ... The shows take place in an arena of collective feminine experience. The form of their practice results from the women's movement and feminist therapy – specifically, the consciousness-raising group as a democratic forum – a place where women create community in the absence of authority by drawing on their social experiences and morality. (Shattuc 1997: 122)

It is an argument which some of the shows' hosts, most notably Oprah Winfrey, have echoed, claiming to 'empower women' (quoted in Squire 1997: 98). 'It is not too far-fetched', comments Patricia Mellencamp, 'to imagine daytime talk as the electronic, syndicated version of consciousness-raising groups of the women's movement' (1992: 218).

Yet on the whole, critics have been ambivalent about these claims. Shattuc concludes that '[e]ssentially daytime talk shows are not feminist', although they 'do represent popular TV at its most feminist' (1997: 136). Mellencamp argues that if talk shows validate women's experiences and emotions, they also produce them as 'abnormalities or scandals', adding that in 'the divisions between daytime and primetime, entertainment and news, the aberrant and the normal (and homosexuality and heterosexuality), taxonomies emblematic of private/public spaces, TV enacts institutional containment – reminiscent of Foucault's definition of the disciplinary society' (1992: 265). So how can we best understand both the shows themselves and the ambivalence of their critics?

First, this is a genre in which notions of 'the real' and 'authenticity' are as central as they are for news. As Grindstaff argues, ' "real" stories told by "ordinary" people are the bedrock of the genre' (1997: 189), and the processes by which stories are sourced, selected and authenticated are very similar to those employed in newsgathering. Yet despite their title, 'talk' in these programmes is on the whole restricted to the host, the 'expert', and occasional interjections by audience members; participants are inarticulate, tearful or aggressive – though in US shows they may on occasion also echo, tentatively, the therapeutic discourse of the 'expert'. This is a 'real' identified with women and the working class: the *body* is the domain in which it operates. As Elspeth Probyn puts it, the talk show 'is ruled by bodies' (1992: 93), and 'the real' of the bodies which it displays is one of emotion and excess. In an essay on 'body genres' in film, Linda Williams argues that what characterises these genres – horror, melodrama and pornography – is a form of bodily excess: 'the body "beside itself" with sexual pleasure, fear and terror'. It is an excess which is rendered not through language but through 'inarticulate cries' and tears, and it is one which invites the spectator into a lack of 'proper' distance, 'a sense of over-involvement in sensation and emotion'. Above all, it is on the bodies of *women* that these excesses have been written: women 'have functioned traditionally as the primary *embodiments* of pleasure, fear and pain'. Williams concludes that the function of these 'low' genres is 'cultural problem solving'; they address 'persistent problems in our culture, in our sexualities, in our very identities'. Their 'solutions' – excessive and performative – do not of course resolve the problems they address, but they do, repetitively, display them in what Williams elsewhere calls a 'frenzy of the visible' (Williams 1991: 2–12; 1990). Within the domain of the televised 'real', we can argue, talk shows offer a similar form of 'problem solving', presenting, as Grindstaff argues, narratives of 'explicit revelation where people . . . "bare it all" for the pleasure, fascination, or repulsion of viewers' (1997: 169).

The comparison of talk shows to other 'low' genres, particularly 'women's genres' has proved attractive to critics. Jane Shattuc describes the talk show as offering a 'melodramatic narrative', in which participants are cast in the role of victim (usually female) or perpetrator (male), and the ideal of 'home' and the fear or pathos of its loss are the strongest themes (1997: 80–1). Livingstone and Lunt prefer the parallel of romance, in which the victim is rescued by the hero (the host, especially when male) with the aid of helpers in the form of both bystanders (the studio audience) and those with knowledge (the 'experts') (1994: 60). Yet a further comparison can be made with the 'grotesque' or 'unruly' female body of comedy, particularly when it is the fat body. Fatness in women, as Kathleen Rowe argues, is a form of 'making a spectacle' of oneself. Both she and Mary Russo argue that this out-of-control body – the 'open, protruding, extended, secreting body', in Russo's words (1988: 219) – can be a figure of transgression, with 'oppositional potential' (Rowe 1997: 82). Yet, as Rowe admits, for working class women, this body is 'more likely to be a source of embarrassment, timidity, and alienation, because the norms of the "legitimate" body – beauty, fitness, and so on – are accepted across class boundaries while the ability to achieve them is not' (1997: 80).

An episode of *Trisha Goddard* (C5, 23 March 2006) shows these narratives at work. The episode features four stories of dysfunctional mother-child relationships, separated by advertising breaks, with a final coda which returns us to the first of the stories. The programme operates conventions common to many talk shows. The participants are brought onstage in turn to sit facing a studio audience, without the protection of the table or desk which would shield a panel of 'experts'. The host, Trisha, moves between stage and audience, often touching the onstage participants and crouching down to speak to them. Another camera takes us backstage, for reaction shots from those yet to be presented, and allows us to see glimpses of the therapeutic process which follows the onstage interactions. In the first story we meet a mother, Ann, whose teenage son, Trisha tells us, 'spends seven hours a day surfing the net to meet strangers for sex'. *His* story is of the isolation felt by a gay teenager who is, he says, searching for 'comfort . . . someone who I can talk to, tell all my troubles to'. But it is *Ann's* situation, that of a mother fearful of losing her child, her emotions manifested in tears and physical symptoms, on which we focus. The 'solution' to this problem of maternal suffering is to forbid him the internet, mend their relationship, and restore her self-esteem through a makeover in which the son will assist. At the end of the programme the pair re-appear, to applause; a newly glamorised Ann feels 'lovely' and, says her son, 'looks beautiful'. They plan to hold a party together.

In the second story the protagonist is a daughter, Sheena, whose mother, she feels, has rejected her. As a child, we learn, she constantly ran away from home. Again, there is a reunion with tears, but, with the help of audience questions, Trisha hints at a history of childhood abuse which led to Sheena's feeling of rejection and history of self-harm. 'A lot of women have been through what you have and come out the other side,' says Trisha. A counsellor takes Sheena by the hand and leads her offstage.

In the third story, a mother is again the protagonist, her daughter the object of concern. Cheryl has spent over £10,000 on cosmetic surgery and halved her body weight. She is now attractive and well dressed; the audience greets the details of her self-transformation with applause. Her daughter, Samantha, is grossly overweight, poorly dressed and dirty: an out-of-control body. 'What do you think of what your mum's achieved?' Trisha asks, without response. Samantha, suggests Trisha, is 'going through a cycle of depression' and probably needs 'some sort of help'. Samantha is enrolled at a gym and given a mood diary. She will return when her weight loss is sufficient to transform her from victim to 'expert'.

Finally, we are presented with a mother who is afraid of her daughter's violent temper. It will, she fears, cause her daughter, Sian, to harm, and lose, her own small children. Here, again, is a body out of control. The cause is revealed to be low self-esteem: 'As a child I wasn't liked', Sian confesses, and in answer to Trisha, reveals that she does not feel that she is a good person. A counsellor is called in and leads the pair offstage. 'Everybody needs their mum with them,' comments Trisha.

As in many of these shows, 'the real' is manifested here not in words (the childhood abuse suggested in the second story is never made explicit; none of the participants is able to articulate their feelings) but through emotional and bodily display (the marks of self-harming which Trisha uncovers on Sheena's arms, the suffocating and tearful embraces). It is presented by a host who combines the status of 'survivor' ('I'm thinking of when *I* was in my most depressed state,' she says to Samantha) and therapist,[8] and displayed for a studio audience composed almost entirely of women. In the show's accompanying booklet, Trisha describes this audience as fulfilling the traditional role of 'extended families and friends [who] were just around the corner and always there to supply advice and support'. But sympathetic though they (and we) may be, it is the staged display of bodily and emotional excess which produces the show as media entertainment ('shocking revelations' are promised by its trailer), and it is the transformation and containment of this excess which provides its narrative structure. The normative values of the show combine the traditional (the family, conventional gender roles, a female community centred on the domestic) with post-feminist ideas of self empowerment through disciplinary bodily practices (the makeover, exercise, cosmetic surgery). But neither the personal nor the everyday is *politicised*.

Strategies of containment

In some shows these personal narratives *are* opened out to become more general statements: Sally Jesse Raphael provides statistics of marital abuse to accompany the personal stories of abuse we see; Oprah Winfrey includes figures on addiction to crystal meth. as background to individual narratives of addiction and recovery. But it is rare to find *testimony*, as Macdonald defines it, in which the voice of individual experience can break through its framing, to challenge the structures of meaning which seek to contain it. More usually, framing discourses are imposed and accepted, from injunctions to self-empowerment and family support, to more authoritative therapeutic discourses and overt disciplinary control. From Trisha's 'You probably need some sort of help' and the injunction of Oprah's expert to 'make a commitment' to recovery, it is a short step to the advice of *Dr Phil* (himself an expert) that 'You've got to take your power back' by 'know[ing] your authentic self', and thence to the shouted instruction of Sally Jesse Raphael's expert, 'You're going to listen to what I have to say', followed by military-style exercises during which the victim of domestic abuse chants, 'We're not taking it no more, we're not living with lies no more . . .' Even more overtly disciplinary, courtroom programmes like *Judge Judy*, in Laurie Ouellette's words, fuse 'an image of democracy . . . with a privatized approach to conflict management and an intensified government of the self', seeking to 'shape and guide the conduct and choices of lower-income women in particular' (2004: 232). Here the set is courtroom rather than stage, the audience respectful and silent, host has become judge, and the discourse demanded of the participants is evidential. Stories of emotional and bodily excess are recounted and sometimes displayed, but they are used, in Ouellette's words, to train participants and viewers to become 'self-disciplining, self-sufficient, responsible, and risk-averting individuals' (2004: 232).

We can see the same structures at work in makeover programmes. C4's *Ten Years Younger* offers to reverse the passage of time for participants (or at least to turn back their 'poll age') through a series of expert interventions: dental and plastic surgery; hair, makeup and fashion training. As a result they will improve both their 'personal life' and, even more important, their careers. As we saw in relation to news, as women age, they become invisible in the public sphere. The *solution* is to change their clothes, their faces and their bodies, the *problem* not one of social structures but of inadequate self-management leading to poor self-esteem. Shirley, then, who is forty-one but, according to an audience of passers by, 'looks fifty-two', has 'sagging skin, Deputy Dawg eyebags and tombstone teeth'. Unlike her exact contemporaries Michelle Pfeiffer, Elle Macpherson and Courtney Cox, she has failed to 'work hard to look good'. She will be restored to an imaginary earlier self, the shameful traces of her present inadequacy erased, and so avoid the horrific future predicted in a series of computer-generated images of her ageing face. But first she must have her grotesque body exposed; her teeth are shown filed to stumps, her skin is peeled back and the fatty lumps on her face are removed one by one and displayed to camera. Finally she is reconstructed, ready for public display: passers by now judge her to be thirty-eight; she is 'a new woman' and, asked to comment, says she is 'speechless'. Her job serving gourmet food is safe.

Like other reality TV programmes, *Ten Years Younger* is constructed as a competition, a race against time to complete a successful transformation. But its material is 'the female body in disarray' (Mellencamp 1992: 274); the time to be beaten that of the ageing process as visible deterioration; the process of transformation a survival guide which is also a training exercise in normalisation. A re-made Shirley is restored to public visibility, but the gendered structures that insist that her visibility (and employment) depends on the appearance of youth have not been challenged. Nor, despite the process of 'mediated visibility' in which the private body has been subjected to a public gaze, have the boundaries between public and private been eroded. As private body, Shirley is fragmented into body parts, each subjected to the disciplinary gaze of the camera; once re-made as public self, the camera retreats, observing her at work with colleagues and clients, not powerful but surviving.

Conclusion: real women and 'mediated visibility'

It may be, then, that we should think of these genres not as a broadening, or indeed a degeneration, of the Habermasian public sphere, but rather as inheritors of the scandal sheets and other forms of scurrilous press popular from the eighteenth century onwards. Jane Shattuc (1997) traces the continuities between these early news-sheets, the penny press of the nineteenth century, the journalistic traditions of the 'sob sisters' of the early American tabloids, and the women's magazine's advice column. In all of these, 'sex, violence, crime and tragedy' dominate, as she demonstrates with a comparison of the contents of an 1884 issue of *The New York World* and those of one week's talk shows during 1994 (1997: 18). Like their predecessors, talk shows are agents of scandal and as such, as James Lull and Stephen Hinerman argue, they *can* become 'a popular forum for public awareness and debate of moral questions' in ways that may cross over into the 'public sphere' function of the media, as watchdog on the politically and economically powerful (1997: 28). But this crossover function is limited, in a number of ways.

First, within these narratives the real people who inhabit them are most likely to be presented, not within what Bill Nichols calls the 'indexical domain of historical time', in which individuals are presented as social and political actors, but rather within the domain of 'the mythical', in which cultural concerns are played out through stories of exemplary or cautionary figures (1991: 243). 'Love rats', addicts, abusers, neglected wives or estranged parents are displayed for us so that we, and the studio audience, can police the boundaries of the normal. 'Why do [these people] have to shout and scream and weep and threaten? Why are they so eager for confrontation that they often walk onstage already bellowing?' asks Lynn Barber of the participants on *Trisha Goddard* (*The Observer*, 23 March 2003), but they must, if they are to serve this 'mythic' function.

Second, the model of resolution these programmes employ is, as we have seen, therapeutic not political. The shame which is so persistently invoked is that of personal failure to live up to gendered or familial norms ('Be a man!' exhorts Jeremy Kyle; 'Why the heck did you get married?' asks Sally Jesse Raphael; 'Do you have a shower or a bath every single day?' demands Trisha). Thus the boundaries between a shared (masculine) political realm of rational discourse and a privatised (feminine) sphere of personal responsibility, guilt and shame are reinforced, not dismantled. The goal is to produce a 'whole' self, but the method, the display of bodily symptoms 'onstage' to a responsive audience, is more reminiscent of the performances of hysteria staged by Freud's precursor as scientist of female neurosis, Jean-Martin Charcot,[9] than it is of feminist 'consciousness-raising'. Extending outwards, these personal problems may indeed become visible as *social* problems, but, as Denise Riley reminds us, this is not necessarily to politicise them. With the development of the 'human sciences' in the nineteenth century, she writes, the categories 'women' and 'society' were seen to form a continuum. Women were seen to be immersed in the social, as both agents and objects of reform, so that 'society' (as opposed to politics, or the rational individual) was seen as always 'already permeated by the feminine' (1988: 15). 'Social issues' thus line up with 'women's issues', as distinct from 'political issues'.

Finally, these programmes are 'low culture'. Andreas Huyssen has drawn attention to the way in which, from the nineteenth century onwards, 'mass culture is somehow associated with woman, while real, authentic culture remains the prerogative of men' (1986a: 47). 'Low' or 'mass' culture, like the social, was seen to be permeated with the feminine; 'high culture', the realm of Habermas's 'literary public sphere', remained masculine. We have seen in the study of news how too much 'feminisation' can lead to its devaluation as an 'objective' form. Within both TV schedules and within the programmes themselves these boundaries are maintained. Thus on one week day, BBC2's *Working Lunch*, 'a daily taste of the latest developments in business and personal finance', features only one female presenter, the consumer affairs re-porter, and only one female 'expert', who speaks on behalf of the British Chamber of Commerce against a change in law which will benefit mainly low-paid women. Following it on ITV1, a women's discussion pro-gramme is called *Loose Women*; its participants discuss wedding-night sex, the value of opera, weight loss, and the issues raised by a current *Coronation Street* storyline. It is the *professional* expertise of the male experts that is referenced in makeover programmes; women are usually given no such introduction. Within BBC2's *The Apprentice*, a ruthlessly competitive context ('It's a dog-eat-dog situation') sees women 'fired' because they are too 'nice', too 'overpowering', or too emotional: 'she jumps up and down, she squawks, she claps her hands, she falls out with people, she stamps, she sulks and she cries' comments *The Guardian* (30 March 2006) on one contestant. *Men* are 'fired' because they are not aggressive enough. Indeed, we can argue that across the very different genres of news and talk shows, real women fulfil essentially the same function: they are, as Margaret Gallagher writes of news, victims, 'ordinary people', embodiments of personal experience, or the voice of popular opinion.

These boundaries, of course, are permeable: personal trauma, as Anita Biressi and Heather Nunn (2005) argue, is worked through in the realm of the public in talk shows and reality television; elsewhere, women *do* appear as 'experts'. Today's public space of 'mediated visibility' is indeed, as John B. Thompson argues, a more open-ended discursive space than the restricted Habermasian public sphere, one in which 'the conse-quences of becoming visible cannot be fully anticipated and controlled' (1995: 247). But the 'frenzy of the visible' which is so often the result reminds us that, as Mellencamp argues, 'TV both traverses *and* maintains

Habermas's and Foucault's divide' between the public and the private (1992: 264), and that for the real women who are displayed there, the visibility which it confers can be far from liberatory.

Notes

1. Nichols 1991. Nichols' reference is to documentary rather than to news.
2. In the *Structural Transformation of the Public Sphere*, first published in 1962, the 'bourgeois public sphere' is presented historically. Later, Habermas was more concerned to stress its status as an 'ideal type' (Habermas 1992: 422).
3. Published between 1870 and 1876, *Woodhull and Claflin's Weekly* stakes its claim to a position in the public sphere, proposing to 'take the highest ground in the diffusion of religion, philosophy and science'; to advocate 'the widest action of the citizen compatible with the dignity of the State'; and to 'treat of all matters freely and without reservation' (http://copperas.com/woodhull/opinions.htm). Topics included investment news, feminism, black suffrage, women's suffrage, racism, classism, and banking fraud. It also served as a platform for Woodhull's candidacy for President of the United States. In 1872, it published the first English translation of *The Communist Manifesto*. It was destroyed through the destruction of Woodhull's personal reputation.
4. It is worth noting that the earliest BBC television news bulletins were broadcast in sound only, the face and body of the newsreader withheld in order to preserve impartiality and the BBC's authority. The newsreaders were always male.
5. For example, Stuart Allan (1997: 308) quotes the new owner of *The New York Times*, Adolph Ochs, who declared in 1896: 'It will be my earnest aim that *The New York Times* give the news, all the news, in concise and attractive form, in language that is parliamentary in good society . . . to give the news impartially, without fear or favour, regardless of any party, sect or interest involved; to make *The New York Times* a forum for the consideration of all questions of public importance, and to that end to invite intelligent discussion from all shades of opinion.'
6. This first edition of the *Ladies Mercury* opens with a firm declaration of separate spheres, announcing that: 'All questions relating to Love etc., are desired to be sent in to the Latine-Coffee-House in Ave-Mary-Lane, to the Ladies' Society there, and we promise that they shall be weekly answered with all the Zeal and Softness becoming to the Sex. We likewise desire we may not be troubled with other Questions relating to Learning, Religion, etc.' (Ballaster et al. 1991: 47).
7. A similar feeling seems to underlie the widely reported comments of former BBC news reporter and presenter Michael Buerk, who complained in August 2005 that the 'shift in the balance of power between the sexes' had gone too far. Buerk complained that broadcasting was being controlled by women, who are now 'the people who decide what we see and hear'. The result was clearly felt to compromise the authority of the BBC.

8. The booklet which accompanies the show is called *Trisha Goddard's Survivor's Guide to Life*. In it, topics such as 'Making a relationship work' and 'Surviving childhood abuse' are treated in turn. Each is described as it relates to 'us' ('Perhaps someone always criticised the way you looked as a child'), a case study is provided, there are details of organisations which can help, and Trisha herself provides a list of therapeutic 'tips'. In the case of two of the topics, Trisha is herself the case study.

9. In a famous picture of Charcot, we see him giving a lecture on hysteria at the La Salpetrière clinic in Paris. We are positioned within the semi-circle of the all-male audience as Charcot stands, finger raised, apparently responding to a questioner. The woman who is the object of his lecture stands with her breasts exposed, her body turned towards us, her eyes closed, apparently in a hypnotically-induced trance. Her body seems both passive and unruly. For the image, see Hall 1997: 52.

5 Technologies of difference

We come to see ourselves differently as we catch sight of our images in the mirror of the machine ... A rapidly expanding system of networks, collectively known as the internet, links millions of people in new spaces that are changing the way we think, the nature of our sexuality, the form of our communities, our very identities. (Turkle 1997: 9)

[W]hat these VR encounters really provide is an illusion of control over reality, nature and, especially, over the unruly, gender and race-marked, essentially mortal body ... In this sense, these new technologies are implicated in the reproduction of at least one very traditional cultural narrative: the possibility of transcendence whereby the physical body and its social meanings can be technologically neutralized. (Balsamo 1995: 229)

Cyberspace depends for its existence on real space, real time, real bodies. Without space/time/bodies the cyber- is inconceivable. It is a metaphor – not a place. Similarly, immersive spaces are not real, and the body's 'experience' is not real. (Hawthorne 1999: 228)

There are no utopian spaces anywhere except in the imagination. (Grosz 2001: 19)

The opening of Sherry Turkle's *Life on the Screen*, quoted above, at once references a familiar conceptual framework in feminist theory – the screen as Lacanian mirror-image, with its illusory promise of self-identity – and declares it redundant. Screen as mirror is replaced by screen as network, and with this shift comes the promise of a collapse not only of familiar binaries (nature/culture, human/machine, real/virtual), but also of the split self of psychoanalysis. In its place is a 'multiple self', 'fluid, and constituted in interaction with machine connections' (Turkle 1997: 15). This self is not, like the 'I' narrated by Irigaray (see Chapter 2), *'frozen* ... on this side of the screen ... paralyzed by all those images, words, fantasies'; on the contrary, it can 'step through the looking glass' to 'navigate virtual oceans, unravel virtual mysteries, . . . engineer virtual skyscrapers' and try out virtual identities (1997: 9). In thus stepping into cyberspace, it also enters a new space of virtual community, no longer alone.

Yet, despite her own self-identification with this transformation, if we look closely at Turkle's vision of the 'virtual worlds' in which, she argues, we now live, the details – navigating virtual oceans, unravelling virtual mysteries, engineering virtual skyscrapers, even trying out virtual identities – seem both familiar and decidedly gendered. They are the imaginary adventures of the unitary male self, designed precisely to confirm that sense of unitary selfhood. A little later in her account, indeed, the image of the screen as mirror reappears. In a 'new variant on the story of Narcissus', she writes, people 'are able to see themselves in the computer' and 'fall in love with the artificial worlds that they have created' (1997: 30). Cyberspace, then, is also a space of dreams and fantasy, and above all of fantasies of 'a new level of control and mastery' (1997: 274). It offers, in Scott Bukatman's words, 'the possibility of a mind independent of the biology of bodies, a mind released from the mortal limitations of the flesh' (2000: 159). It is difficult to avoid the conclusion that, despite Turkle's own careful non-gendering of the process she describes, these fantasies belong to a very specific masculine tradition, in which a vision of disembodied transcendence coincides with a position of mastery, and the body is not so much transmuted as repressed.

This chapter examines the relationship between feminism, women and new media technologies. In it I consider both claims that new technologies have profoundly changed not only gendered identities but embodiment itself, and the counter-argument, suggested in the quotation from Balsamo above, that they represent, rather, a continuation of existing power relations and the re-articulation of traditional cultural narratives. Throughout this account, as is evident in the quotations above, the three terms around which this book has been so far organised – the image, narrative, and the real – remain crucial in thinking about the media as technologies of difference.

Technologies of gender: cinema

> In the first moments of the history of cinema, it is the technology which provides the immediate interest: what is promoted and sold is the experience of the machine, the apparatus. (Heath 1980: 1)

Technologies of Gender is the title of a collection of essays on 'Theory, Film and Fiction' by Teresa de Lauretis. De Lauretis begins from Foucault's concept of sexuality as a 'technology of sex', proposing that 'gender, too, both as representation and as self-representation, is the product of various social technologies, such as cinema, as well as institutional discourses, epistemologies, and critical practices' (1989: ix).

'Technology' in her account, then, is used in a sense which, in Kathleen Woodward's words (1999: 282), is 'primarily metaphorical': to describe the workings of a set of practices which produce specific cultural effects, effects that will be inscribed on, and lived through, the body. Yet insofar as de Lauretis' account concerns the 'technology' or 'apparatus' of cinema, her definition also includes the idea of technology in the term's narrower, more literal sense, and it is an account which has been drawn upon by later theorists writing about the impact of new media technologies on the gendered body, most notably Anne Balsamo (1996). Since, too, the relationship of computer as screen to its precursor, cinema, is one which returns repeatedly to trouble theorists of new media technologies, it is here that I shall begin.

For de Lauretis, the 'sex-gender system' is 'both a sociocultural construct and a semiotic apparatus, a system which assigns meaning (identity, value, prestige, location in kinship, status in the social hierarchy etc) to individuals within society' (1989: 5). Gender, then, is a lived reality produced in and through representations, both the public representations of a specific socio-technological apparatus like cinema, and the self-representations through which we construct our identities. Caught up in relations of power, and produced in spaces of mediated visibility (de Lauretis cites the spaces of cinema, narrative and theory), this gender-as-representation can nevertheless never fully contain women's lived reality. Women are always 'both inside and outside gender, at once within and without representation' (1989: 10). It is a position which gives rise to the 'doubled vision' of feminism; and for de Lauretis, this is a position which, however uncomfortable, *must* be retained:

> We cannot resolve or dispel the uncomfortable condition of being at once inside and outside gender either by desexualizing it (making gender merely a metaphor, a question of *difference*, of purely discursive effects) or by androgynizing it . . . (De Lauretis 1989: 11)

To flatten out sexual difference by displacing it onto a 'purely textual figure' is, she writes, both to deny the reality of women as historical subjects, and to lose that point of resistance which constitutes the possibility of a view from 'elsewhere' and the construction of a different cultural narrative.

De Lauretis' strictures here concern male-centred postmodern theory. But we can apply them equally well both to the literalisation of such theory in masculine fantasies of techno-sexual transcendence in cyber-space, and to similar fantasies in some 'cyberfeminist' accounts. Other feminist accounts of cinema as apparatus/technology are equally sug-gestive in this respect. Here I want to point to three such accounts. The first is Linda Williams' account of the prehistory of pornography in the origins of cinema, in *Hard Core* (1990). Like de Lauretis, Williams draws on the work of Foucault, but also on the account of the birth of cinema by Jean-Louis Comolli. For Comolli, as for de Lauretis, cinema is above all a 'social machine'. Technically possible long before its formal invention, cinema appears as part of the intensification of the 'field of the visible' in the second half of the nineteenth century. It is a period, he writes, which 'lives in a sort of frenzy of the visible', in which 'the whole world becomes visible at the same time as it becomes appropriatable' (1980: 122–3). At once science and spectacle, surveillant power and fetishistic pleasure, proto-cinematic moving images such as those of Eadweard Muybridge constitute both 'the construction of better machines of observation to measure and record bodies now conceived themselves as machines' and 'an unanticipated pleasure attached to the visual spectacle of lifelike moving bodies'. Thus 'the power exerted over bodies *in* technology is rendered pleasurable *through* technology' (Linda Williams 1990: 38–9). In the process, argues Williams, women are constructed as the objects rather than subjects of vision, through the first halting cinematic narratives that 'will facilitate seeing [the] previously hidden further truths' of the female body (1990: 45). Williams' account is important because it refuses to locate the to-be-looked-at-ness of woman in prior psychic structures to be explained *through* psychoanalysis. Instead, it insists that both psycho-analysis as science and cinema as visual pleasure are the products of a specific historical and social conjuncture,[1] in which new technologies of the visible become the means by which nature/the social/woman can be fully known, mastered, and – via the camera – penetrated. It is a point worth returning to in considering the claims made for both techno-science and the pleasures of cyberspace in later accounts.

Comolli's account of the origins of cinema theorises the cinematic apparatus through the familiar psychoanalytic mechanism of disavowal. The advent of the 'photographic machine', he writes, in fact displaces the human eye from its position of privilege and mastery, a loss/lack which is disavowed both via the power which is accorded the *camera*, as extension of human vision, in definitions of cinema (masking the importance of more 'invisible' processes such as editing and processing), and through the persuasiveness of the 'reality effects' which it produces. The cinema screen's illusion of reality *seems* to confirm for us the truth of human vision. Disavowal – 'knowing but not wanting to know' – is thus for

Comolli a crucial source of pleasure in narrative, or fictional, cinema. In a passage which strikingly prefigures later accounts of virtual reality gaming – accounts which are often constructed in perceived opposition to the passivity attributed to the cinematic or televisual spectator – he describes these pleasures:

> There is ambivalence, play. The spectacle is always a game, requiring the spectators' participation not as 'passive, 'alienated' consumers, but as players, accomplices, masters of the game even if they are also what is at stake . . . Different in this to ideological and political representations, spectatorial representations declare their existence as simulacrum and, on that contractual basis, invite the spectator to *use* the simulacrum to fool him or herself. (1980: 140)

Despite these similarities, Comolli's conclusions are ones seldom drawn by writers on new technologies, as Kevin Robins has observed. For Comolli, what is offered by the simulacra of cinema to the complicit player/spectator is an illusion of mastery which masks an actual lack/loss, both of the real which the cinematic illusion purports to (re)present, and of the unified self which it appears to reinforce. Imagined as 'a combination of the objectivity of the physical world with the unlimitedness and the uncensored content normally associated with dreams or imaginations' (Lanier, quoted in Robins 1995: 139), cinema's successor, cyberspace, is a space, suggests Robins, in which both the body and threats to the notion of a unified self 'can be denied or disavowed, and coherence sustained through the fiction of protean imagination'. It is, he adds, 'not new in this respect' (1995: 142–3).

Disavowal, fantasy and regression: these are the mechanisms through which male theorists of cinema like Comolli, Jean-Louis Baudry and Christian Metz explained the 'cinematic apparatus'. Yet, heavily dependent on psychoanalytic theory though these explanations are, they nevertheless, as Mary Ann Doane writes, 'find it necessary to desexualize' the Freudian scenario, in which disavowal functions specifically to enable the male child to deal with *sexual difference* (1999: 30). In the accounts of both Comolli and Metz, what the cinematic spectator both recognises and disavows is not the Freudian conception of female difference or 'lack', but the 'absence' or 'lack' which characterises the projected images of the cinema screen. Yet, as Doane points out, whilst the work of Laura Mulvey and other feminist film theorists succeeds in re-sexualising the mechanism of disavowal, returning it to its Freudian meaning of sexual difference, it does this largely within the sphere of representation, through a concern with the figure of Woman as site of textual meaning. In Doane's insistence that the 'fantasmatic ground of cinema itself' (1999:

23) needs to be reconceptualised in these terms, we can find the second account of cinema as apparatus/technology which is suggestive in thinking about new media technologies.

For Comolli, it was the equation of cinema with the *camera* which allowed the fantasy of the centrality of human vision and mastery to be maintained in the age of mechanical reproduction. But of course this is also a fantasy of *masculine* power. Against the phallic connotations of the camera can be set the feminine connotations of the screen: as mirror, barrier, and veil; as shiny reflective surface and as troubling concealment of a mystery to be penetrated.[2] Judith Mayne has written of this 'ambivalence of the screen' which, simultaneously threshold and obstacle, transparent and translucent, seems to function for the male spectator as both 'the mother and the self' (1990: 39, 43). Both the screen itself and its substitute, the veil, appear frequently as tropes *within* the cinematic text, as both Mayne and Doane have observed. Writing of the use of the veil in close-ups of the woman in cinema, Doane argues that, in its translucence, the veil 'both allows and disallows vision', intercepting the space between camera and woman, 'forming a *second screen*' (1991: 49, original italics). But, as she also comments, the screen itself also frequently figures within cinematic representations, as the veiled space of the maternal/feminine, whose horror/seduction is concealed/eroticised by the screen's deceptive doubleness. Doane draws her examples[3] from science fiction where, as she writes, the terms woman, machine and screen are commonly conflated. An image advertising a May 2006 episode of the BBCTV science fiction series, *Dr Who* provides a recent example. Here, the episode's male author poses, cup of tea in hand, before a bank of television screens on which are displayed the two aspects of woman/machine/screen figured in the episode: those of helpless victim and devouring monster. The first has her face/identity (her 'essence') devoured by, and then imprisoned behind, the screen, whilst her faceless body is reduced to an automaton. The second is identified *with* the screen, an ever-hungry mouth which seeks to 'gorge' on its/her television-viewing victims.[4]

For a far more self-reflexive exploration of the meanings of the screen we can turn to Michael Powell's *Peeping Tom* (1960). Here, the failure of the cameraman protagonist, Mark, to maintain his identification with masculine distance and control is signified by his regressive identificatory movement from camera to screen. Having filmed and killed his female victims with the apparatus of camera/tripod/mirror, Mark is nevertheless persistently drawn away from his position as spectator-director of the resulting footage, and towards the cinema screen and its extreme close-up of his victim's gaping mouth. Seeking both merging and re-absorption, he finds to his despair that 'the lights faded too soon'. Whilst he may temporarily achieve the merging he desires, as the projected image of his victim plays across his body as well as the screen, the screen as maternal/feminine ultimately retains its mystery.

In the screen spaces of virtual reality and cyberspace, the centrality of the camera, or what Kaja Silverman calls 'the camera . . . internal to [the] screen' (1996: 196), is replaced by the fantasy of a more direct penetration of/immersion in the computer's virtual world. But the metaphors of screen as mirror (Turkle) and screen as veil (Plant 1995) persist, to be augmented by the now central metaphor for that which the screen veils/ reveals: the 'matrix', a term whose origins lie in the Latin *mater* – mother or womb. As Sadie Plant puts it, 'Today, both woman and the computer screen the matrix, which also makes its appearance as the veils and screens on which its operations are displayed' (1995: 46).

The third of the accounts of cinema as apparatus/technology to which I want to draw attention is that of the 'bachelor machines' described by Constance Penley (1989). The machines of which Penley writes appear in both scientific and imaginative discourses of the nineteenth and twentieth centuries: anthropomorphised apparatuses through which various aspects of psychic, social or embodied existence could be explained or imagined. The bachelor machine, she writes,

> is typically a closed, self-sufficient system. Its common themes include frictionless, sometimes perpetual motion, an ideal time and the magical possibility of its reversal (the time machine is an exemplary bachelor machine), electrification, voyeurism and masturbatory eroticism, the dream of the mechanical reproduction of art, and artificial birth or reanimation. (Penley 1989: 57)

No matter how complicated the machine becomes, however, 'the control over the sum of its parts rests with a knowing producer who therefore submits to a fantasy of closure, perfectibility, and mastery' (1989: 58). For Penley, the 'bachelor machine' is a perfect term for cinema, both as technological, social and psychical apparatus, and as object of fantasy for its male theorists. It is a machine, she writes, following de Certeau, which 'does not tend to write the woman' (1989: 57).

What is interesting here in Penley's account of cinema as bachelor machine is the way in which it ranges across a number of discourses: scientific (Freud's reliance on machine metaphors for his descriptions of the workings of the psyche); technological (cinema as producer of powerful reality effects); theoretical (Baudry's view of cinema as 'a faultless technological simulacrum' of the workings of the psyche); and imaginative (she describes both literary and artistic creations). Across them all runs a common fantasy: a homeostatic model of the self in which 'all circulating energy is regulated, balanced, controlled' (Penley 1989: 61), a model replicated in cinema, explained in film theory, and fantasised, in the form of anthropomorphised machines, in literature and art. It is a model both *of* the male self and created *by* that self, infinitely reproducing a fantasy of unity and control both imaginatively and technologically, a model in which embodiment, and particularly embodied sexual difference, is absent. In Penley's description quoted above, we can see many of the characteristics of a later techno-scientific culture.

The small screen

Between cinema and the computer screen stands television, an apparatus saturated in connotations of the feminine, as a number of feminist critics have pointed out. From Raymond Williams onwards, it has been television's 'interminable flow (of images and sounds, their endlessly disappearing present)' and its 'explosion of messages, signs, endless traces of meaning' (Heath 1990: 267, 275), which have dominated discussions of the medium. In contrast to cinema, it has not been the camera which has functioned synecdochically as its representative, but rather the screen. Thus for Williams, it is an 'apparently casual and miscellaneous flow' which constitutes the 'television experience' (Raymond 1990: 111, 93). For Stephen Heath, television is 'saturation, overloading, neutralization'; 'its extension, its availability, its proximity' all function to absorb the viewer into the screen: 'I become part of the network, the circulation' (1990: 297, 292–3). These metaphors of 'flow' and 'saturation', descriptions of the suffocating closeness, the excessive availability and empathy which television induces, and accounts of its distracted, dreaming viewer, all serve to identify television with an irrational, passive and enveloping femininity.

For Jean Baudrillard, television is 'the ultimate and perfect object' for contemporary culture (1985: 127). In it, differences and distances are collapsed. Representation gives way to 'simulation' in which we have 'models of the real without origin or reality' (Baudrillard 1994: 1), and simulation, as we have seen in Chapter 2, is identified with femininity. Any reality which cannot be absorbed into television now seems like 'a kind of archaic envelope, a vestige of human relations whose very survival remains perplexing' (Baudrillard 1985: 129). History is similarly effaced, becoming a random collection of images without cause or effect, absorbed into television's sense of 'total instantaneity' (1985: 133). The separation of public and private is collapsed: 'the most intimate processes of our life become the virtual feeding ground of the media', whilst at the same time, 'the entire universe comes to unfold arbitrarily on your domestic screen' (1985: 130). Even the distance between subject and object is effaced, as we are absorbed into this world of the screen.

For Baudrillard, however, the metaphor of the screen extends beyond television. In the postmodern era, he writes, the television has become 'control screen and terminal', so that each individual becomes 'a terminal of multiple networks', a 'pure screen, a switching center for all the networks of influence' (1985: 127, 128, 133). Elsewhere, this 'dissolution of TV in life, dissolution of life in TV' is seen as an invasion – 'viral, endemic, chronic' – of our genetic coding itself, so that it is not only the distance between the real and the virtual which has disappeared, but that between the screen and the self:

> Now, one must conceive of TV along the lines of DNA as an effect in which the opposing poles of determination vanish, according to a nuclear contraction, retraction, of the old polar schema that always maintained a minimal distance between cause and effect, between subject and object: precisely the distance of meaning, the gap, the difference . . . (Baudrillard 1994: 31)

This nightmare vision of the collapse of the boundaries of the self in the screen, and the invasion of the body by technology, is also, as Tania Modleski (1986) has pointed out, a vision of the body as feminised. It is, writes Baudrillard, 'too great a proximity, the unclean promiscuity of everything which touches, invests and penetrates without resistance, with no halo of private protection, not even his own body, to protect him anymore' (1985: 132).

Narratives of the new

In Baudrillard's description of the screen we can see television – as multiple 'switching centre', as 'network', as an effect of coding which replicates that of DNA and is subject to viral invasion – already becoming computer. These continuities have been noted by a number of writers on new technologies, whilst others in effect produce them, through the images of flow and distraction, mirroring, absorption, instantaneity and simulation which they employ. At the same time, however, it is the *newness* of new technologies and the epoch they inaugurate which is constantly emphasised. For Manuel Castells, this 'new world' of the 'network society' has as key characteristics 'a culture of real virtuality constructed by a pervasive, interconnected, and diversified media system' and 'the transformation of the material foundations of life, space and time' (2004: 1–2). To Sherry Turkle, the 'age of the internet' means the erosion of boundaries 'between the real and the virtual, the animate and the inanimate, the unitary and the multiple self'. From 'scientists trying to create artificial life to children "morphing" through a series of virtual personae', she finds evidence of 'fundamental shifts in the way we create and experience human identity' (1997: 10). Sarah Kember writes that this is a 'posthuman' era, one enmeshed, 'at all levels of materiality and metaphor, with information, communication and biotechnologies and with other non-human actors' (2003: vii). In an article in the *Times Higher Education Supplement* of 12 May 2006, Terry Sejnowski, head of the computational neurobiology laboratory at the Salk Institute for Biological Studies in the US, writes that the 'growth of the internet over recent decades more closely resembles biological evolution than engineering', with the difference that what took humans hundreds of millions of years of evolution has been achieved by the computer in only thirty-seven years. With the aid of the internet, Sejnowski writes, 'I have achieved omniscience for all practical purposes' (2006: 14).

For Katherine Hayles, however, it is important to understand these accounts of 'how we became posthuman' in terms of *narrative*. Like Somers and Gibson, whose work was discussed in Chapter 2, Hayles argues that structuring many of these accounts, and running across the discourses of science as well as cultural theory and cultural texts, is an underpinning metanarrative: 'a metanarrative about the transformation of the human into a disembodied posthuman' (1999: 22). It is important to understand this 'teleology of disembodiment' *as* narrative, rather than as the 'analytically driven systems theory' (1999: 22) as which it presents itself, she writes, because narrative, in its contingency and particularity, always resists the kinds of abstraction claimed by theoretical systems. In what follows, I shall follow Hayles in structuring this account of new media technologies around a number of central, overlapping narratives, though mine do not mirror those of Hayles. But I also want to argue that each of these narratives is organised around a key image, an image which in each case carries gendered connotations. Precisely because of these connotations, these images in turn become contested sites: at once sites for the repression of sexual difference and opportunities for its reassertion by feminist critics. As Michèle le Doeuff argues (2002)[5] images cannot be fully absorbed by the system that deploys them; they can always be mobilised in other, potentially contradictory ways.

The network

For Felix Stalder, Manuel Castells' theory of the network society provides 'the single most comprehensive framework' through which to understand 'a world reconstituting itself around a series of networks strung around the globe on the basis of advanced communication technologies'. It is, he suggests, 'the lone contender as the grand narrative of the present' (Stakter 2006: 1). Castells argues that the end of the twentieth century saw the transformation of material culture by 'a new technological paradigm organized around information technologies' (2000: 28). By information technologies, he means 'the *converging set* of technologies in micro-electronics, computing (machines and software), telecommunications/broadcasting, and opto-electronics' (original emphasis), together with 'genetic engineering and its expanding set of developments and applications' (2000: 29). In this new 'Information Age', the dominant form of social organisation is the network, so that politics, economics, social and cultural forms all function through global networks made possible by the new convergence of communication technologies. Thus, the 'inclusion/exclusion in networks, and the architecture of relationships between networks, enacted by light-speed-operating information technologies, configure dominant processes and functions in our societies' (2000: 501). Power is no longer fixed in hierarchies, but flows through networks which are structured through protocols rather than chains of command. But networks can also function as expressions of new collective identities, both resistant and transformative, and these identities, too, are pervasive in the network society.

For Castells, the network functions as both technological actuality and over-arching metaphor. Its double-edged possibilities refer back to the twin origins of the internet, first in the work of the 'technological warriors' of the US Defense Department's Advanced Research Projects Agency, who sought to prevent a Soviet takeover or destruction of US communications through the creation of a networked system which could not be controlled by any centre, and second in the efforts of a 1960s computer counterculture, for which dispersal and universal access were ideological goals (2000: 49). As *metaphor*, its identification with the dispersed flows of power has its origins in the work of Michel Foucault, for whom:

> Power must be analysed as something which circulates or rather as something which functions in the form of a chain. It is never localised here or there, never in anybody's hands, never appropriated as a commodity or piece of wealth. Power is employed and exercised through a net-like organisation. And not only do individuals circulate between its threads; they are always in the position of simultaneously undergoing and exercising this power. (Foucault 1980: 98)

But in its 'softer' sense, 'network' also has feminine connotations, as we can see in the following quotation from Castells, where he seeks to describe the oppositional possibilities of the network society for feminist groups. These reside, he writes, in 'the rapid diffusion of ideas in a globalized culture, and in an interrelated world, where people and experience travel and mingle, quickly weaving a hyperquilt of women's voices throughout most of the planet' (2004: 195). This is a very different account of networking from those cited above, reminding us that a network was originally a fabric made of netted threads, later woven or 'webbed', its female-identified techniques both tactile and social. As Castells notes, women, unlike men, 'do . . . well in networking' (2004: 292). This is an etymology which has been exploited by cyberfeminists like Sadie Plant, for whom the computer 'emerges out of the history of weaving, the process so often said to be the quintessence of women's work' (1995: 46). Just as in weaving there is no division between 'the weaver, the weaving, and the woven', she writes, so too touch dominates in the networks of hypermedia, where communication is always 'a matter of getting in touch, a question of contact, contagion, transmission, reception and connectivity' (1996: 179). For Plant, then, the future of cyberspace is not the phallic dream of 'total control and autonomy' but 'a dispersed, distributed emergence composed of links between women, women and computers, computers and communication links, connections and connectionist nets' (1996: 182).

For those male theorists for whom the metaphor of the network is central, its feminine connotations can be drawn upon whilst remaining unacknowledged. Through a series of images which Kevin Robins describes as 'images . . . of maternal-familial containment' (1995: 149), for example, Howard Rheingold depicts the Net as a means of rekindling a sense of family and rebuilding feelings of community. In Rheingold's vision, cyberspace can become not only 'one of the informal public places where people can rebuild the aspects of community that were lost when the maltshop became the mall' (1994: 25–6), but also an 'electronic agora' through which we can 'revitalise citizen-based democracy' and 'the public sphere' (1994: 14). These are families and communities without bodies and without sexual difference, however, and like the malls which he deplores, Rheingold's virtual successor to the communal meeting places of the past effaces their material, embodied presence even whilst invoking it in a series of idealised, nostalgic images.

In other uses of the network metaphor this effacement of the gendered body is more thorough and more systematic. In actor-network theory (ANT), the image of the network is extended to include the social, the institutional and the conceptual, as well as the technological. Originating as a sociology of science and technology, it argues that scientific knowledge is not the result of a privileged and objective scientific method, or of a set of ideas, but of 'a process of "hetero-geneous engineering" in which bits and pieces from the social, the technical, the conceptual and the textual are fitted together' (Law 2003: 2). This notion of 'a network of heterogeneous materials' is then extended, to become a theory of 'agents, social institutions, machines and organisations' (2003: 2). All are seen to operate through networks of connections between humans, technologies and objects, networks in which the human is neither the only source of agency nor analytically distinct from the non-human. As a theory of power, actor-network theory once again draws on the work of Foucault, since it sees power as always relational and always distributed. It is most radical, however, as a theory of agency. Drawing on structural theories of narrative (see Greimas 1987), it argues that agency is not the property of an individual but is instead a *function*, a putting into motion, whether within a text or an institution, a function which is always the effect of a network of heterogeneous, interacting materials. My agency as writer here, for example, is the effect of a network involving my computer and its software, a publishing institution, paper, print and so on. To attribute agency only to the human aspect of this network, argues John Law, is to obscure both the importance of non-human aspects of this agency (I could not have the identity of *author* of this chapter without these aspects) and the increasingly permeable boundaries between people and machines. At the same time, these contributing entities – humans, machines, texts, institutions – are themselves the effects of complex and heterogeneous networks.

In this account, the functioning of network as metaphor is stretched to its limits. Everything, from bodily symptom to global capitalism, dis-solves upon examination into network, so that agency, conceived as action in time, dissolves into spatial extension, becoming indistinguish-able from structure, and embodiment becomes simply one kind of 'black box'[6] – to be opened up and its patterned threads revealed. In this process, the body, no longer sexually specific, located in time and space, location of subjectivity or knowledge, is abstracted, attenuated into the sexless, techno-social movements of the network. Gendered relations of power, like those of class or race, become invisible, or even impossible to conceptualise within this framework, since power differentials between human actors *matter* no more than relationships between non-human (or human and non-human) actors. Yet, infinitely dispersed and largely unmentioned as they are, gender and sexuality for this reason also remain unexamined, to occur infrequently as apparently naturalised markers of human identity. When John Law suggests as an aside that '[p]erhaps it is only in lovemaking that there is interaction between unmediated human bodies' (2003: 3), we can also suspect that this lack of examination masks a more fundamental conservatism.

If networks can be global and technological, or social and relational, they can also be biological. Felix Stalder (2006: 170–1) points out that Castells' concept of the network owes much to models developed in the natural sciences, particularly those of Fritjof Capra. Capra's concept of 'the web of life' argues that discovering 'the fundamental building blocks of life' such as DNA does not help us to understand 'the vital integrative actions of living organisms'. These must be conceptualised not as materials or codes but as complex *systems*, which are always integrated wholes, and therefore much more than the sum of their parts. To understand life, therefore, what we must understand are contexts – themselves a form of 'weaving together' – and relationships: the way in which specific systems maintain both themselves, through their internal relationships, and their relationships with surrounding larger systems. Capra's key metaphor is the network conceived as web. The web of life, he writes, is an ancient idea, conveying the 'interwovenness and interdependence of all phenomena'. As systems thinkers have increasingly used 'network models' to understand systems at all levels, however, this has led to a new insight that 'the network is a pattern that is common to all life' (Capra 1997).

Life as network/web, a matter of relationships and the 'weaving together' of contexts: this is a feminised model, very different from the heroic narratives which dominate writing on genetics, whether in the form of the narrative of the 'selfish gene' (Dawkins 1976), struggling to establish dominance, or in that of DNA's 'code-breakers', who are seen to have cracked 'the code of life',[7] or even deciphered 'the language of God'.[8] Its feminised nature is articulated by Morwena Griffiths, who uses the same metaphor to construct a feminist model of the self. 'Spiders make webs', she writes,

> which are nearly invisible until the dew falls on them. They are made with threads stronger than steel and take their shape from the surrounding circumstances and from the spider herself. Second, women have traditionally made webs: knitting, tapestry, crochet and lace. Their creations are constrained by the circumstances of their making but they bear the marks of the maker . . . Many webs can be seen as wholes or as a conglomeration of parts. Which perspective is used depends on the purpose of the looking . . . Third, and last, the abstract noun, 'web' refers to something which is complex. It is intricate, interlaced, with each part entangled with the rest and dependent on it. (Griffiths 1995: 2)

Yet, if Capra's notion, with its talk of 'nurturing', of 'nature's communities', of 'weaving together', and of 'interdependence', seems deliberately to evoke this lineage, the history of systems theories which he sketches involves very different emphases. The key concepts of systems thinking, he writes (1997), 'were developed in the 1920s and 1930s', and became 'actual systems *theories*' (original emphasis) in the 1940s. Foremost amongst these is cybernetics, whose central concern was 'patterns of communication, especially in closed loops and networks'. This in turn led to 'the concepts of feedback and self-regulation, and then later onto self-organisation' (autopoiesis) (1997). It is in cybernetics that the network model, in the words of Katherine Hayles, 'loses its body' (1999: 4). Writing in 1948, the mathematical physicist and military researcher Norbert Wiener proposed that the body should be seen as a communications network whose successful operation is based on 'the accurate reproduction of a signal' (1954: 15, quoted in Tomas 1995: 24). Life, then, becomes *information*, and information is disembodied, an electronic system in which self-regulation and self-organisation is a matter of electronic signals. Once the nervous system is seen as a form of information processing, its similarity with the machine becomes its defining feature. As Katherine Hayles comments, 'Henceforth, humans were to be seen primarily as information-processing entities who are *essentially* similar to intelligent machines' (1999: 7, original emphasis). And if both living organisms and machines are primarily information processing and communications networks, then they become not only equivalent – so that terms like 'neural net' can apply equally to the central nervous system and to mathematical or computational models – but also fundamentally linked, via a common communications language. 'Life' is then redefined, to include the intelligent machine. As Wiener commented, 'now that certain analogies of behavior are being observed between the machine and the living organism, the problem as to whether the machine is alive or not is, for our purposes, semantic and we are at liberty to answer it one way or another as best suits our convenience' (1954: 32). Twenty years after the publication of Wiener's *Cybernetics: or Control and Communication in the Animal and the Machine*, David Tomas notes an art exhibition's definition of cybernetics as 'a science of control and communication in complex electronic machines like computers and the human nervous system' (1995: 30). By 1996, Marvin Minsky can argue that 'The most important thing about each person is the data, and the programs in the data that are in the brain. And some day you will be able to take all that data, and put it on a little disk, and store it for a thousand years, and then turn it on again and you will be alive in the fourth millennium or the fifth millennium' (quoted in Hayles 1999: 244–5).

In an essay on television, Peter Larsen defines the function of metaphor as one of 'mapping':

> A metaphor works by transferring the structure of a (familiar) field of experience to another (unfamiliar), one, regardless of whether there are common denominators between the two fields or not. And . . . spatial or 'orientational' metaphors are the most common of all, something which presumably has to do with the fact that mental mapping is 'grounded' in fundamental bodily experiences. (Larsen 1999: 119)

In the elevation of the network to totalising metaphor, binding global systems, social structures, information/communication technologies, the human body and life itself, it acquires an *authorising* function – as Felix Stalder perhaps suggests when he argues for Castells' network theory as the latest 'grand narrative'. In this, it is aided by the fact that so many of its uses originate in the discourses of science and technology. In the process, however, analogies slide into firm connections, and specificities and differences are obscured. The result is not only the process which Katherine Hayles and David Tomas trace, in which human embodiment is lost in the move to see humans as information-processing machines, but also one in which embodied *differences* are repressed. Many of the applications of the concept of network discussed here draw on the feminine connotations of the term, only to substitute an abstract and disembodied system based on what Castells calls 'the information technology paradigm' (2000: 75). The feminine connotations serve then to *naturalise* this model, and to position it within a teleology in which the natural (feminine) network (webs, weaving, the interconnectedness of nature) *necessarily* becomes the electronic network (abstract, mathematical, a matter of multi-level electronic systems). Cyberfeminists like Sadie Plant have sought to reclaim the metaphor, and with it the notion of information technologies as 'self-organizing, self-arousing systems' (1995: 58) which the metaphor has authorised, by insisting on its origins. 'The computer was always a simulation of weaving', Plant writes, 'threads of ones and zeros riding the carpets and simulating silk screens in the perpetual motions of cyberspace' (1995: 63). But the electronic network which she seeks to reclaim retains its abstraction, and in identifying women with the matrix/womb of cyberspace, she participates in the fantasy of disembodiment, even if it is disembodiment conceived as subversion: 'Every software development is a migration of control, away from man, in whom it has been exercised only as domination, and into the matrix, or cyberspace' (1995: 62). In this vision, woman once again becomes screen, the interface 'between man and matter, . . . the actual and the virtual' (1995: 63). The male network theorists, meanwhile, remain outside their theoretical creations, and in control. From Minsky's fantasy of achieving eternal life by downloading consciousness into a computer, and Sejnowski's conviction that with the aid of the internet he has achieved omniscience, to the following vision from Hans Moravec, an engineering-based roboticist, man as God-the-Father retains his centrality:

> Today, our machines are still simple creations, requiring the parental care and hovering attention of any newborn, hardly worthy of the word 'intelligent'. But within the next century they will mature into entities as complex as ourselves, and eventually into something transcending everything we know – in whom we can take pride when they refer to themselves as our descendents. (quoted in Adam 1998: 167)

The screen

In Baudrillard's writing we have already seen the screen become computer. In his nightmare vision of 'the ecstasy of communication', in which representation has given way to simulation and the screen has become 'a non-reflecting surface, an immanent surface where operations unfold – the smooth operational surface of communication' (1985: 127), the screen devours the real, the unconscious and the (male) body. There is no real beyond the screen which, in turn, is a 'terminal of multiple networks' (1985: 128). The shift being described here is one in which the screen is no longer seen as a 'window' on to anything outside itself; instead it is the threshold to an interiorised, though infinite, space: to 'cyberspace' or 'virtual reality'.

The two terms 'cyberspace' and 'virtual reality' are not equivalent, though in practice they are often used interchangeably. Cyberspace is the electronic matrix in which the simulations of virtual reality operate; virtual reality systems are a means to access that space. Among the applications of virtual reality, Alison Adam lists

> (a) computer games with people rather than cartoon characters; (b) computer generated films involving simulated people in simulated worlds; (c) interactive dramas where the user could be involved in a scene rather than just watching it; (d) simulation based learning and training; and (e) virtual reality worlds populated by simulated people. (Adam 1998: 143)

All involve an 'immersion' in cyberspace in which the boundaries between the human and the virtual are eroded. Yet the term itself, as Elizabeth Grosz points out, betrays an anxiety. This is a real, she writes, which is 'not quite real, not an "actual real," a "really real" but a real whose reality is at best virtual. An equivocation in and of the real. An apparent rather than an actual "real"' (2001: 80). It is a real stripped of matter and embodiment which nevertheless insists on its claims to *be a* 'real'. Manuel Castells prefers the term 'real virtuality' and Zoë Sofia 'virtual corporeality', but both substitutes strain equally against the oxymoronic coupling they incorporate.

For Baudrillard, the response to this immersion is a mix of horror and fascination: this new scene is, he writes, 'ecstatic and obscene' (1985: 132). It is a response which has been replicated in science fiction, where films from *Videodrome* (1982) to *Strange Days* (1995) and *Existenz* (1999) have depicted Baudrillard's 'unclean promiscuity of everything which touches, invests and penetrates without resistance'. Elsewhere, however, the world of virtual reality is seen differently, as 'a world without rules and controls, without borders and boundaries, a world where everything is possible'. In this description from Morpheus in *The Matrix* (1999), we find echoed the vision of Howard Rheingold, who writes:

> Imagine immersing yourself in an artificial world and actively ex-
> ploring it, rather than peering in at it from a fixed perspective through
> a flat screen in a movie theatre, on a television set, or on a computer
> display. Imagine that you are the creator as well as the consumer of
> your artificial experience, with the power to use a gesture or a word to
> remold the world you see and hear and feel . . . The . . . computer
> models that constitute a VR system make it possible, today, to
> immerse yourself in an artificial world and to reach in and reshape
> it. (Rheingold 1991: 16)

In Rheingold's vision, immersion has become exploration and above all *power*: the power to create experience, and to perform an effortless reshaping of the world according to desire. It is a vision that occurs again and again in writing on virtual reality, from the games and MUD players interviewed by Sherry Turkle, who report liking to 'put myself in the role of a hero' or wanting to 'feel like a master of the universe' (1997: 189, 68), to scientific fantasies of omniscience. It is a vision of mastery in a body-free universe, what Grosz calls a 'fantasy of disembodied self-containment . . . a megalomaniacal attempt to provide control in a world where things tend to become messy, complicated or costly' (2001: 42–3). In virtual reality, writes Sherry Turkle, 'we self-fashion and self-create'; people can 'build a self by cycling through many selves' (1997: 178–80).

This notion of *cycling through* identities is suggestive. In cyberspace the explorer can try on any number of self-created identities, crossing not only the boundaries of gender but also those separating human and non-human. Yet ultimately the disembodied self remains intact, *cycling through* the virtual landscape of possible identities.

It is also a self which, despite its cross-dressing, remains firmly gendered. The vision of a disembodied and *therefore* powerful self, as Grosz points out, is 'a luxury only afforded the male subject' (2001: 43). In cyberspace gendered characteristics remain firmly intact, even if they are worn by cross-dressers. In Turkle's investigations, women who play men learn to be confident and competitive; men who play women learn passivity and co-operation; on-line harassment and rape occur. Turkle quotes one MUD rapist: 'MUDs are somewhere you can have fun and let your "hidden" self out . . . We don't do it to make people feel victimized . . . we do it for fun . . . The victim didn't actually mind, she thought it was somewhat humorous' (1997: 252–3). Similarly, fantasies of virtual sex betray their masculine origins, as in this from Rheingold:

> Picture yourself a couple of decades hence, dressing for a hot night in the virtual village . . . You slip into a lightweight (eventually, one would hope, diaphanous) bodysuit, something like a bodystocking, but with the kind of intimate snugness of a condom . . . Depending on what numbers you dial and which passwords you know and what you are willing to pay (or trade or do), you can find one partner, a dozen, a thousand, in various cyberspaces that are no farther than a telephone number. (1991: 346)

Fifteen years after Rheingold's vision, typing 'virtual sex games' into my internet search machine, I get a site advertising 'Interactive cyberbabes at your fingertips'; 'Hear the girls moan and scream when YOU bring them to climax!' it promises. Clicking on the invitation to acquire a 'free virtual reality babe', I get a choice of 'VirtualFems'. A VirtualFem, I learn, is a 'Virtual Girlfriend who lives inside your computer; she will do anything you ask, understands plain English, and speaks to you out loud!' Scrolling down, I find the latest 'industry news': 'If you haven't heard, there is a new online multi-user game featuring hard-core sex!' The review assures me of its value: 'We're talking some really wicked and twisted stuff, gobs of sex, back stabbing, murder, rape, kidnapping, payoffs, dirty money, your imagination is the limit! . . . After you pump your first load in some hooker's ass, (or whatever you personal fantasy is) you'll be coming back to play every day'.[9]

In the descriptions above, the space of the screen is a space to be penetrated, one in which the disembodied but clearly masculine self enacts often eroticised fantasies of masculine control. But, as Deborah Lupton points out, and Baudrillard demonstrates, this identification of the screen with the feminine also produces anxieties. The computer brings the threat of infection:[10] like television, its seductive screen can be seen as bringing danger into the home, threatening the family. And as matrix or womb, argues Lupton, it can threaten to engulf the self. Computer users, she writes,

> are both attracted towards the promises of cyberspace, in the utopian freedom from the flesh, its denial of the body ... but are also threatened by its potential to engulf the self and expose one's vulnerability to the penetration of enemy others. As with the female body, a site of intense desire and emotional security but also threatening engulfment, the inside of the computer body is dark and enigmatic, potentially leaky, harbouring danger and contamination, vulnerable to invasion. (Lupton 1995: 111)

In the words of the virtual sex games review quoted above, 'you are *sucked into* a fantasy world unlike anything you've ever experienced' (my emphasis). Alongside the fantasy of infinite power and a pleasure without effects or consequences, then, runs a barely acknowledged fear of *loss* of control within the feminised space of the screen. It is this which cyberfeminists like Sadie Plant emphasise when they argue that 'both woman and computer screen the matrix' (1995: 46), and that both threaten to engulf.

This cultural identification of screen with womb, like that of electronic network with 'the web of life', both contributes to and receives authorisation from the discourses of science. If Artificial Intelligence was able to equate organism with machine by arguing that both were *essentially* self-organising electronic systems characterised by a flow of information, Artificial Life makes a similar move. Defined by Chris Langton as 'life made by Man rather than by Nature', Artificial Life (or Alife) is

> a new discipline that studies 'natural' life by attempting to recreate biological phenomena from scratch within computers and other 'artificial' media. Alife complements the traditional analytic approach of traditional biology with a synthetic approach in which, rather than studying biological phenomena by taking apart living organisms to see how they work, one attempts to put together systems that behave like living organisms ... By extending the horizons of empirical research in biology beyond the territory currently circumscribed by life-as-we-know-it, the study of Artificial Life gives us access to the domain of life-as-it-could-be ... (Langton 2004)

By modelling the behaviour of living organisms in computer simulations which, through the use of complex feedback loops, produce behaviour which was unanticipated by the programmer, Alife seeks to model evolutionary processes. More than this, however, like the systems theorists discussed earlier, in separating the 'logical form' of an organism from its material embodiment and arguing that 'aliveness' is a property of the former not the latter (Langton 1989: 1), Alife researchers can claim to have created life itself. For Langton, then, 'Artificial Life will be *genuine* life – it will simply be made of different stuff than the life that has evolved here on Earth' (1989: 33).

In the examples available on Alife websites,[11] the screen is the bounded space in which the Alife forms move. Looking at them, we seem to be gazing into the embodied space/womb of nature, but here the screen has become the body, and the life-forms are simulations with no existence outside the screen. Continuing to gaze, we may also feel that we have seen these images before: in one of the films about 'life before birth' which, in taking us inside the woman's body, promise to 'shed new light on the miracle of life'. This is not surprising since these films rely on similar technology, the 'footage' of the developing foetus which we see being in fact largely a computer-generated simulation. *Life Before Birth,*[12] first screened in Britain on Channel 4 on 7 April 2005, provides an example. 'Revolutionary 3-D and 4-D ultrasound imagery sheds light on the delicate, dark world of a fetus as never before', the DVD sleeve of the US version tells us. These technologies make it possible, continues the commentary, to open up for the first time 'a window on the womb'. Yet, as the website of MillTV makes clear, most of these images were generated electronically:

> After months of research, courtesy of 4D ultrasound scans, medical books and pictures of mummified foetuses, MillTV developed ana-tomically accurate CG recreations of month-four and month-seven foetuses. In total, it took the team six months to generate between 110 and 120 shots, each one multi-layered for shadowing, depth of field and colour correction flexibility. MillTV also designed biological graphics for the programme, including nerves and cells.[13]

'Leading, edgy post production work is what we do best at MillTV', comments the head of MillTV. 'Building CG humans and recreating convincingly organic movements and looks is always a challenge, espe-cially when you're dealing with something as hidden as a foetus.' Some of the results are remarkably like the Alife images available elsewhere.

A number of feminist critics have commented on the parallels between foetal imagery and images of man in space, so that the mother's womb seems to become 'empty space' and the foetus 'an autonomous, atomized mini-space hero' (Petchesky 2000: 176). It is a parallel echoed in *The Scotsman*'s review of *Life Before Birth*, which comments that the 'programme took us in a logical progression, from faffing about in the fallopian tube through the nine months of preparation for Mission To Earth' (McNeil 2005). In these images the mother's body disappears, and the solitary, autonomous foetus acquires individuality, selfhood, and, implicitly, rights. Unusually, the foetus in *Life Before Birth* is female, though she is programmed by the 'set of instructions' which are her genes, and develops out of the heroic journey of the triumphant sperm: 'The journey is so long and arduous that only a handful will survive . . . There are no prizes for coming second'. Yet even this female foetus is voiced, in the television version of the programme, by poet Roger McGough. It is McGough, not the programme's female voiceover, who speaks the triumph of the successful sperm and the egg's fertilisation – 'I have passed from isn't into is' – and McGough who, contemplating the possibilities of genetic variation, wonders, 'Will I be St Francis of Assisi or Al Capone?' The effect is curiously dislocating, as if, in its separation from the mother and acquisition of individuality, this female foetus must *become* male.

As the commentary of *Life Before Birth* tells us, 'The mother provides the shelter and the basics . . . but the real star of the show is the foetus'. This foetus is both a solitary creature which 'evolves in darkness' and 'the star of the show', the mother's body both sheltering womb and stage/ screen for its performance. Two parallels seem important here. The first is with the computer-generated forms of Alife, indistinguishable from the images of cells and nerves produced in this documentary. Once analogy becomes sameness on our screens, then Alife can indeed seem a form of 'life itself', just as the images generated by MillTV can indeed seem to be the result of 'peering into the womb'. The second, noted above, is between the screen and the female body. This mother's body is fragmented, so that we do not see her face; usually only her pregnant belly fills the screen. As she stands motionless, a moving image of the growing foetus is superimposed on her body; we can see both its movements and its facial expressions. The woman's body becomes, then, both container and screen, a membrane to be penetrated by the camera which goes *behind* the screen and into the void, and the site of projection of the foetal images. As many critics have pointed out, techniques of foetal imaging become a form of disciplinary surveillance of the pregnant body, what Rosalind Petchesky calls a '*panoptics of the womb*' (2000: 180, original emphasis), positioning the woman within a regime of professional investigation and 'care', and making her always secondary to the 'star of the show', the foetus. But, as her body becomes a 'window on the womb', it is also robbed of its materiality. The troubling embodied nature of sexual difference can be set aside; the reality, however virtual, is what is *on* the screen.

Commenting on the visual nature of cyberspace, Elizabeth Grosz writes:

> We were all already completely visually immersed, even before the advent of cyberspace. Cyberspace has become embodied in the screen not accidentally or contingently but because of the visualized nature of our culture and its prevailing pleasures. The technology predicated on an economy of watching has been pervasive for at least half a century. (Grosz 2001: 23)

In order to understand cyberspace, she returns us to existing understandings of two key elements: the screen image and the virtual. The real, she writes, is saturated with the virtual; as both ideas and simulacra, it is the precondition of culture. It is through the virtual – our mirrored image – that we acquire a sense of who we are: 'An external image presents us with an image of ourselves. This is the structure of identification: I make myself like the image of myself' (2001: 24). Thus the virtual was always already a part of our subjectivity before it became literalised in cyberspace. As fantasised screen image it accounts for the fascination of both cinema and television, though it did not originate with them. The narcissistic pleasure offered by cyberspace is therefore both a continuation of these pleasures and their intensification. Its promise of disembodiment is also a fantasy of re-embodiment, through an autogenesis whose imagined body remains male. But subjectivity, she points out, is anchored in the body: the body in the screen is a projection of the body outside the screen. Faced with a situation in which the screen in its newest incarnation once more functions, as Virginia Woolf famously wrote of women, to reflect 'the figure of man at twice its natural size' (1993: 32), we need, as Grosz does, to re-anchor it in the material and the embodied. To accept the identification of woman with screen, as does, for example, Sadie Plant, will not be enough to unsettle this fantasised reflection, however subversive our intent.

The cyborg

Cybernetics, which arose out of military research, conceptualised the essence of sentient activity as command, control and communication. Both living organisms and machines were seen as primarily information processing and communications networks, functioning through coding, feedback and response. From the beginning, then, cybernetics researchers not only envisaged but also built what Wiener called 'life-imitating automata'. These were machines which possessed both 'effector organs (analogous to arms and legs in human beings)' and 'sense organs, such as photoelectric cells and thermometers'. The latter would enable not only detection of the surrounding context but also feedback, which would in turn permit what we might think of as 'a conditioned reflex', but what could equally well be designated as 'learning'. Finally, these automata must possess 'the central decision organs' and a means of storing information, which would be 'analogous to the memory of a living organism' (Wiener 1954, quoted in Tomas 1995: 25). In this description, we can see Wiener humanise the automaton, attributing to it arms, legs, senses, memory and the capacity to learn. But we can also see the beginnings of a re-imaging of the human body, so that it becomes just one of many organisational systems, to be described in the language of electronics. Once this has occurred, the notion of *boundary* between human and machine gives way to that of *interface*, and the idea of an organism which is *both* human *and* machine becomes a possibility.

The term cyborg (cybernetic organism), referring to 'self-regulating man-machine systems' (Clynes and Kline 1995: 30), first appears in 1960. In a paper which applied cybernetic theory to the problems experienced by the human body during space travel, Manfred E. Clynes and Nathan S. Kline proposed that, faced with the problems of adapting human bodies to alien environments, it is the body not the environment which should be adapted. Through the use of devices which would sense the need for intervention and then, via biochemical, surgical or electronic modifications, supply the necessary adjustment, bodily self-regulation could be achieved without the need for conscious intervention. The cyborg would thus incorporate and extend the body's own homeostatic systems, to 'provide an organizational system in which such robot-like problems are taken care of automatically and unconsciously, leaving man free to explore, to create, to think, and to feel' (Clynes and Kline 1995: 31). The aim, insisted Clynes in a later interview, was to improve human beings' adaptability via a form of 'participant evolution'. It was not in any way to alter their 'essential identity', their gender, or their sexuality (Clynes 1995: 48–53).

The concept of the cyborg, then, arises out of cybernetics, and is therefore bound up with the notion of the network – Donna Haraway writes of its positioning as a 'node' within 'the scary new networks which I have called the informatics of domination' (1991b: 161), and elsewhere acknowledges the influence of actor-network theory in her own deployment of the term (Penley and Ross 1991: 3). As fantasised post-human being, it also represents a technological incarnation of the simulated body of cyberspace: a fluid, multiple, flexible being without bodily limitations, a boundary figure which is both human and non-human. Fantasies of bodily transcendence in cyberspace are, writes Sherry Turkle, 'cyborg dreams' (1997: 264). Increasingly, then, the figure of the cyborg has come to stand for all forms of imagined post-human self-hood. Cyborgs, write Gray, Mentor and Figueroa-Sarriera in their introduction to *The Cyborg Handbook* (1995), 'are everywhere and multiplying' (1995: 2), and they are increasingly difficult to define. Gray et al. list four 'cyborgology centers' – the military, medicine, entertainment and work – and four functions of cyborg technologies, which stretch across their real and imagined figurations. Cyborg technologies may, they write, be *restorative*, replacing lost organs, or *normalising* – both functions of their medical applications. They may be *reconfiguring*, as in the bodily permutations of cyberspace. Finally, they may be *enhancing*, improving the performance of human agents, a function which stretches across medicine, the military, 'work', and the imagined beings of popular culture.

It is in the sphere of what Gray et al. call 'entertainment' – advertising, films, television, video and internet games – that the figure of the cyborg is most familiar to us. In the replicants, androids, and genetically modified creatures of science fiction cinema, we can see various manifestations of the cyborg concept. Yet what is most striking about these creatures, as Claudia Springer points out, is that whilst the boundaries between human and non-human are 'enthusiastically explored' in these films, the boundaries of gender and sexuality remain firmly in place: 'In a world without human bodies, the films tell us, technological things will be gendered and there will still be a patriarchal hierarchy' (1999: 41, 48). We can recall the repeated, uncomfortable insistence of the founder of the cyborg concept, Manfred Clynes, when interviewed in 1995, that

> the idea of the cyborg in no way implies an it. It's a he or a she. It is either a male or female cyborg; it's not an it. It's an absurd mistake . . . The genes and the chromosomes already determine sex, and the brain circuitry expresses that sexuality . . . No, no . . . the cyborg, per se – talking now of men or women who have altered themselves in various cyborgian ways – in no way has that altered their sexuality . . . it hasn't altered their essential identity. (1995: 48–9)

Clynes' over-insistence here, and his emphasis on an *essential* sexual identity, offer a mirror of the hyper-gendered creations of popular culture. This is clearest in what Springer calls the 'attempt to preserve the masculine subject as a cyborg' in films like *Robocop* (1987) or the

Figure 5.1 Adidas boots, in *FHM*, April 2006

Terminator series (1984, 1991, 2003), films which suggest, she argues, 'that there is an essential masculinity that transcends bodily presence' (1999: 48). In these films, the male body is hard, impregnable, an exaggerated version of the muscular male physique. As critics have pointed out, the embodiment of the cyborg in the built physique of Arnold Schwarzenegger reinforces this notion of an *essential* and rigid masculinity, insisting, as does Clynes, on the impermeability of the boundary of gender: 'It is either a male or female cyborg; it's *not* an it' (emphasis added). It is a figure repeated constantly in advertising. In an advertisement for Adidas boots in *FHM* of April 2006, for example (see Figure 5.1), we find the 'assembled' quality of the boot mirrored in the assembled male figure: a hypermasculine cyborg pictured in aggressive action against a background suggestive of electronic space. His human face, however, is not only gendered but 'raced': action, aggression, bodily skills all remain essential qualities of the black male.

The female cyborg is equally firmly gendered. From the female robot in Fritz Lang's *Metropolis* (1926) to the 'genetically-engineered alien creature' of *Species* (1995), who penetrates and then sexually devours her male victims, the female cyborg, once escaped from masculine control, is both irresistibly seductive and infinitely deadly. As Andreas Huyssen writes, 'the male fantasy of the machine-woman' both reproduces and intensifies the double image of woman as both docile and obedient *and*

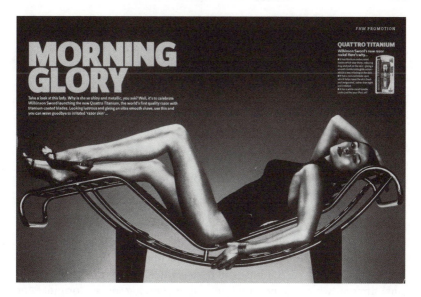

Figure 5.2 Wilkinson Sword, in *FHM*, April 2006

threateningly sexual and out of control (1986b: 73). In one of the images of 'bachelor machines' which Constance Penley reproduces in her essay on cinema as 'bachelor' apparatus, the male scientist is pictured as reality behind the Pygmalion myth, his electronic machine giving life to the sculptor's fantasy (Penley 1989: 56). It is an image – of the technologically constructed female figure, first safe *in vitro* within the scientifically created womb-space, then, released, a monstrous threat to her male creators – that recurs in recent films, from *Species* to *Alien Resurrection* (1997). The issue of *FHM* of April 2006, which featured the image of a male cyborg, provides a similarly ambivalent image of its female equivalent. Here a 'shiny and metallic' woman lies draped seductively, but with a suggestion of menace, along the surface of Wilkinson's new Quattro titanium razor (see Figure 5.2); she is its blade. 'Looking lustrous' and 'giving a smooth comfortable glide action', this blade-woman is also extremely dangerous.

Today, however, the most frequently quoted *theoretical* deployment of the concept of the cyborg is that of Donna Haraway. Haraway is acutely aware of the cyborg's origins in cybernetics, with its 'translation of the world into a problem of coding', in the service of a military-industrial complex built on 'command-control-communication-intelligence' (1991b: 164). Her feminist appropriation of the cyborg figure acknowledges both its metaphorical nature and the power of such 'body imagery' in constructing a world view (1991b: 173). Her 'Cyborg Manifesto' therefore represents a very deliberate and *public* attempt to mobilise this most powerful of metaphors in the service of a very different narrative and politics. The cyborg, she writes, is a 'boundary creature', a 'monster': an 'excessive and dislocated figure' in a post-human and therefore post-gender world (1991c: 21–5). It disturbs the boundaries of Western thought, being both (and neither) mind/body, human/machine, nature/culture, whole/part, and (or) self/other. The cyborg is embodied but not unitary; a figure of blurred boundaries and subject to regeneration rather than (re)birth, it cannot be fixed within such dualisms. Nor can it be explained by unitary myths of origin or fixed within Oedipal narratives of identity and sexual difference. It has never been innocent; nor has it 'fallen'. It cannot be objective or self-identical; it is always partial and situated. Constructed at specific points of intersection within the global network, it is historically and locally specific but globally connected.

The figure of the cyborg offers, in short, a liberatory 'myth of political identity' which is both feminist and post-gender. Its central concept of an embodiment which is not tied to the reclaiming of an 'original' or 'authentic' body – 'a kind of disassembled and reassembled, postmodern collective and personal self' (1991b: 163) – is attractive because it sidesteps traditional identifications of women with a natural corporeality. But if it is a vision which has engaged and excited other feminist writers, it has also proved troubling, and I want to turn now to some of its more troubling aspects.

The first of these concerns the precise sense in which the cyborg can be said to be embodied. Once the body is no longer *lived* but 'disassembled and reassembled', the concept of an embodied subjectivity becomes impossible to maintain. A body which is multiple and fragmented, transgressive and shifting, subject to neither pain nor ageing, is, suggests Susan Bordo, 'no body at all' (1990: 145). Neither, suggests Rosi Braidotti, can we be quite sure that it is 'sexed' (2002: 243). Haraway's cyborg is a feminist concept; she links it with the 'hyphenated identities' of postcolonial women, whose identities cannot be fixed within straightforward binaries of gender, race, nation or class, but are always multiple and partial. Nevertheless her cyborg, in being beyond gender, seems also to be beyond embodied sexual difference, sexuality, and the unconscious – beyond, therefore, any feminist politics grounded in lived experience and subjectivity. In an interview with Constance Penley in 1991, Haraway insisted that her cyborg is indeed female, but she added, 'the cyborg is a bad girl, she is really not a boy. Maybe she is not so much bad as she is a shape-changer . . . She is a girl who's trying not to become woman' (Penley and Ross 1991: 20). The 'girl who's trying not to become a woman' is of course a familiar figure within popular culture, from the girl-heroes of children's fiction to Clarice Starling in *The Silence of the Lambs* (1991). Adventurous, investigative, a 'tom-boy', she can be the narrative's hero precisely because she is *not* yet a woman.[14] Once a woman, she will become, in de Lauretis' words, 'female-obstacle-bound-ary-space' (1984: 121), and she will also become that most disturbing and potentially threatening of bodies: the sexual and potentially maternal female body.

The second aspect of Haraway's vision that has troubled feminist critics is its distance from the ways in which the technologically extended or enhanced body is *actually* produced and imagined within contemporary culture. Vivian Sobchack writes of her own transformation into 'cyborg woman' following a leg amputation. But the resulting prosthesis, she writes, has neither transformed her into a 'techno-body' nor liberated her from gender: 'Prosthetically enabled, I am, nonetheless, not a cyborg . . . Without my lived-body to live it, the prosthetic exists as part of a body without organs – a techno-body that has no sympathy for human suffering, cannot understand human pleasure and, since it has no conception of death, cannot possibly value life' (1995: 210, 213). Contemporary surgical interventions promise a technologically transformed body: freed from vulnerability, ageing, death; rejuvenated; sexually enhanced. But this fetishisation of 'the body that we *have*', writes Sobchack, is a fantasy grounded in the devaluation of 'the body that we *are*' (1995: 211). It is, she comments, 'hardly what Donna Haraway had in mind' (1995: 208).

'They had their perfect church, but not their perfect bodies', says the voiceover in UK Channel 5's *Bride and Grooming*, one of the growing number of reality shows that combine the promises of cosmetic surgery with the fascinations of the screen. As engaged couples prepare to undergo plastic surgery in order to produce the 'perfect bodies' necessary for a perfect wedding, computer-generated images simulate the promised facial transformations. Surgeon and groom watch; it is *this* transformation that delights: 'It's amazing!' During the surgery itself, the body and face are fragmented and marked (the nose, the eyelids, the belly, the breasts), then cut, carved, broken, filled. As we gaze, the surgeon also watches on screen the operation he performs. It is a process in which, as Anne Balsamo writes, 'the material body comes to embody the characteristics of technological images' (1996: 56). But the final image we see is of the wedding, the public record of a 'dream come true'. As with Haraway's cyborg, these are images which represent both cultural fantasies and material transformations, but they are transformations performed in the service of highly conservative gendered ideals.

Tammy (*Bride and Grooming*, 11 May 2006) has been thinking about having breast implants 'since I was about fifteen'; she wants 'a Cinderella style' and a 'more feminine nose'. Her groom Rob will also have implants; his now more manly chest will 'give him the confidence he craves' (*Bride and Grooming*, 11 May 2006). For these couples, many in their thirties or forties and marrying for the second or third time, the 'perfect' traditional wedding is something both wholly 'natural' and to be achieved only through technological intervention. The body must be normalised, time and lived experience erased, and the limits of the 'body that we are' denied. Patricia Holland writes that the wedding photograph is so powerful because its 'familiar structure is able to contain the tension between the longed-for ideal and the ambivalence of lived experience' (1991: 4). Here it works also to disavow the technological interventions on which it is dependent, and to reassert the rightness of traditional gendered norms.

The final question about Haraway's cyborg figure concerns the utopian qualities attached to its *newness*. Jennifer Gonzalez has pointed out that the image of the cyborg, though not named as such, dates back at least to the eighteenth century. It is not, she writes, 'a simulacrum which signifies only itself', but rather a cultural image which is already saturated in meaning (2000: 59). Cyborg images are evidence of cultural anxieties; they cannot 'float above the lingering, clinging past of differences, histories, stories, bodies, places' (2000: 64). Gendered female for the most part, they have also functioned consistently as images of the racially 'other', the product of 'miscegenation'. The persistence of this image of the ' "exotic" and vindictive cyborg who passes . . . as simply human' (2000: 70) reminds us, writes Gonzalez, that the figure of the cyborg will not resolve issues of social and cultural power. Nor, she adds, do cyborg bodies yet 'function as radical alternatives' (2000: 71).

Haraway's cyborg, therefore, is a problematic figure. Nevertheless there *is* something transgressive about the cyborg, as both its popular incarnation as *excessively* gendered body and Manfred Clynes' repeated and uncomfortable protestations of its gendered 'normality' confirm. The radical potential which Haraway mobilises, however, lies neither in its image of female-as-machine, since that has a long and far from radical history, nor in its evasion of the Oedipal romance – for that seems to be a fantasy. Rather, it lies in the importance of the cyborg image to the techno-scientific project of re-imaging the human body as information processing system. Michèle le Doeuff (2002) has suggested that images which are used to sustain a philosophical system always simultaneously *undo* that system, because their meanings can never be fully contained. Haraway's is a sustained attempt to *undo* what she calls a 'heavily militarized, communications-system-based technoscience' (Penley and Ross 1991: 6), through the appropriation and reworking of one of its dominant metaphors, for the telling of a very different story.

Conclusion

As Katherine Hayles has argued, structuring contemporary discourses of techno-science is an underpinning metanarrative of disembodiment. It is a disembodiment which Hayles calls 'posthuman', but which is also, importantly, post-gender. Like the philosophical systems which le Doeuff analyses, its contributory strands are underpinned by central, organising metaphors. These function to pull together, into a single totalising vision, a narrative of transformation which is at once techno-logical, cultural and fantasised. Looked at closely, what is most evident in these contemporary narratives is their *continuity* with older stories of masculine transcendence and feminine embodiment. What is *new* about their promises, however, is their claim to a literal, technological truth. The network, the screen and the cyborg all literalise fantasies in which technology becomes the privileged space of a dream of transcendence. 'The body we *are*' is transcended as its boundaries are effaced, and gender, and therefore feminism, becomes irrelevant. Metaphors, how-ever, are slippery tools, undoing the systems they sustain. Feminist critics have reappropriated and reworked them in different ways, and with varying degrees of success, but always with the aim of reinserting them within the context of embodied experience.

Notes

1. Lisa Cartwright makes a similar argument, when she writes that 'the cinematic apparatus can be considered as a cultural technology for the discipline and management of the human body, and that the long history of bodily analysis and surveillance in medicine and science is critically tied to the history of the development of the cinema as a popular cultural institution and a technological apparatus' (1995: 3).
2. Kaja Silverman notes the metaphors which psychoanalytic theorist Jacques Lacan uses to characterise the screen as 'stain', 'envelope', 'mask', 'double', 'semblance' and 'thrown-off skin'. See Silverman 1996: 196.
3. In her earlier work Doane analyses the function of the screen within melodrama. See Doane 1987: 155–75.
4. Episode of *Dr Who* screened on 27 May 2006 on BBC1.
5. See Chapter 2 for a fuller account of le Doeuff's argument.
6. A 'black box' is a stabilised network which then becomes 'naturalised', so that it appears to be a single entity.

7. The company deCODE Genetics, for example, uses the slogan 'decoding the language of life' on its corporate website.
8. A phrase used by Francis S. Collins, Director of the National Human Genome Research Institute at the National Institutes of Health in Bethesda, Maryland.
9. Website at http://www.virtualsexgames.com/inside.html
10. See Ross 1991. Ross argues that the metaphors of illness, viral infection and disease which are used of computers link the body of the computer with the body threatened by AIDS, quoting a *Saturday Night Live* host: 'Remember, when you connect with another computer, you're connecting to every other computer that computer has ever connected to' (1991: 108).
11. See http://www.calresco.org/pic4/img4.htm
12. The programme is available on DVD as *In the Womb*. The DVD version is without the voice and poetry of Roger McGough.
13. See http://www.ukpost.org.uk/news/articles.htm?aId=195
14. See, for example, Mulvey 1989b and Clover 1989 and 1992.

6 Conclusion: everyday readings

[T]he text-context dualism constructs a conceptual and methodological gulf which is unbridgeable within the terms of any of the systems of thought sustaining it. (Kuhn 1988: 5)

It's not true, I think, to say at the center of the encoding/decoding model is the Cartesian subject; it's already a decentered subject. But it's still a sort of cognitive decentered subject; it's still a subject with a lot of interpretive codes going on. But it's not yet a subject with an unconscious. When it becomes a subject with an unconscious in which textuality also involves the pleasurable response, or the pleasurable consumption of the text, it's very hard to know, empirically, how you then go about finding that out in some observable, behaviourally identifiable way. (Hall 1994: 273)

Interpreting interpretations is viciously circular. (Staiger 1993: 153)

In this final short chapter I want to return to an issue which has recurred throughout this book: that of the relationship between the meanings produced by and in the text and the meanings, uses and pleasures produced by and in its audience. Early research, as we have seen, struggled with the contradiction between the *pleasures* produced by popular genres aimed at women – the pleasures of self-recognition, of finding women placed centre-stage, of participation in a shared 'women's culture' – and the sense that these genres simultaneously act to contain women within the accepted bounds of femininity. Feminist researchers sought to establish female *agency*, to insist that women do *not* simply slip into what Beverley Skeggs (1997: 102) calls the 'uninhabitable' position of femininity in their viewing of media texts. Yet, in seeking, in consequence, to revalue 'women's genres' as more complex, contradictory and potentially open textual spaces than ideological criticism had suggested, such research risked both an essentialising of the category 'woman' (women *can* be defined by and in the genres aimed at them), and a confinement of feminist research to what Charlotte Brunsdon has called the 'girlzone' of popular culture aimed at women (1997: 169). It also tended to reproduce both the gendered public knowledge/popular culture divide, and to reinforce the identification of mass culture with the feminine which has been so pervasive in Western cultural theory. The theoretical tools on which feminist critics have drawn in order to prise open these circular structures of devaluation have varied. Pierre Bourdieu's concepts of taste cultures, cultural competences and 'the popular aesthetic' have been used,[1] as has the Bakhtinian notion of the carnivalesque.[2] All of these, however, tend to place 'women's genres' in an *inherently* subordinate and oppositional – if potentially dialogic – relationship to 'dominant' masculine cultures and, once again, to 'fix' categories of sexual difference. A more useful, because less rigid, approach has been the turn to theories of discourse which Annette Kuhn has advocated.[3] 'Discourse', writes Diane Macdonell (1986), 'is social. The statement made, the words used and the meanings of the words used, depends on where and against what the statement is made' (1986: 1). This concept of discourse draws on Volosinov's concept of the 'multi-accentuality' of the sign. '[I]n the alternating lines of a dialogue,' argues Volosinov, 'the same word may figure in two mutually clashing contexts . . . Actually, any real utterance, in one way or another or to one degree or another, makes a statement of agreement with or negation of something' (1973: 80). Thus, not only is dialogue the primary condition of discourse, but different social groups produce differently organised discourses. Discourse, then, is historically and socially specific. The kind of speech used to describe an event will depend on the precise context in which it is used and the social positioning of the speaker. This means that discourses are connected to institutions (medical discourse or legal discourse, for example), to ways of understanding or forms of knowledge, and to power. 'In any institution', writes Macdonell, 'there is a distribution and a hierarchy of discourses' (1986: 2).

Discourses, then, produce knowledge(s) and are the product of power relations. In any given society they will be ordered both hierarchically and in opposition, but these power relations may shift, allowing different discourses to shift, intersect and acquire dominance. Such a perspective allows the linking of the textual, the institutional and the social (text, context and audience), since all are constituted in discourse. As Kuhn argues, '[r]epresentations, contexts, audiences and spectators would then be seen as a series of interconnected social discourses, certain discourses possessing greater constitutive authority at specific moments than others'. Such a model, she argues, would permit 'relative autonomy for the operations of texts, readings and contexts, and also allow [ ] for contradictions, oppositional readings and varying degrees of discursive authority' (1987: 347). In addition, it permits theorisation of the complexities of articulation between gender and other discursive categories noted by some researchers. As Ang and Hermes note, we are 'always multiply positioned in relation to a whole range of discourses' (1990: 320), so that we never respond *simply* as women and at times our primary point of identification may not be that of gender. Thus Andrea Press (1990), for example, could note radical differences between the responses of middle-class and working-class women to the soap opera *Dynasty* despite elements of commonality in their positioning. And Jacqueline Bobo (1995), interpreting the positive readings of Spielberg's *The Color Purple* made by her black female respondents, despite their recognition that Spielberg's reframing of Alice Walker's novel represents 'a throwback to prior demeaning depictions of black women' (1995: 86), points to the importance of the extra-textual discursive context which black women brought to the film.

Finally, the use of discourse as a framing concept allows recognition of the complexities of the position of the feminist researcher in studies of women's responses to media texts. In her study of women's use of the VCR in the domestic setting, Ann Gray writes of the overlapping but nevertheless different subject positions occupied by Gray herself and the women she interviews. With them she shares a background as a working-class white woman, but despite this common history, she now writes from a very different position, that of the 'woman who is an academic researcher and teacher' (1992: 34). She also reminds us that both she *and* the women in her study are producers of interpretations – not straightforward reflections – of experience:

> The interview data upon which this project depends has . . . been subjected to a double interpretation: the first is the interpretation which the women bring to their own experience, and the one which they share with me, whilst the second is the interpretation I make of what they say. Their interpretations depend on their subject position and the discourses to which they have access and through which their subjectivities are constructed. My interpretation depends on these things also, with the important addition of a theoretical and conceptual discourse, which constitutes the framework of my analysis. (Gray 1992: 33–4)

The feminist researcher, then, occupies a no less *partial* (in both its senses) position than her respondents. Conversely, as Janet Bergstrom and Mary Ann Doane emphasise, neither does the positioning of her subjects as 'ordinary women' provide her research with 'an automatic epistemological guarantee' (1989: 11). Experience, as Beverley Skeggs writes, is 'at once always already an interpretation' (1995: 17). The feminist researcher in turn interprets the experiences and understandings of her subjects according to the academic and political frameworks of interpretation available to her. In so doing, she, like other producers of 'legitimate' discourse, is engaged in a discursive process which is bound up in power relations. Unlike those accounts which make claims to 'objectivity', however, she is both reflexively implicated in the experiences and understandings she interprets and aware of her participation in what Ien Ang calls 'a *politics of interpretation*' (1989: 105, original emphasis).

Pleasure, desire and fantasy

An explanatory framework based on concepts of discourse and discursive formations can, then, enable a conceptual bridging of the gap between texts and audiences. It can see audience readings as always complex, always historically situated and always interpretive; and it can conceptualise the intersection of discursive positionings with *power*: in relationships both between texts/producers and audiences, and between the interpretive audience and the (doubly) interpretive researcher. Yet, as the quotation from Stuart Hall at the start of this chapter suggests, it does not quite get us to an understanding of pleasure, particularly pleasure in the *visual*, or of the relationship between texts and desire and fantasy, or, finally, of audiences' embodied *uses* of (their readings of) media texts. In what follows I want to suggest that, though Annette Kuhn's recent work on 'cinema and cultural memory' explicitly points us once again towards theories of discourse as an explanatory framework (2002: 5), in fact her work suggests other conceptual framings which are more useful in understanding these more troubling aspects of audience readings.

Kuhn's recent work is on cinema and *memory*, and it is in her reflections on the workings of memory that we find tentative answers to some of the questions posed above. 'The language of memory does seem to be above all a language of images', she writes, so that it functions 'in much the same way as the dreamwork', sharing with dreams and fantasies the ability to condense and displace our desires and fears into powerful images (1995: 160). Cinema, too, functions at least in part as 'an apparatus in which the spectator is caught up in a set of psychical processes centring around vision' (2002: 146). Thus in discussion some of her informants (2002: 206) talk about the shared fantasies ('imagining that you was the female in the film') which were a central part of their viewing pleasures in the 1930s. These fantasies of transformation, rooted in desire, have as their 'content, form and context' the experience of cinema viewing, but they are then re-lived, re-enacted (in fantasy or play), and recounted amongst friends.

Thus this involvement in the cinematic moment also stretches both forwards and back. Stretching back, it evokes other, buried images and desires. Stretching forward, it is constitutive – as identificatory ideal – of our sense of self, a sense of self which can then be projected forwards into our daily living. And, as Kuhn writes, 'the dreams themselves remain in memory, powerful and pleasurable' (2002: 133).

But Kuhn also reminds us that memory 'is always already secondary revision' (1995: 158). It is bound up, that is, in narrative: in both the personal stories that we tell ourselves and others, and in the culturally sanctioned narratives which constitute media texts, and which help to shape our more personal stories. Audience responses are themselves, of course, always a form of 'memory text', and therefore always also a form of 'secondary revision'. When Kuhn suggests that memory texts are 'imagistic' and 'metaphorical', but that they are then 'wrought into a "telling" that is . . . linear, syntagmatic' and 'shaped by conventions that are in their nature collectively held' (2000: 188–91), she is also giving us a way of thinking about our responses to media texts. These responses, too, are bound into and yet – because they involve unconscious processes – also evade those 'collectively held' public narratives 'of history, of a culture' (Hall 1987: 44) which shape their telling and through it our sense of identity.

Kuhn's work on cinema memories also insists on the importance of 'the embodied quality of spectatorial engagements with cinema' (2002: 206). Her respondents always frame their accounts of the 'fantasy space' of cinema within a very precisely detailed description of its everyday setting, so that fantasy is always grounded 'in the mundane' (2002: 185). Further, their memories clearly indicate that 'the pleasure of looking at the cinema screen is but a small part of an all-encompassing somatic, sensuous and affective involvement in the cinema experience' (2002: 147). And finally, this embodied response acquires a performative aspect in the young women's enactment of what Jackie Stacey has called 'identificatory practices' (1994: 171). Cinema and its stars, Kuhn writes, became 'a site of identifications or a template for imitations' (2002: 110), as young women in the inter-war years used their imitations of stars' appearances (hair, clothes, makeup) to negotiate the limitations of 1930s working-class femininity, exploring through these processes of identificatory performance 'modes of feminine identity unavailable to previous generations' (2002: 110).

As Kuhn's respondents make clear, such promises usually remained unfulfilled, so that their memories are often tinged with 'a sense of lack or disappointment' (2002: 110). Yet, if this reflection suggests the material, discursive and subjective limitations on these women's power to both imagine and perform 'new ways of being a woman' (2002: 133), it also insists on their agency. We are returned here to Teresa de Lauretis' rethinking of identity as a process of appropriation, interpretation and re-telling, in which, she argues, we appropriate public narratives (and images) and rework them through fantasy, returning them to the public world 'resignified, rearticulated discursively and/or performatively' (1994: 308). Kuhn's female respondents enact all of these processes, but they also remind us of the constraints within which such active agency must operate. The sedimented categories of class and gender limit not only these women's opportunities but also the forms which their fantasies can take.

Kuhn's respondents are concerned with cinema viewing in the 1930s, but I would argue that the explanatory framework I have outlined here, centring on image and fantasy, their re-articulation in discourse and narrative, and the embedding of these narratives in the embodied and the everyday, is equally applicable to the understanding of our relationships with new media technologies. The virtual, as Elizabeth Grosz reminds us, is nothing new: we 'did not have to wait for the computer screen . . . to enter virtual space'. In both memory and fantasy, we have lived 'in its shadow more or less continually' (2005: 105). Nor, as I have suggested, are its discourses and narratives new: as both screen narrative and grand, or meta-narrative, the discourses of cyberspace re-work existing cultural narratives. Finally, we can argue that consideration of its uses and users must, if it is to be of value, return us to a consideration of the embodied and the everyday. As one recent piece of research on video game-play reminds us, its pleasures are not – or not only – about fantasies of transcendence. Instead, they are embodied and social:

> [the] pleasure of talking about the game, the pleasure of disseminating that game into other conversations . . . [t]he pleasure of narrating or performing what is pleasurable about gaming within the interview scenario, and the pleasure of performing knowledge about or aligning yourself to a fan base about any one game. (Thornham 2006)

Like the pleasures recounted by Kuhn's interviewees, these are pleasures marked by categories of class and gender, insisting on agency but characterised by constraints. In contemporary landscapes of media use, categories of the 'new' and the 'post' promise resolution, or at least *supercession*, of these issues. Yet familiar tensions in fact remain: between structure and agency, between woman as social category and femininity as cultural fiction, between image and narrative, between fantasy and lived reality, between texts and their readers and readers and their researchers. These tensions, and their accompanying questions about identity, desire, subjectivity and power, have structured thinking about the relationship between women, feminism and media; they need to be constantly kept in play.

Notes

1. See Ang's *Watching Dallas* (1985) for use of this term.
2. Mikhail Bakhtin's concept of popular carnival is that of a space outside everyday power structures, in which social hierarchies are temporarily overturned in an atmosphere of laughter and play to produce 'a world inside out' (Bakhtin 1965: 11).
3. Kuhn's first articulation of this framework was in 'Women's Genres', first published in 1984. Most recently, she has employed it in her study of cinemagoing in the 1930s, *An Everyday Magic: Cinema and Cultural Memory* (2002).

Bibliography

Adam, Alison (1998), *Artificial Knowing: Gender and the Thinking Machine*, London and New York: Routledge.

Alcock, Beverley and Robson, Jocelyn (1990), 'Cagney and Lacey Revisited', *Feminist Review* no. 35, pp. 42–53.

Allan, Stuart (1997), 'News and the Public Sphere: Towards a History of Objectivity and Impartiality', in Bromley, Michael and O'Malley, Tom (eds), *A Journalism Reader*, London: Routledge, pp. 296–329.

Ang, Ien (1985), *Watching Dallas: Soap Opera and the Melodramatic Imagination*, London: Methuen.

Ang, Ien (1988), 'Feminist Desire and Female Pleasure: On Janice Radway's *Reading the Romance*', *Camera Obscura* 16, pp. 178–91.

Ang, Ien (1989), 'Wanted: Audiences. On the Politics of Empirical Audience Studies', in Seiter, Ellen, Borchers, Hans, Kreutzner, Gabrielle and Warth, Eva-Maria (eds), *Remote Control: Television, Audiences and Cultural Power*, London and New York: Routledge, pp. 96–115.

Ang, Ien (1990), 'Melodramatic Imaginations: Television Fiction and Women's Fantasy', in Brown, Mary Ellen (ed.), *Television and Women's Culture: The Politics of the Popular*, London: Sage, pp. 75–88.

Ang, Ien and Hermes, Joke (1991), 'Gender and/in Media Consumption', in Curran, James and Gurevitch, Michael (eds), *Mass Media and Society*, London: Edward Arnold, pp. 307–28.

Arthurs, Jane (2003), '*Sex and the City* and Consumer Culture: Remediating Postfeminist Drama', *Feminist Media Studies* 3: 1, pp. 83–98.

Baehr, Helen (ed.) (1980), *Women and Media*, Oxford: Pergamon Press.

Baehr, Helen (1981), 'Women's Employment in British Television', in *Media, Culture and Society*, 3: 2, 125–34.

Bakhtin, Mikhail (1965), *Rabelais and his world*, trans. Iswoy, Cambridge, MA: MIT Press.

Ballaster, Ros, Beetham, Margaret, Frazer, Elizabeth and Hebron, Sandra (1991), *Women's Worlds: Ideology, Femininity and the Woman's Magazine*, Basingstoke: Macmillan.

Balsamo, Anne (1995), 'Forms of Technological Embodiment: Reading the Body in Contemporary Culture', in Featherstone, Mike and Burrows, Roger (eds), *Cyberspace/Cyberbodies/Cyberpunk*, London: Sage, pp. 215–37.

Balsamo, Anne (1996), *Technologies of the Gendered Body*, Durham and London: Duke University Press.

Battersby, Christine (1998), *The Phenomenal Woman*, Oxford: Polity.

Baudelaire, Charles [1863] (1995), 'The Painter of Modern Life', in *The Painter of Modern Life and other Essays*, ed. and trans. J. Mayne, London and New York: Phaidon Press, second edition.

Baudrillard, Jean (1985), 'The Ecstasy of Communication', in Foster, Hal (ed.), *Postmodern Culture*, London: Pluto, pp. 126–34.

Baudrillard, Jean (1990), *Seduction*, trans. Brian Singer, Basingstoke: Macmillan.

Baudrillard, Jean (1994), *Simulacra and Simulation*, trans. Sheila Faria Glaser, Ann Arbor: University of Michigan Press.

Belsey, Catherine (1980), *Critical Practice*, London: Methuen.

Benhabib, Seyla (1992), 'Models of Public Space: Hannah Arendt, the Liberal Tradition, and Jürgen Habermas', in Calhoun, Craig (ed.), *Habermas and the Public Sphere*, Cambridge, MA: MIT Press, pp. 73–98.

Benjamin, Walter (1973), *Charles Baudelaire: A Lyric Poet in the Era of High Capitalism*, trans. Harry Zohn, London: New Left Books.

Benjamin, Walter [1931] (1979), 'A Small History of Photography', in Benjamin, Walter, *One-Way Street*, trans. Edmund Jephcott and Kingsley Shorter, London: Verso, pp. 240–57

Benjamin, Walter (1986), *Reflections*, ed. and intro. Peter Demetz, New York: Schocken Books.

Benjamin, Walter [1936] (1999), 'The Work of Art in the Age of Mechanical Reproduction', in Benjamin, Walter, *Illuminations*, ed. and intro. Hannah Arendt, trans. Harry Zorn, London: Pimlico, pp. 211–44.

Berger, John (1972), *Ways of Seeing*, Harmondsworth: Penguin.

Berger, John (1991), *About Looking*, New York: Vintage Books.

Bergstrom, Janet and Doane, Mary Ann (1989), 'The Female Spectator: Contexts and Directions', *Camera Obscura* 20–1, pp. 5–27.

Biressi, Anita and Nunn, Heather (2005), *Reality TV: Realism and Revelation*, London: Wallflower Press.

Bobo, Jacqueline (1995), *Black Women as Cultural Readers*, New York: Columbia University Press.

Bondebjerg, Ib (1996), 'Public Discourse/Private Fascination: Hybridization in "True-life-story" Genres', *Media, Culture & Society* 18: 1, pp. 27–45.

Bordo, Susan (1989), 'The Body and the Reproduction of Femininity', in Bordo, Susan and Jaggar, Alison M. (eds), *Gender/Body/Knowledge: Feminist Reconstructions of Being and Knowing*, New Brunswick and London: Rutgers University Press, pp. 13–33.

Bordo, Susan (1990), 'Feminism, Postmodernism, and Gender-Scepticism', in Nicholson, Linda J. (ed.), *Feminism/Postmodernism*, New York and London: Routledge, pp. 133–56.

Bordo, Susan (1993), *Unbearable Weight: Feminism, Western Culture, and the Body*, London: University of California Press.

Bordo, Susan (1997), *Twilight Zones: The Hidden Life of Cultural Images from Plato to O.J.*, London: University of California Press.

Bourdieu, Pierre (1986), 'The Aristocracy of Culture', in Collins, Richard et al. (eds), *Media, Culture and Society: A Critical Reader*, London: Sage, pp. 164–93.

Bowlby, Rachel (1985), *Just Looking: Consumer Culture in Dreisen, Gissing and Zola*, London: Methuen.

Bowlby, Rachel (1987), 'Modes of Modern Shopping: Mallarme at the *Bon Marché*, in Armstrong, N. and Tennenhouse, L. (eds), *The Ideology of Conduct: Essays in Literature and the History of Sexuality*, New York and London: Methuen, pp. 185–205.

Braidotti, Rosi (1994), *Nomadic Subjects: Embodiment and Sexual Difference in Contemporary Feminist Theory*, New York: Columbia University Press.

Braidotti, Rosi (2002), *Metamorphoses: Towards a Materialist Theory of Becoming*, Cambridge: Polity.

Braithwaite, Ann (2002), 'The Personal, the Political, Third-wave and Post-feminisms', *Feminist Theory* 3: 3, pp. 335–44.

Bridge, M. Junior (1995), 'What's News?', in Lont, Cynthia M. (ed.), *Women and Media: Content/Careers/Criticism*, Belmont: Wadsworth Publishing Co., pp. 15–28.

Brooks, Ann (1997), *Postfeminisms: Feminism, Cultural Theory and Cultural Forms*, London: Routledge.

Brown, Mary Ellen (1994), *Soap Opera and Women's Talk*, London: Sage.

Brunsdon, Charlotte (1978), 'It is well known that by nature women are inclined to be rather personal', in Women's Studies Group, CCCS, *Women Take Issue: Aspects of Women's Subordination*, London: Hutchinson, pp. 18–34.

Brunsdon, Charlotte (1996), 'A Thief in the Night: Stories of Feminism in the 1970s at CCCS', in Morley, David and Kuan-Hsing Chen (eds), *Stuart Hall: Critical Dialogues in Cultural Studies*, London: Routledge, pp. 276–86.

Brunsdon, Charlotte (1997), *Screen Tastes: Soap Opera to Satellite Dishes*, London: Routledge.

Brunsdon, Charlotte (2000), *The Feminist, the Housewife, and the Soap Opera*, Oxford: Oxford University Press.

Bukatman, Scott (2000), 'Terminal Penetration', in Bell, David and Kennedy, Barbara (eds), *The Cybercultures Reader*, London: Routledge, pp. 149–74.

Burgin, Victor [1977] (2003), 'Looking at Photographs', in Wells, Liz (ed.), *The Photography Reader*, London: Routledge, pp. 130–7.

Busby, Linda J. (1975), 'Sex-Role Research on the Mass Media', in *Journal of Communication*, Autumn 1975, pp. 107–31.

Butcher, Helen, Coward, Ros, Evaristi, Marcella, Garber, Jenny, Harrison, Rachel and Winship, Janice (1974), *Images of Women in the Media*, Stencilled Occasional Paper, Centre for Contemporary Cultural Studies, University of Birmingham.

Butler, Judith (1990), *Gender Trouble: Feminism and the Subversion of Identity*, New York and London: Routledge.

Butler, Judith (1995), 'Burning Acts – Injurious Speech', in Parker, Andrew and Sedgwick, Eve Kosofsky (eds), *Performativity and Performance*, New York: Routledge, pp. 197–227.

Butler, Judith (1997a), *The Psychic Life of Power*, Stanford, CA: Stanford University Press.

Butler, Judith (1997b), *Excitable Speech: A Politics of the Performative*, London and New York: Routledge.

Butler, Judith (2004), *Undoing Gender*, New York: Routledge.

Byrne, Bridget (2003), 'Reciting the Self: Narrative Representations of the Self in Qualitative Interviews', *Feminist Theory*, 4: 1, 29–49.

Campbell, Beatrix (1988), *Unofficial Secrets*, London: Virago.

Capra, Fritjof (1997), 'The Web of Life', The Schrödinger Lectures, 10 September 1997, http://www.tcd.ie/Physics/Schrodinger/Lecture3.html.

Carter, Cynthia (1998), 'When the "Extraordinary" becomes "Ordinary": Everyday News of Sexual Violence', in Carter, Cynthia, Branston, Gill and Allan, Stuart (eds), *News, Gender and Power*, London: Routledge, pp. 219–32.

Cartwright, Lisa (1995), *Screening the Body: Tracing Medicine's Visual Culture*, Minneapolis and London: University of Minnesota Press.

Castells, Manuel (2000), *The Information Age: Economy, Society and Culture*, vol. I, *The Rise of the Network Society*, 2nd edn, Oxford: Blackwell.

Castells, Manuel (2004), *The Information Age: Economy, Society and Culture*, vol. II, *The Power of Identity*, 2nd edn, Oxford: Blackwell.

Caughie, John (2000), *Television Drama: Realism, Modernism, and British Culture*, Oxford: Oxford University Press.

Cavarero, Adriana, 2000), *Relating Narratives: Storytelling and Selfhood*, London: Routledge.

Chodorow, Nancy (1978), *The Reproduction of Mothering: Psychoanalysis and the Sociology of Gender*, Berkeley, Los Angeles and London: University of California Press.

Citron, Michelle, Le Sage, Julia, Mayne, Judith, Rich, B. Ruby, Taylor, Anna Marie, and the editors of *New German Critique* (1978), 'Women and Film: A Discussion of Feminist Aesthetics', *New German Critique* 13, pp. 83–107.

Clark, Danae (1990), '*Cagney & Lacey:* Feminist Strategies of Detection', in Brown, Mary Ellen (ed.), *Television and Women's Culture*, London: Sage, pp. 117–33.

Clover, Carol J. (1989), 'Her Body, Himself: Gender in the Slasher Film', in Donald, James (ed.), *Fantasy and the Cinema*, London: BFI, pp. 91–133.

Clover, Carol J. (1992), *Men, Women and Chainsaws: Gender in the Modern Horror Film*, London: BFI.

Clynes, Manfred E. (1995), 'An Interview with Manfred E. Clynes', conducted by Chris Hables Gray, in Gray, Chris Hables (ed.), *The Cyborg Handbook*, New York and London: Routledge, pp. 43–53.

Clynes, Manfred E. and Kline, Nathan S. (1995) [1960], 'Cyborgs and Space', in Gray, Chris Hables (ed.), *The Cyborg Handbook*, New York and London: Routledge, pp. 29–33.

Comolli, Jean-Louis (1980), 'Machines of the Visible', in de Lauretis, Teresa and Heath, Stephen (eds), *The Cinematic Apparatus*, Basingstoke and London: Macmillan, pp. 121–42.

Constable, Catherine (2005), *Thinking in Images*, London: BFI.

Coote, Anna and Campbell, Beatrix (1982), *Sweet Freedom: The Struggle for Women's Liberation*, London: Pan.

Corner, John (1991), 'Meaning, Genre and Context: the Problematics of "Public Knowledge" in the New Audience Studies', in Curran, James and Gurevitch, Michael (eds), *Mass Media and Society*, London: Edward Arnold, pp. 267–84.

Corner, John (1992), 'Presumption as Theory: "realism" in television studies', *Screen*, vol. 33, no. 1, pp. 97–102.

Corner, John (1995), *Television Form and Public Address*, London: Edward Arnold.

Coward, Rosalind (1984), *Female Desire: Women's Sexuality Today*, London: Paladin.

Creedon, Pamela J. (ed.) (1989), *Women in Mass Communication: Challenging Gender Values*, London: Sage.

Cronin, Anne M. (2000), *Advertising and Consumer Citizenship*, London and New York: Routledge.

Curran, James (1991), 'Mass Media and Democracy: A Reappraisal', in Curran, James and Gurevitch, Michael (eds), *Mass Media and Society*, London: Arnold, pp. 82–117.

D'Acci, Julie (1987), 'The Case of *Cagney and Lacey*', in Baehr, Helen and Dyer, Gillian (eds), *Boxed In: Women and Television*, London: Pandora, pp. 203–26.

D'Acci, Julie (1994), *Television and the Case of* Cagney and Lacey, Chapel Hill, NC: University of North Carolina Press.

Davies, Kath, Dickey, Julienne and Stratford, Teresa (eds) (1987), *Out of Focus: Writings on Women and the Media*, London: The Women's Press.

Dawkins, Richard (1976), *The Selfish Gene*, Oxford: Oxford University Press.

De Beauvoir, Simone [1949] (1988), *The Second Sex*, London: Pan Books.

De Lauretis, Teresa (1984), *Alice Doesn't: Feminism, Semiotics, Cinema*, Basingstoke and London: Macmillan.

De Lauretis, Teresa (1986), 'Feminist Studies/Critical Studies: Issues, Terms and Contexts', in de Lauretis (ed.), *Feminist Studies/Critical Studies*, Bloomington and Indianapolis: Indiana University Press, pp. 1–19.

De Lauretis, Teresa (1989), *Technologies of Gender: Essays on Theory, Film, and Fiction*, Basingstoke and London: Macmillan.

De Lauretis, Teresa (1990), 'Upping the Anti (sic) in Feminist Theory', in Hirsch, Marianne and Fox Keller, Evelyn (eds), *Conflicts in Feminism*, New York and London: Routledge, pp. 255–70.

De Lauretis, Teresa (1994), *The Practice of Love: Lesbian Sexuality and Perverse Desire*, Bloomington and Indianapolis: Indiana University Press.

Delmar, Rosalind (1986), 'What Is Feminism?', in Mitchell, Juliet and Oakley, Ann (eds), *What Is Feminism?*, Oxford: Blackwell, pp. 8–33.

Dickey, Julienne (1987), 'Women for Sale – the Construction of Advertising Images', in Davies, Kath, Dickey, Julienne and Stratford, Teresa (eds), *Out of Focus: Writings on Women and the Media*, London: The Women's Press, pp. 74–7.

Doane, Mary Ann (1984), 'The "woman's Film": Possession and Address', in Doane, Mary Ann, Mellencamp, Patricia and Williams, Linda (eds), *Re-Vision: Essays in Film Criticism*, Los Angeles: American Film Institute, pp. 67–82.

Doane, Mary Ann (1987), *The Desire to Desire: The Woman's Film of the 1940s*, Basingstoke and London: Macmillan.

Doane, Mary Ann (1991), *Femmes Fatales: Feminism, Film Theory, Psychoanalysis*, New York and London: Routledge.

Doane, Mary Ann (1999), 'Technophilia: Technology, Representation, and the Feminine', in Wolmark, Jenny (ed.), *Cybersexualities*, Edinburgh: Edinburgh University Press, pp. 20–33.

Dyer, Richard, Lovell, Terry, and McCrindle, Jean [1977] (1993), 'Soap Opera and Women', in Gray, Ann and McGuigan, Jim (eds), *Studying Culture*, London: Edward Arnold, pp. 35–41.

Eley, Geoff (1992), 'Nations, Publics, and Political Cultures: Placing Habermas in the Nineteenth Century', in Calhoun, Craig (ed.), *Habermas and the Public Sphere*, Cambridge, MA: MIT Press, pp. 289–339.

Ellmann, Mary (1968), *Thinking about Women*. New York: Harcourt.

Elsaesser, Thomas (1987), 'Tales of Sound and Fury: Observations on the Family Melodrama', in Gledhill, Christine (ed.), *Home is Where the Heart is: Studies in Melodrama and the Woman's Film*, London: BFI, pp. 43–69.

Faludi, Susan (1992), *Backlash: The Undeclared War Against Women*, London: Chatto & Windus.

Feuer, Jane (2001), 'Situation Comedy, Part 2', in Creeber, Glen (ed.), *The Television Genre Book*, London: BFI, pp. 67–70.

Felski, Rita (2000), *Doing Time: Feminist Theory and Postmodern Culture*, New York and London: New York University Press.

Fiske, John (1987), *Television Culture*, London: Methuen.

Foucault, Michel (1980), *Power/Knowledge: Selected Interviews and other Writings, 1972–77*, ed. C. Gordon, Brighton: Harvester.

Fraser, Nancy (1989), *Unruly Practices: Power, Discourse and Gender in Contemporary Social Theory*, Cambridge: Polity.

Fraser, Nancy (1992), 'Rethinking the Public Sphere: A Contribution to the Critique of Actually Existing Democracy', in Calhoun, Craig (ed.), *Habermas and the Public Sphere*, Cambridge, MA: MIT Press, pp. 109–42.

Freud, Sigmund [1900] (1976), *The Interpretation of Dreams*, trans. James Strachey, London: Penguin.

Freud, Sigmund (1993), 'Medusa's Head', in *Sexuality and the Psychology of Love*, ed. Philip Rieff, New York: Collier Books (Macmillan), pp. 212–13.

Friedan, Betty [1963] (1965), *The Feminine Mystique*, London: Penguin.

Friedman, Leslie J. (1977), *Sex Role Stereotyping in the Mass Media: An Annotated Bibliography*, New York: Garland Press.

Gallagher, Margaret (1980), *Unequal Opportunities: The Case of Women and the Media*, Paris: UNESCO.

Gallagher, Margaret (1985), *Unequal Opportunities: Update*, Paris: UNESCO.

Gallagher, Margaret (2001), *Gender Setting: New Agendas for Media Monitoring and Advocacy*, London: Zed Books.

Gallagher, Margaret (2006), *Who Makes the News? Global Media Monitoring Project 2005*, www.whomakesthenews.org.

Galtung, Johan and Ruge, Mari (1973), 'Structuring and Selecting News', in Cohan, Stanley and Young, Jock (eds), *The Manufacture of News*, London: Constable, pp. 52–63.

Garnham, Nicholas (1995), 'The Media and the Public Sphere', in Boyd-Barrett, Oliver and Newbold, Chris (eds), *Approaches to Media*, London: Arnold, pp. 245–51.

Gledhill, Christine (1984), 'Developments in Feminist Film Criticism', in Doane, M. A., Mellencamp, P. and Williams, L. (eds), *Re-Vision: Essays in Film Criticism*, Los Angeles: American Film Institute, pp. 18–48.

Gledhill, Christine (1987a), 'The Melodramatic Field: An Investigation', in Gledhill, Christine (ed.), *Home is Where the Heart is: Studies in Melodrama and the Woman's Film*, London: BFI, pp. 5–39.

Gledhill, Christine (1987b), 'Introduction', in *Home is Where the Heart is: Studies in Melodrama and the Woman's Film*, London: BFI, pp. 1–4.

Gonzalez, Jennifer (2000), 'Envisioning Cyborg Bodies: Notes from Current Research', in Kirkup, Gill et al. (eds), *The Gendered Cyborg*, London and New York: Routledge, pp. 58–73.

Gray, Ann (1992), *Video Playtime: The Gendering of a Leisure Technology*, London and New York: Routledge.

Gray, Chris Hables, Mentor, Steven, and Figueroa-Sarriera, Heidi J. (1995), 'Cyborgology: Constructing the Knowledge of Cybernetic Organisms', Introduction to Gray, Chris Hables (ed.), *The Cyborg Handbook*, New York and London: Routledge, pp. 1–13.

Greer, Germaine [1970] (1971), *The Female Eunuch*, St Albans: Granada Publishing.

Greimas, A. J. (1987), *On Meaning: Selected Writings in Semiotic Theory*, trans. Paul J. Perron and Frank H. Collins, Minneapolis: University of Minnesota Press.

Griffiths, Morwena (1995), *Feminisms and the Self: The Web of Life*, London and New York: Routledge.

Griffiths, Morwena and Whitford, Margaret (eds) (1988), *Feminist Perspectives in Philosophy*, Basingstoke: Macmillan.

Grimshaw, Jean (1986), *Philosophy and Feminist Thinking*, London: University of Minnesota Press.

Grindstaff, Laura (1997), 'Producing Trash, Class and the Money Shot: A Behind-the-scenes Account of Daytime TV Talk', in Lull, James and Hinerman, Stephen (eds), *Media Scandals*, Cambridge: Polity, pp. 164–202.

Grosz, Elizabeth (1990), *Jacques Lacan: A Feminist Introduction*, London: Routledge.

Grosz, Elizabeth (1994), *Volatile Bodies: Towards a Corporeal Feminism*, Bloomington and Indianapolis: Indiana University Press.

Grosz, Elizabeth (2001), *Architecture from the Outside*, London: MIT Press.

Grosz, Elizabeth (2005), *Time Travels: Feminism, Nature, Power*, Durham and London: Duke University Press.

Habermas, Jürgen (1984), 'The Public Sphere: An Encyclopedia Article', in *New German Critique*, Autumn, pp. 49–55.

Habermas, Jürgen (1989), *The Structural Transformation of the Public Sphere*, Cambridge: Polity.

Habermas, Jürgen (1992), 'Further Reflections on the Public Sphere', in Calhoun, Craig (ed.), *Habermas and the Public Sphere*, Cambridge, MA: MIT Press, pp. 421–61.

Hall, Stuart (1973), *Encoding and Decoding in the Television Discourse*, Stencilled Occasional Paper No. 7, Centre for Contemporary Cultural Studies, University of Birmingham.

Hall, Stuart (1980), 'Encoding/decoding', in Hall, Stuart, Hobson, Dorothy, Lowe, Andrew, and Willis, Paul (eds), *Culture, Media, Language*, London: Hutchinson, pp. 128–38.

Hall, Stuart (1986), 'Media Power and Class Power', in Curran, James, Ecclestone, Jake, Oakley, Giles and Richardson, Alan (eds), *Bending Reality: The State of the Media*, London: Pluto Press, pp. 5–14.

Hall, Stuart (1987), 'Minimal Selves', ICA Documents 6, *Identity, The Real Me: Postmodernism and the Question of Identity*, London: ICA, pp. 44–6.

Hall, Stuart (1994), 'Reflections upon the Encoding/Decoding Model: An Interview with Stuart Hall', in Cruz, Jon and Lewis, Justin (eds), *Viewing, Reading, Listening: Audiences and Cultural Studies*, Boulder, CO: Westview Press, pp. 253–74.

Hall, Stuart (1997), 'The Work of Representation', in Hall, Stuart (ed.), *Representation: Cultural Representations and Signifying Practices*, London: Sage, pp. 13–64.

Hall, Stuart, Critcher, Chas, Jefferson, Tony, Clarke, John and Roberts, Brian (1978), *Policing the Crisis: Mugging, the State, and Law and Order*, Basingstoke and London: Macmillan Education.

Hall, Stuart, Held, David and McLennan, Gregor (1992), 'Introduction', in Hall, Held and McLennan (eds), *Modernity and its Futures*, Cambridge: Polity, pp. 1–11.

Hamilton, Peter (1992), 'The Enlightenment and the Birth of Social Science', in Hall, Stuart and Gieben, Bram (eds), *Formations of Modernity*, Cambridge: Polity, pp. 17–58.

Haraway, Donna (1991a), 'Situated Knowledges', in *Simians, Cyborgs, and Women*, London: Free Association Books, pp. 183–201.

Haraway, Donna (1991b), 'A Cyborg Manifesto', in *Simians, Cyborgs, and Women*, London: Free Association Books, pp. 149–81.

Haraway, Donna (1991c), 'The Actors are Cyborg, Nature is Coyote, and the Geography is Elsewhere: Postscript to "Cyborgs at Large"', in Penley, Constance and Ross, Andrew (eds), *Technoculture*, Minneapolis: University of Minnesota Press, pp. 21–6.

Hawthorne, Susan (1999), 'Cyborgs, Virtual Bodies and Organic Bodies: Theoretical Feminist Responses', in Hawthorne, Susan and Klein, Renate (eds), *CyberFeminism: Connectivity, Critique and Creativity*, Melbourne: Spinifex, pp. 213–49.

Hayles, Katherine (1999), *How We Became Posthuman*, Chicago & London: University of Chicago Press.

Heath, Stephen (1980), 'The Cinematic Apparatus: Technology as Historical and Cultural Form', in de Lauretis, Teresa and Heath, Stephen (eds), *The Cinematic Apparatus*, Basingstoke and London: Macmillan, pp. 1–13.

Heath, Stephen (1987), 'Male Feminism', in Jardine, Alice and Smith, Paul (eds), *Men in Feminism*, London: Methuen, pp. 1–32.

Heath, Stephen (1990), 'Representing Television', in Mellencamp, Patricia (ed.), *Logics of Television*, London: BFI, pp. 267–302.

Hobson, Dorothy (1980), 'Housewives and the Mass Media', in Hall, Stuart, Hobson, Dorothy, Lowe, Andrew and Willis, Paul (eds), *Culture, Media, Language*, London: Hutchinson, pp. 105–14.

Hobson, Dorothy (1982), *'Crossroads': The Drama of a Soap Opera*, London: Methuen.

Hobson, Dorothy (2003), *Soap Opera*, Oxford: Polity.

Holland, Patricia (1987), 'When a Woman Reads the News', in Baehr, Helen and Dyer, Gillian (eds), *Boxed In: Women and Television*, pp. 133–50.

Holland, Patricia (1991), 'Introduction: History, Memory and the Family Album', in Spence, Jo and Holland, Patricia (eds), *Family Snaps: The Meanings of Domestic Photography*, London: Virago, pp. 1–14.

Huyssen, Andreas (1986a), 'Mass Culture as Woman: Modernism's Other', in Huyssen, *After the Great Divide: Modernism, Mass Culture and Postmodernism*, Basingstoke and London: Macmillan, pp. 44–62.

Huyssen, Andreas (1986b), 'The Vamp and the Machine: Fritz Lang's *Metropolis*', in Huyssen, *After the Great Divide: Modernism, Mass Culture and Postmodernism*, Basingstoke and London: Macmillan, pp. 65–81.

Irigaray, Luce [1977] (1985), *This Sex Which is Not One*, trans. Catherine Porter, Ithaca: Cornell University Press.

Jacobus, Mary (1979), 'The Difference of View', in Jacobus, M. (ed.), *Women Writing and Writing about Women*, London: Croom Helm, pp. 10–21.

Jaddou, Liliane and Williams, Jon (1981), 'A theoretical contribution to the struggle against the dominant representations of women', *Media, Culture and Society* 3, pp. 105–24.

Janus, Noreene (1977), 'Research on Sex Roles in the Mass Media', in *Insurgent Sociologist* 7, pp. 19–31.

Johnston, Claire (ed.) (1973), *Notes on Women's Cinema*, Screen Pamphlet 2, London: Society for Education in Film and Television.

Kaplan, Cora (1986), *Sea Changes: Essays on Culture and Feminism*, London: Verso.

Kaplan, E. Ann (1983), *Women and Film: Both Sides of the Camera*, New York and London: Methuen.

Kaplan, E. Ann (1997), *Looking for the Other: Feminism, Film, and the Imperial Gaze*, London: Routledge.

Kember, Sarah (2003), *Cyberfeminism and Artificial Life*, London: Routledge.

Kennedy, Barbara (2000), 'Cyberfeminisms: Introduction', in Bell, David and Kennedy, Barbara (eds), *Cybercultures: A Reader*, London: Routledge, pp. 283–90.

Kibbey, Ann (2005), *Theory of the Image: Capitalism, Contemporary Film, and Women*, Bloomington and Indianapolis: Indiana University Press.

Kuhn, Annette (1985a), *The Power of the Image: Essays on Representation and Sexuality*, London: Routledge & Kegan Paul.

Kuhn, Annette (1985b), 'Lawless Seeing', in *The Power of the Image: Essays on Representation and Sexuality*, London: Routledge & Kegan Paul, pp. 19–47.

Kuhn, Annette (1987), 'Women's Genres: Melodrama, Soap Opera and Theory', in Gledhill, Christine (ed.), *Home is Where the Heart is: Studies in Melodrama and the Woman's Film*, London: BFI, pp. 339–49.

Kuhn, Annette (1988), *Cinema, Censorship and Sexuality 1909–1925*, London and New York: Routledge.

Kuhn, Annette (1995), *Family Secrets*, London: Verso.

Kuhn, Annette (2000), 'A Journey Through Memory', in Radstone, Susannah (ed.), *Memory and Methodology*, Oxford and New York: Berg, pp. 179–96.

Kuhn, Annette (2002), *An Everyday Magic: Cinema and Cultural Memory*, London and New York: I. B. Tauris.

Kustow, Lis (1972), 'Television and Women', in Wandor, Michelene (ed.), *The Body Politic: Writings from the Women's Liberation Movement in Britain 1969–1972*, London: Stage 1, pp. 60–71.

Langton, Christopher (ed.) (1989), *Artificial Life*, Redwood City, CA: Addison-Wesley.

Langton, Chris (2004), 'What is Artificial Life?', at http://zooland.alife.org/.

Laplanche, Jean and Pontalis, Jean-Bertrand (1986), 'Fantasy and the Origins of Sexuality', in Burgin, Victor, Donald, James and Kaplan, Cora (eds), *Formations of Fantasy*, London and New York: Routledge, pp. 5–34.

Lara, Maria Pia (1998), *Moral Textures: Feminist Narratives in the Public Sphere*, Cambridge: Polity.

Larsen, Peter (1999), 'Imaginary Spaces: Television, Technology and Everyday Consciousness', in Jostein Gripsrud (ed.), *Television and Common Knowledge*, London: Routledge, pp. 108–21.

Law, John (2003), 'Notes on the Theory of the Actor Network: Ordering, Strategy and Heterogeneity', Centre for Science Studies, Lancaster University, at http://www.comp.lancs.ac.uk/sociology/papers/Law-Notes-on-ANT.pdf.

Le Doeuff, Michèle (2002), *The Philosophical Imaginary*, trans. Colin Gordon, London and New York: Continuum.

Leavis, F. R. [1930] (1994), 'Mass Civilisation and Minority Culture', in Storey, John (ed.), *Cultural Theory and Popular Culture: A Reader*, Hemel Hempstead: Harvester Wheatsheaf, pp. 12–20.

Lentricchia, Frank (1983), *Criticism and Social Change*, Chicago and London: University of Chicago Press.

Lister, Martin [1995] (2003), 'Introduction to the Photographic Image in Digital Culture', in Wells, Liz (ed.), *The Photography Reader*, London: Routledge, pp. 218–27.

Livingstone, Sonia and Lunt, Peter (1994), *Talk on Television*, London: Routledge.

Long, Elizabeth (1989), 'Feminism and Cultural Studies', *Critical Studies in Mass Communication*, 6, pp. 427–35.

Lotz, Amanda (2001), 'Postfeminist Television Criticism: Rehabilitating Critical Terms and Identifying Postfeminist Attributes', in *Feminist Media Studies* 1: 1, pp. 105–21.

Lull, James and Hinerman, Stephen (1997), 'The Search for Scandal', in Lull, James and Hinerman, Stephen (eds), *Media Scandals*, Cambridge: Polity, pp. 1–33.

Lupton, Deborah (1995), 'The Embodied Computer/User', in Featherstone, Mike and Burrows, Roger (eds), *Cyberspace/Cyberbodies/Cyberpunk*, London: Sage, pp. 97–112.

Lury, Celia (1993), *Cultural Rights: Technology, Legality and Personality*, London: Routledge.

MacCabe, Colin (1981), 'Realism and the Cinema: Notes on some Brechtian Theses', in Bennett, Tony et al. (eds), *Popular Television and Film*, London: BFI, pp. 216–35.

Macdonald, Dwight [1957] (1994), 'A Theory of Mass Culture', in Storey, John (ed.), *Cultural Theory and Popular Culture: A Reader*, Hemel Hempstead: Harvester Wheatsheaf, pp. 29–43.

Macdonald, Myra (1998), 'Publicizing the Personal: Women's Voices in British Television Documentaries', in Carter, Cynthia, Branston, Gill and Allan, Stuart (eds), *News, Gender and Power*, London: Routledge, pp. 105–20.

Macdonell, Diane (1986), *Theories of Discourse: An Introduction*, Oxford: Blackwell.

McGrath, Roberta (1987), 'Re-reading Edward Weston', in *Ten.8*, 27, pp. 26–35.

McGrath, Roberta (2002), *Seeing her Sex: Medical Archives and the Female Body*, Manchester: Manchester University Press.

McLaughlin, Lisa (1998), 'Gender, Privacy and Publicity in "Media Event Space"', in Carter, Cynthia, Branston, Gill and Allan, Stuart (eds), *News, Gender and Power*, London: Routledge, pp. 71–90.

McLaughlin, Lisa and Carter, Cynthia (2001), 'Editors' Introduction', *Feminist Media Studies*, 1: 1, pp. 5–10.

McNay, Lois (2000), *Gender and Agency: Refiguring the Subject in Feminist and Social Theory*, Oxford: Polity.

McNeil, Robert (2005), 'Unsettling view through window on the womb', *The Scotsman*, 8 April 2005, at http://news.scotsman.com/topics.cfm?tid=814&id=369082005.

McRobbie, Angela (2004), 'Post Feminism and Popular Culture', *Feminist Media Studies*, 4: 3, pp. 255–64.

Marc, David (1989), *Comic Visions: Television Comedy and American Culture*, New York: Blackwell.

Mayne, Judith (1990), *The Woman at the Keyhole: Feminism and Women's Cinema*, Bloomington and Indianapolis: Indiana University Press.

Mellencamp, Patricia (1986), 'Situation Comedy, Feminism and Freud: Discourses of Gracie and Lucy', in Modleski, Tania (ed.), *Studies in Entertainment*, Bloomington and Indianapolis: Indiana University Press, pp. 80–95.

Mellencamp, Patricia (1992), *High Anxiety: Catastrophe, Scandal, Age, and Comedy*, Bloomington and Indianapolis: Indiana University Press.

Metz, Christian [1985] (2003), 'Photography and Fetish', in Wells, Liz (ed.), *The Photography Reader*, London: Routledge, pp. 138–45.

Miller, Nancy (1990), 'The Text's Heroine: A Feminist Critic and her Fictions', in Hirsch, Marianne and Fox Keller, Evelyn (eds), *Conflicts in Feminism*, New York and London: Routledge, pp. 112–20.

Mitchell, Juliet (1971), *Woman's Estate*, Harmondsworth: Penguin.

Mitchell, W. J. T. (1986), *Iconology: Image, Text, Ideology*, Chicago and London: University of Chicago Press.

Modleski, Tania (1984), 'The Search for Tomorrow in Today's Soap Operas', in Modleski, *Loving with a Vengeance: Mass Produced Fantasies for Women*, New York and London: Methuen, pp. 85–109.

Modleski, Tania (1986), 'Femininity as Mas(s)querade: a Feminist Approach to Mass Culture', in MacCabe, C. (ed.), *High Theory/Low Culture*, Manchester: Manchester University Press, pp. 37–52.

Modleski, Tania (1991), *Feminism Without Women: Culture and Criticism in a 'Postfeminist' Age*, London: Routledge.

Moers, Ellen [1976] (1978), *Literary Women*, London: The Women's Press.

Morgan, Janet (1986), 'The BBC and the Concept of Public Service Broadcasting', in MacCabe, Colin and Stewart, Olivia (eds), *The BBC and Public Service Broadcasting*, Manchester: Manchester University Press, pp. 22–31.

Morley, David (1980), *The 'Nationwide' Audience*, London: BFI.

Morse, Margaret (1986), 'The Television News Personality and Credibility: Reflections on the News in Transition', in Modleski, Tania (ed.), *Studies in Entertainment: Critical Approaches to Mass Culture*, Bloomington and Indianapolis: Indiana University Press, pp. 55–79.

Mulvey, Laura (1979), 'Feminism, Film and the *Avant-garde*', in Jacobus, Mary (ed.), *Women Writing and Writing about Women*, London: Croom Helm, pp. 177–95.

Mulvey, Laura (1989a), 'Visual Pleasure and Narrative Cinema', in Mulvey, *Visual and Other Pleasures*, Basingstoke and London: Macmillan, pp. 14–26.

Mulvey, Laura (1989b), 'Notes on Sirk and Melodrama', in Mulvey, *Visual and Other Pleasures*, Basingstoke and London: Macmillan, pp. 39–44.

Mulvey, Laura (1989c), 'Afterthoughts on "Visual Pleasure and Narrative Cinema" inspired by King Vidor's *Duel in the Sun* (1946)', in Mulvey, *Visual and Other Pleasures*, Basingstoke and London: Macmillan, pp. 29–38.

Murray Eddings, Barbara (1980), 'Women in Broadcasting (US) *de jure, de facto*', in Baehr, Helen (ed.), *Women and Media*, Oxford: Pergamon Press, pp. 1–13.

Negra, Diane (2004), ' "Quality Postfeminism?": Sex and the Single Girl on HBO', *Genders* Issue 39, http://www.Genders.org.

Nichols, Bill (1991), *Representing Reality*, Bloomington and Indianapolis: Indiana University Press.

Nichols, Bill (1994), *Blurred Boundaries: Questions of Meaning in Contemporary Culture*, Bloomington and Indianapolis: Indiana University Press.

Nietzsche, Friedrich (1968), *The Will to Power*, ed. and trans. W. Kaufman, New York: Vintage Books.

Ouellette, Laurie (2004), ' "Take Responsibility for Yourself": *Judge Judy* and the Neoliberal Citizen', in Murray, Susan and Ouellette, Laurie (eds), *Reality TV: Remaking Television Culture*, New York: New York University Press, pp. 231–50.

Penley, Constance (1989), 'Feminism, Film Theory, and the Bachelor Machines', in Penley, *The Future of an Illusion*, London: Routledge, pp. 57–80.

Penley, Constance and Ross, Andrew (1991), 'Cyborgs at Large: Interview with Donna Haraway', in Penley and Ross (eds), *Technoculture*, Minneapolis: University of Minnesota Press, pp. 1–20.

Petchesky, Rosalind Pollack (2000), 'Foetal Images: The Power of Visual Culture in the Politics of Reproduction', in Kirkup, Gill et al. (eds), *The Gendered Cyborg*, London and New York: Routledge, pp. 171–92.

Plant, Sadie (1995), 'The Future Looms: Weaving Women and Cybernetics', in Featherstone, Mike and Burrows, Roger (eds), *Cyberspace/Cyberbodies/Cyberpunk*, London: Sage, pp. 45–64.

Plant, Sadie (1996), 'On the Matrix: Cyberfeminist Simulations', in Shields, Rob (ed.), *Cultures of Internet*, London: Sage, pp. 170–83.

Pollock, Griselda [1977] (1987), 'What's Wrong with Images of Women?', in Betterton, Rosemary (ed.), *Looking On: Images of Femininity in the Visual Arts and Media*, London: Pandora, pp. 40–8.

Pollock, Griselda (1988), *Vision and Difference: Femininity, Feminism and the Histories of Art*, London: Routledge.

Porter, Dennis (1977), 'Soap Time: Thoughts on a Commodity Art Form', *College English* 38, pp. 782–8.

Potter, Dennis (1984), *Waiting for the Boat: Dennis Potter on Television*, London: Faber and Faber.

Press, Andrea (1990), 'Class, Gender and the Female Viewer: Women's Responses to *Dynasty*', in Brown, Mary Ellen (ed.), *Television and Women's Culture*, London: Sage, pp. 158–80.

Probyn, Elspeth (1992), 'Theorizing Through the Body', in Rakow, Lana F. (ed.), *Women Making Meaning: New Feminist Directions in Communication*, New York: Routledge, pp. 83–99.

Radner, Hilary (1995), *Shopping Around: Feminine Culture and the Pursuit of Pleasure*, New York and London: Routledge.

Radway, Janice [1984] (1987), *Reading the Romance*, London: Verso.

Rakow, Lana F. (1989), 'Feminist Studies: The Next Stage', in *Critical Studies in Mass Communication* 6, pp. 209–14.

Rakow, Lana F. and Kranich, Kimberlie (1996), 'Woman as Sign in Television News', in Marris, Paul and Thornham, Sue (eds), *Media Studies: A Reader*, 2nd edn, Edinburgh: Edinburgh University Press, pp. 663–75.

Rheingold, Howard (1991), *Virtual Reality*, New York and London: Touchstone.

Rheingold, Howard (1994), *The Virtual Community: Finding Connection in a Computerised World*, London: Secker and Warburg.

Ricoeur, Paul (1991a), 'The Human Experience of Time and Narrative', in Valdés, Mario, J. (ed.), *A Ricoeur Reader: Reflection and Imagination*, New York: Harvester Wheatsheaf, pp. 99–116.

Ricoeur, Paul (1991b), 'Life: A Story in Search of a Narrator', in Valdés, Mario, J. (ed.), *A Ricoeur Reader: Reflection and Imagination*, New York: Harvester Wheatsheaf, pp. 425–37.

Riley, Denise (1988), *'Am I that Name?' Feminism and the Category of 'Women' in History*, Basingstoke: Macmillan.

Riley, Denise (1992), 'A Short History of Some Preoccupations', in Butler, Judith and Scott, Joan (eds), *Feminists Theorize the Political*, London: Routledge, pp. 121–9.

Robins, Kevin (1995), 'Cyberspace and the World We Live In', in Featherstone, Mike and Burrows, Roger (eds), *Cyberspace/Cyberbodies/Cyberpunk*, London: Sage, pp. 135–55.

Rose, Jacqueline (1986), *Sexuality in the Field of Vision*, London: Verso.

Ross, Andrew (1991), 'Hacking Away at the Counterculture', in Penley, Constance and Ross, Andrew (eds), *Technoculture*, Minneapolis: University of Minnesota Press, pp. 107–34.

Rowbotham, Sheila (1973), *Woman's Consciousness, Man's World*, Harmondsworth: Penguin.

Rowe, Kathleen K. (1997), 'Roseanne: Unruly Woman as Domestic Goddess', in Brunsdon, Charlotte, D'Acci, Julie and Spigel, Lynn (eds), *Feminist Television Criticism: A Reader*, Oxford: Clarendon Press, pp. 74–83.

Russo, Mary (1988), 'Female Grotesques: Carnival and Theory', in de Lauretis, Teresa (ed.), *Feminist Studies/Critical Studies*, Basingstoke: Macmillan, pp. 213–29.

Sejnowski, Terry (2006), 'I, Internet: Will www switch on to itself?', in *The Times Higher Education Supplement*, 12 May, p. 14.

Shafer, Roy (1981), 'Narration in the Psychoanalytic Dialogue', in Mitchell, W. J. T. (ed.), *On Narrative*, Chicago and London: University of Chicago Press, pp. 25–49.

Shattuc, Jane (1997), *The Talking Cure: TV, Talk Shows and Women*, New York: Routledge.

Showalter, Elaine (1977), *A Literature of Their Own: British Women Novelists from Brontë to Lessing*, Princeton: Princeton University Press.

Showalter, Elaine (1979), 'Towards a Feminist Poetics', in Jacobus, Mary (ed.), *Women Writing and Writing about Women*, London: Croom Helm, pp. 22–41.

Silverman, Kaja (1996), *The Threshold of the Visible World*, New York and London: Routledge.

Skeggs, Beverley (1995), 'Introduction', in Skeggs, Beverley (ed.), *Feminist Cultural Theory: Process and Production*, Manchester and New York: Manchester University Press, pp. 1–29.

Skeggs, Beverley (1997), *Formations of Class and Gender*, London: Sage.

Smith, Sharon [1972] (1999), 'The Image of Women in Film: Some Suggestions for Future Research', in Thornham, Sue (ed.), *Feminist Film Theory: A Reader*, Edinburgh, Edinburgh University Press, pp. 14–19.

Sobchack, Vivian (1995), 'Beating the Meat/Surviving the Text, or How to Get Out of this Century Alive', in Featherstone, Mike and Burrows, Roger (eds), *Cyberspace/Cyberbodies/Cyberpunk*, London: Sage, pp. 205–14.

Sofia, Zoë (1999), 'Virtual Corporeality: A Feminist View', in Wolmark, Jenny (ed.), *Cybersexualities*, Edinburgh: Edinburgh University Press, pp. 55–68.

Somers, Margaret R. and Gibson, Gloria D. (1994), 'Reclaiming the Epistemological "Other": Narrative and the Social Constitution of Identity', in Calhoun,
Craig (ed.), *Social Theory and the Politics of Identity*, Oxford: Blackwell, pp. 37–99.

Spender, Dale (1986), *Mothers of the Novel*, London: Pandora.

Springer, Claudia (1999), 'The Pleasure of the Interface', in Wolmark, Jenny
(ed.), *Cybersexualities*, Edinburgh: Edinburgh University Press, pp. 34–54.

Squire, Corinne (1997), 'Empowering Women? The *Oprah Winfrey* Show', in
Brunsdon, Charlotte, D'Acci, Julie and Spigel, Lynn (eds), *Feminist Television
Criticism: A Reader*, Oxford: Clarendon Press, pp. 98–113.

Stacey, Jackie (1994), *Star Gazing: Hollywood Cinema and Female Spectatorship*,
London and New York: Routledge.

Staiger, Janet (1993), 'Taboos and Totems: Cultural Meanings of *The Silence of the
Lambs*', in Collins, Jum, Radner, Hilary and Collins, Ava Preacher (eds), *Film
Theory Goes to the Movies*, New York and London: Routledge, pp. 142–54.

Stalder, Felix (2006), *Manuel Castells: The Theory of the Network Society*, Cambridge:
Polity.

Steedman, Carolyn (1986), *Landscape for a Good Woman*, London: Virago.

Steedman, Carolyn (1992), *Past Tenses: Essays on Writing, Autobiography and History*,
London: Rivers Oram Press.

Steenland, Sally (1995), 'Content Analysis of the Image of Women on Television', in Lont, Cynthia M. (ed.), *Women and Media: Content/Careers/Criticism*,
Belmont and London: Wadsworth Publishing Co., pp. 179–89.

Stuart, Andrea (1990), 'Feminism: Dead or Alive?', in Rutherford, Jonathan (ed.),
Identity: Community, Culture, Difference, London: Lawrence and Wishart, pp. 28–
42.

Thompson, John B. (1995), *The Media and Modernity*, Cambridge: Polity.

Thornham, Helen (2006), 'Bodies @ Play: Negotiated Performances and Game-
play', unpublished paper.

Thornham, Sue (1994), 'Feminist Interventions: *Prime Suspect 1*', *Critical Survey* 6:
2, pp. 226–33.

Thornham, Sue (2001), *Feminist Theory and Cultural Studies*, London: Arnold.

Thornham, Sue (2002), '"A Good Body": The Case of/for Feminist Media
Studies', *European Journal of Cultural Studies*, 6: 1, pp. 75–94.

Tomas, David (1995), 'Feedback and Cybernetics: Reimaging the Body in the
Age of Cybernetics', in Featherstone, Mike and Burrows, Roger (eds), *Cyber-
space/Cyberbodies/Cyberpunk*, London: Sage, pp. 21–43.

Treichler, Paula A., and Wartella, Ellen (1986), 'Interventions: Feminist Theory
and Communication Studies', in *Communication* 9, pp. 1–18.

Tuchman, Gaye (ed.) (1978a), *Hearth and Home*, New York: Oxford University
Press.

Tuchman, Gaye (1978b), 'Introduction: The Symbolic Annihilation of Women
by the Mass Media', in Tuchman, G. (ed.), *Hearth and Home*, New York: Oxford
University Press, pp. 3–38.

Tuchman, Gaye (1979), 'Women's Depiction by the Mass Media', *Signs: Journal
of Women in Culture and Society* 4: 3, pp. 528–42.

Tulloch, John (1990), *Television Drama: Agency, Audience and Myth*, London: Routledge.

Turkle, Sherry (1997), *Life on the Screen: Identity in the Age of the Internet*, New York: Touchstone.

UNESCO (1979), *Mass Media: The Image, Role and Social Conditions of Women*, Paris, Reports and Papers on Mass Communication.

Van Zoonen, Liesbet (1988), 'Rethinking Women and the News', *European Journal of Communication* 3: 335–53.

Van Zoonen, Liesbet (1991), 'A Tyranny of Intimacy? Women, Femininity and Television News', in Dahlgren, Peter and Sparks, Colin (eds), *Communication and Citizenship: Journalism and the Public Sphere*, London: Routledge, pp. 217–35.

Van Zoonen, Liesbet (1994), *Feminist Media Studies*, London: Sage.

Volosinov, Valentin [1929] (1973), *Marxism and the Philosophy of Language*, New York: Seminar Press.

Walkerdine, Valerie (1991), 'Behind the Painted Smile', in Spence, Jo and Holland, Patricia (eds), *Family Snaps: The Meanings of Domestic Photography*, London: Virago, pp. 35–45.

Wandor, Michelene (1990), *Once a Feminist: Stories of a Generation*, London: Virago, 1990.

Ware, Cellestine (1970), *Woman Power: The Movement for Women's Liberation*, New York: Tower Publications.

Warner, Michael (1992), 'The Mass Public and the Mass Subject', in Calhoun, Craig (ed.), *Habermas and the Public Sphere*, Cambridge, MA: MIT Press, pp. 377–401.

Weston, Edward [1964] (2003), 'Seeing Photographically', in Wells, Liz (ed.), *The Photography Reader*, London: Routledge, pp. 104–8.

Whitford, Margaret (1991), *Luce Irigaray: Philosophy in the Feminine*, London: Routledge.

Wiener, Norbert (1954), *The Human Use of Human Beings: Cybernetics and Society*, 2nd edn, New York: Doubleday Anchor.

Williams, Kevin (1998), *Get me a Murder a Day! A History of Mass Communication in Britain*, London: Arnold.

Williams, Linda (1990), *Hard Core*, London: Pandora.

Williams, Linda (1991), 'Film Bodies: Gender, Genre and Excess', *Film Quarterly* vol. 44, no. 4, pp. 2–13.

Williams, Raymond (1977), *Marxism and Literature*, Oxford: Oxford University Press.

Williams, Raymond (1979), *Politics and Letters: Interviews with New Left Review*, London: New Left Books.

Williams, Raymond (1990), *Television: Technology and Cultural Form*, London: Routledge.

Williamson, Judith (1978), *Decoding Advertisements*, London: Marion Boyars.

Winship, Janice (1978), 'A Woman's World: *Woman* – An Ideology of Femininity', in Women's Studies Group, CCCS, *Women Take Issue: Aspects of Women's Subordination*, London: Hutchinson, pp. 133–54.

Winship, Janice (1980), 'Sexuality For Sale', in Hall, Stuart, Hobson, Dorothy, Lowe, Andrew and Willis, Paul (eds), *Culture, Media, Language*, London: Hutchinson, pp. 217–23.

Winship, Janice (2001), 'Consuming Women: Winning Women?', in Miles, Steven, Meetham, Kevin and Anderson, Alison (eds), *The Changing Consumer: Markets and Meanings*, London, Routledge, 2001, pp. 25–40

Wolf, Naomi (1993), *Fire with Fire: The New Female Power and How it will Change the Twenty-First Century*, New York: Random House.

Women and Film (1972), 'Overview', *Women and Film* 1, pp. 3–6.

Women's Studies Group, CCCS (1978), 'Women's Studies Group: Trying to Do Feminist Intellectual Work', in Women's Studies Group, *Women Take Issue: Aspects of Women's Subordination*, London: Hutchinson, pp. 7–17.

Women's Studies Group, CCCS (1978), *Women Take Issue: Aspects of Women's Subordination*, London: Hutchinson.

Woodhull, Victoria and Claflin, Tennessee (1972), 'Virtue: What it is and What it is Not', in Schneir, Miriam (ed.), *Feminism: The Essential Historical Writings*, New York: Vintage Books, pp. 143–8.

Woodward, Kathleen (1999), 'From Virtual Cyborgs to Biological Time Bombs: Technocriticism and the Material Body', in Wolmark, Jenny (ed.), *Cybersexualities*, Edinburgh: Edinburgh University Press, pp. 280–94.

Woolf, Virginia (1993) [1929]: *A Room of One's Own*, in Barrett, Michèle (ed.), *A Room of One's Own and Three Guineas*, Harmondsworth: Penguin, pp. 1–114.

Index